A Universal Child?

A Universal Child?

ROGER SMITH

palgrave
macmillan

First published 2010 by
PALGRAVE MACMILLAN

Palgrave Macmillan in the UK is an imprint of Macmillan Publishers Limited,
registered in England, company number 785998, of Houndmills, Basingstoke,
Hampshire RG21 6XS.

Palgrave Macmillan in the US is a division of St Martin's Press LLC,
175 Fifth Avenue, New York, NY 10010.

Palgrave Macmillan is the global academic imprint of the above companies
and has companies and representatives throughout the world.

Palgrave® and Macmillan® are registered trademarks in the United States,
the United Kingdom, Europe and other countries.

ISBN-13: 978–1–4039–0784–4   hardback
ISBN-13: 978–1–4039–0785–1   paperback

This book is printed on paper suitable for recycling and made from fully
managed and sustained forest sources. Logging, pulping and manufacturing
processes are expected to conform to the environmental regulations of the
country of origin.

A catalogue record for this book is available from the British Library.

A catalog record for this book is available from the Library of Congress.

10 9 8 7 6 5 4 3 2 1
19 18 17 16 15 14 13 12 11 10

Printed in China

Contents

Acknowledgements and Dedication

First, thanks as usual to Catherine Gray and her colleagues at Palgrave Macmillan who have made the publishing process as easy and painless as ever. Thanks also to Linda Auld and Susan Dunsmore for all their work on the practicalities of making the end product look so impressive.

In addition, though, I must pay huge credit to Lorraine Harding for sharing the idea, all the early work on the book and her comments on the continuing project with me – the overall shape of the book is based on her initial proposal and much of the content of the early chapters draws heavily on her draft material. Not only was it a very well conceived idea, but her initial work gave the book its impetus and sense of purpose which I hope I have not undermined too seriously in my attempts to bring it to fruition.

Finally, in view of the title, I should dedicate the book to Emma, Claire and Daniel.

Introduction:

The Disputed Child

A 'working definition' of childhood

Childhood is something about which most people have an opinion. We have all experienced it, and this seems somehow to endow us all with a degree of expertise. In addition to the vast pool of 'common sense' knowledge of the subject, and almost certainly because of the intense level of collective interest, it is a subject which is very widely researched and contested across a range of academic disciplines. Inevitably, as a consequence, different forms of substantive 'knowledge' about childhood have emerged. These do not necessarily coincide, either in the ways we think about childhood or in what we believe to be true about it. As a result, childhood is extensively 'disputed'.

Ideas and arguments about what it is to be a child are the principal focus of this book, along with the evidence associated with these. As this exploration progresses, it is necessary for us to acknowledge and keep in perspective our own preconceptions about children and childhood. On the other hand, in order to start somewhere, we need to establish a provisional definition of the subject matter. What is a child? Which members of the population are viewed and treated as children? And when? Who are 'our' children? (Mine are all in their late teens and early twenties, but I still think of them as my 'children'.) Who thinks of her/himself as a child? It would clearly be presumptuous at this stage to claim any degree of certainty about the answers to these questions, even if they did not contradict each other. In practice, though, many aspects of daily life are directly informed by assumptions which we take to be 'good enough for the time

1

being'. In the same way, in order to engage in the kind of discussion I want to pursue here, it is necessary to make some attempt at drawing up a working definition of the key terms to be used.

First impressions suggest that this is likely to be a fairly fruitless exercise given the huge divergence in children's lives depending on their place(s) in space and time, or characteristics such as gender, ethnicity and even size. In this case, it hardly seems worth considering the question of whether there are any common features or shared experiences connecting them. And yet, there are counter-arguments, as we shall see, which suggest that childhood is a distinct phenomenon, recognizable aspects of which are shared exclusively by all those to whom the term applies. In this case, a core common definition of children and childhood is not only feasible, but absolutely essential to the task of furthering our knowledge and understanding.

The aim of the present book is to tease out the elements of these opposing arguments and, in the end, to reach some form of (tentative) synthesis. By taking an integrated approach to the subject, I hope to offer some potentially fruitful ways of thinking about and dealing with those members of society whom we will no doubt continue to think of as 'children'.

Increasingly, too, we are reminded that children themselves have a vested interest in these discussions. Younger people certainly have their own views about who is a child and what constitutes childhood specifically, which may or may not coincide with those of adults:

> First I stayed in a playground, then in a childcare institution, now I am in kindergarten and then I will go to school and then to work, and then I will stop working and I will be free all day because I am growing old.
>   (Hans, 6 years old, quoted in Eide and Winger, 2005)

This, indeed, is a fairly conventional account of the anticipated life course from one child's point of view. For some though, expected trajectories and relationships are not so easily mapped out:

> Young caring transgresses the social construct of 'children' as a group occupying distinctly the realm of 'childhood', where they have the right to physical and emotional sustenance, protection from harm, and where they are allowed to make the gradual transition to 'adulthood'. Indeed, when children undertake caring at what might be deemed an inappropriate age, they occupy a distinctly 'adult' realm simply on account of what they do.
>   (Aldridge and Becker, 2002, p. 211)

As is clear from this, what being a child involves is not always straightforwardly predictable.

For the moment, though, my aim is rather more modestly to determine where to begin. On what basis might we be able to draw up some kind of criteria which delimit the subject in some way? We could, for example, rely on formal legal definitions, on physiological characteristics, on 'status', or simply on chronological age. Unfortunately, of course, the results do not coincide. For instance, we know that in law and policy the boundaries of childhood are variably defined within and between jurisdictions. The age of criminal responsibility varies substantially, even among the relatively 'developed' countries of Europe, ranging from 8 in Scotland to 18 in Belgium and Luxembourg (Muncie and Goldson, 2006, p. 200). Implicit in these variations are competing judgements about the dividing line between childhood and adulthood and, by extension, about some of the essential characteristics of children themselves.

The need to start with some form of provisional classification does require compromise, then. The most readily available and most widely accepted framework is offered by the United Nations Convention on the Rights of the Child which incorporates both an age-based definition (those between birth and the age of 18), and an internationally agreed compendium of rights and protections. This, in turn, implicitly incorporates a whole range of assumptions about children's specific characteristics and their 'evolving capacities' (Lansdown, 2005, p. 3). This working definition leaves plenty of space for further examination of the distinct elements of children's 'evolution', and how these may interact, both at the individual level, and in their social and environmental contexts. It does not appear to prejudge unduly the central question of what children share in common, and on what bases they are bound to differ.

As the book progresses, I will develop a series of proposals about the commonalities of childhood based partly on the principle of 'evolving capacities', so this may indeed be a useful place from which to embark on this exercise.

The structure of the book

The book is structured into three parts. Part I presents the initial chapters on theoretical aspects of childhood that offer an analytical framework for the subsequent discussion of childhood 'in context' that appears in Part II. Part III draws on these discussions to reconsider the question of whether and to what extent aspects of childhood and children's lives are fixed and determined (universal), or whether they are contingent and contextual, or, indeed, whether they are a bit of both. The aim is to provide a clearer basis for further analysis and debate about what it means to be a child.

Chapter 1 sets the ball rolling by critically examining a number of influential 'positions' on the subject which may be identified in historical and contemporary discussions about childhood and what the term entails.

Chapters 2 and 3 reflect further on emerging ideas about children in time and space. In the first of these, we will consider concepts and analyses of childhood in different historical periods, drawing on by now well-known sources such as Ariès (1962), Pollock (1983) and Cunningham (1995). The aim will be to examine what, if anything can be learned about change and continuity in childhood across changing social forms, both in terms of the experiences of children and the ways in which they are and have been conceptualized. It will also be of interest here to reflect on the different ways in which children and young people have experienced 'time' historically (as reflected in changing patterns of education and employment, for example).

In Chapter 3, the focus shifts to variations in 'space', including different societies, cultures, classes and communities. While it will be selective, given the space available, use will be made of certain important anthropological sources (Whiting, 1963; Erikson, 1965, for example), which helpfully illustrate the impact on children of different forms of social and cultural organization. It will also be helpful to consider here, as in the previous chapter, how children themselves experience 'space', and how their lives may be influenced by certain assumptions about where they should (and should not be) and how their spaces are managed and controlled (Moss and Petrie, 2002).

Developing these initial discussions further, Chapter 4 revisits the question of how childhood is conceptualized and studied. Drawing on the evidence of the previous chapters, we will be able to gain a fuller insight into the continuing and unresolved arguments over what is natural and constant about children and their development, and what is socially structured and therefore variable across differing 'childhoods'. While the chapter will counter-pose alternative disciplinary traditions for analytical purposes, it will establish that they need not be mutually exclusive. The basis for an effective understanding of children and their experiences may depend on integrating apparently opposing theoretical and empirical perspectives.

Part II of the book will move from this essentially theoretical discussion to consider what we know from contemporary evidence, how childhood is shaped, and indeed, how children themselves make sense of and respond to significant experiences (Smith, 2000a). Chapter 5 reflects on the impact of state and social policies, and their different meanings for children depending on their circumstances and characteristics, including culture, disability and ethnicity, for example. It will be noted that there is a considerable degree of ambiguity in the way in which the state engages with the young. Universalist assumptions are clearly tempered by a range of assessment mechanisms and interventions which create real and substantial differences between children, individually and collectively.

However, the state is not the only powerful influence on the lives of children, or those around them. Chapter 6 broadens the discussion to consider how patterns of consumption (Gunther and Furnham, 1998) and 'marketization' also play a significant part in their experience and emerging systems of belief and patterns of identity. Gender, for example, may be shaped as much by this kind of factor as biological development or genetic influences.

It would also be an omission in the contemporary era not to consider the relationship between children and the media (Hodge and Tripp, 1986; Holland, 2004, for instance). While children are often considered by the media to be passive recipients of broadcast messages, their responses and active engagement with media inputs are also important in helping us to understand the processes of 'development' and construction in which children's lives are constantly engaged. This is the central theme of Chapter 7. One of the 'universal' features of childhood is the constant ability of young people to interpret and reconstruct their worlds in light of the messages they receive.

The final part of the book will return to the underlying question of what is constant in childhood, and what is, in fact, dependent on changing social patterns. The starting point in Chapter 8 will be an examination of the processes by which adult ways of seeing and shaping the world both define, and to an extent problematize, children and young people (Qvortrup, 1994). Children have largely been addressed according to the objectives held for them by adults, rather than as a group with its own interests and body of rights. In this sense, childhood has been seen as a means to an end – a form of preparation or apprenticeship for full adult status. This may be reflected in the ways in which children's bodies are viewed as immature and incomplete (Prout, 2005). This perspective has resulted in a particular concern with the predictable and measurable attributes of children, ranging from physical characteristics to educational targets. In this sense, certain universalizing assumptions are incorporated into 'common-sense' ideas about normal growth and development at the expense of recognizing and valuing diversity, for instance, in relation to disability.

In Chapter 9, the focus will be reversed, and we will give priority to the child's view. Much recent work has emphasized the child's perspective, both in research and policy (Christensen and James, 2000; Lewis and Lindsay, 2000; Franklin, 2002b; John, 2003). We will draw on this here, in order to gain a fuller understanding of the depth and variety of children's lived experience, as well as their capacity to make sense of and create their own social worlds (Corsaro, 1997). This does not mean, of course, that there are not common features to their processes of acquiring understanding and making sense, but it will provide a much more nuanced picture of the means by which children achieve these outcomes.

These reflections will enable us in Chapter 10 to return to the underlying question of what are the common (universal) features of the experience of being a child, and what can be clearly identified as differential and largely socially constructed elements. We will consider the question: to what extent is there some constant core to childhood? If so, where might this be located: in the child or in the social processes which conceptualize and classify the distinctive features of childhood? Where universal features are identified, how can we hold these in balance with those aspects of childhood which are variable and reflect wider social diversities? What conceptual frameworks or analytical tools would be most useful in this context? We can draw the conclusion that there are certain 'universal' features of childhood which can be seen as key determinants of children's lives, represented by the terms physical growth; increasing competencies; inexperience; and vulnerability. However we encapsulate these central aspects of childhood itself, it is important that we treat them as organizing principles in relation to which variations of experience and context must also be taken into account. Other features commonly associated with childhood, such as dependence, formative learning and maturation, are more problematic, and incorporate a number of value judgements which may lead to unsustainable assumptions about children's lives and needs.

The concluding discussion summarizes the key themes and findings of the book in order to sketch out an agenda for future attempts to analyse and understand childhood. It is accepted that, for many of the reasons explored here, attempts will continue to be made to categorize and define children for the foreseeable future. It is thus important, also, to set out a number of key (and universal) principles which should underpin such activities, including features such as the recognition of diversity and the crucial importance of appreciating things from children's own point of view.

Part I

Theoretical Aspects of Childhood

1

Alternative Perspectives on Childhood

Seeking the truth about childhood

Children and childhood are self-evidently both a matter of major social concern and of academic controversy. They represent the collective future of humanity, but at the same time their behaviour is often experienced as either baffling or threatening. Finding ways of making sense of children's lives and their actions will continue to be a matter of keen interest to society, policy-makers, politicians, community leaders and academics for the foreseeable future. At the same time, children themselves have an obvious interest in the quality of their own lives and the ways in which they are affected by their individual experiences and wider social influences. One of the significant developments of recent years has been an emerging emphasis on children's citizenship and rights, and the place of childhood as a distinctive life-stage, rather than merely as a rehearsal for adulthood. This is also a double-edged debate, with some advocates insisting that children have been oppressed for generations, and should be given a greater say over their own lives; while, on the other hand, there are those who feel that most of the world's ills can be traced to a collective over-indulgence of children specific to contemporary society. They are, quite literally, 'spoiled', it is believed, not just by their parents, but by liberal modern social practices in general. The nature and experience of childhood thus constitute a hotly contested and highly politicized issue.

It is one that is further complicated by the necessary distinction between 'childhood' and 'children'. 'Childhood' can be conceptualized as a process and a life stage, which may or may not be socially constructed and mediated. 'Children' comprise the population of young people (for present purposes, all those under the age of 18) who live through this phase of human existence, experiencing it differently depending on their individual characteristics, experiences and social contexts. The distinction between the two forms of categorization is made across and between a variety of academic disciplines, being captured by one social historian as the difference 'between children as human beings and childhood as a shifting set of ideas' (Cunningham, 1995, p. 1).

In relation to historical discourses, this is clearly an important differentiation to make. It is easier to provide an account of how *childhood* has been defined and viewed from adult perspectives, because adult accounts tend to be the source of available evidence, than to describe directly how *children* actually lived in specific eras, or changed and developed during the course of their lives. Their own accounts are much less readily accessible, despite the survival of a 'scattering' of material of this kind (Cunningham, 2006, p. 74). Anthropologists, on the other hand, may be able to offer different and distinctive insights into these questions because of the greater ease with which they are able to gain access to children's first-hand accounts or cultural productions. Thus, it is immediately apparent that quite fundamental definitional issues reflect differing and sometimes competing perspectives and modes of understanding of children and childhood, in both academic and social and political spheres.

For example, the emerging emphasis on children and their rights associated with some social scientists can be seen as reflecting a committed position which identifies idealized and often normative notions of 'childhood' as being oppressive to children. Conventional constructions of 'childhood' may therefore be said to disadvantage actual children. Holt (1974) was a key early proponent of this perspective, likening childhood to a prison, whose constraints children should be encouraged to resist and escape from. Franklin (1995), on the other hand, describes childhood as a social construct which is mythologized as a 'golden age', worry-free and full of fun.

Whichever of these idealized constructions is held, however, they share the tendency to separate childhood and adulthood, and thus to impose another set of limitations on children's worlds. Modern conceptions of childhood may be seen as stifling and restrictive, to the extent that they exclude children from participation in a whole range of 'adult' activities; their ideas and feelings are relatively devalued, and education in preparation for adult roles and tasks is treated as the major portion and most important aspect of their lives (see, for example, Smith, 2000b).

Contemporary developments in the sociology of childhood have tended to follow a similar line. It has been argued that constructions of childhood need to be distinguished from the concrete realities of children's lives, and studied critically in their own right as social phenomena (for example, James *et al.*, 1998). One important consequence of this has been the recognition of children, too, as social actors who make sense of and reinterpret their own childhoods, rather than simply and unconsciously following prescribed developmental pathways. Their perceptions and feelings must therefore be accorded the same degree of validity as others; and prior assumptions, especially those which problematize children from an adult perspective must be called into question.

Childhood is thus a terrain of alternative 'discourses' which make competing claims to capture the reality of children's lives and development: 'While everyday discourses of childhood seek to explain the "truth" of childhood, [we should] aim to explain and deconstruct those very discourses that have established taken-for-granted 'truths' about childhood' (James *et al.*, 1998, p. 9).

Of course, questioning existing assumptions and 'ways of seeing' children and childhood does not imply that we should automatically reject these, but it is clear that emerging sociological perspectives are critical of established forms of knowledge, as might be expected. Nonetheless, it remains problematic to contest, as some do, that 'childhood' (or any other social phenomenon) is purely a construct, deriving its meaning and content solely from the interpretations and beliefs of human actors (Berger and Luckman, 1967, for example).

All the same, a distinction is clearly made, whereby children, individually and collectively, and their lives, feelings and experiences are one thing, while (external, adult) concepts and representations of childhood are another. Within these representations are held to lie a range of beliefs (or 'knowledge') and attitudes, including some which stereotype children in various ways. Taken to its extreme, the adoption of fixed positions of this kind means that children are liable to be systematically misrepresented in the ways in which they are 'known', and such distorted images can, in the end, be positively damaging to them, in the same way in which racism, sexism, disablism, homophobia and other oppressive assumptions have a harmful impact.

Despite this, critical perspectives seek to avoid taking an explicit position *a priori*, but maintain only that accepted ways of thinking about and understanding children must be seen as distinct from children's realities. However, this begs a number of further questions, as to the relationship between perceptions and concrete reality, and the ways in which these can be investigated.

Here, of course, we are at the point of entering wider-ranging debates about the nature of knowledge itself, and the relationship between what we know and how we know it which will probably always remain contentious. For the moment, however, this serves merely to remind us that the critical sociological perspective must itself be open to question. Are ideas about children and childhood really as abstract, arbitrary and disconnected from the essential reality of their lives as is sometimes implied? Can childhood be reduced to merely 'a variable of social analysis' (Prout and James, 1997, p. 8)? Or, alternatively, are there some common features of children's lives which may be found across different social contexts and differing 'childhoods'? In other words, is there a necessary and consistent relationship between the actual experiences of children and the phenomenon of childhood, notwithstanding the various ways in which that term is interpreted and socially defined? Are these constructions therefore contingent on some underlying reality which depends on being young, and which distinguishes this life stage from others, such as adulthood and old age? Is there an objective basis for 'generational' differences (Mannheim, 1952)? Social constructions of childhood may thus reflect something observable and generalizable about being a child; perhaps then the key question for us is not whether or not there exists such a relationship, but what it is, and how we can investigate it. For example, there are common assumptions across societies and cultures about childhood transitions, which may be based on underlying developmental or biological changes, and these may, indeed, be mirrored in other animals (Prout, 2005, p. 102). So, while it may be recognized that social constructions of childhood are in evidence and are influential, they may also be seen as derived, albeit partially, from the lived experience of children, and their specific 'location' (Mannheim, 1952, p. 288). In other words, there is held to be a material basis to childhood, which is distinct from, but interacts with its construction through a range of social forces: 'Childhood studies, if they are to be a genuinely interdisciplinary field, must step beyond the nature–culture dualism. They cannot claim that childhood is 'cultural' and bracket out all that is 'biological' or vice versa' (Prout, 2005, p. 111).

Taking this approach to the subject represents a substantial challenge, which this book will attempt to meet, albeit tentatively. I cannot claim to offer definitive answers to such perennial questions, but it will be very important to explore this interface fully, and to consider what it might mean for 'children' and 'childhood' in the present day.

Why do we worry about our children?

Before moving on to consider some of the tensions in current thinking and research about children, it may help to reflect, too, on an important social and political question which inevitably forms the backdrop to what follows, and this is the extent to which children (and young people) have been, and remain a source of fear and concern to society as a whole. This is arguably the strongest impetus behind our consideration of essentially academic questions about how we define and understand the lives of children. We are driven by the collective need to find solutions to a persistently vexing social problem. Of course, the intensity of the problem also gives rise to more highly politicized and less reflective arguments and discussions than we might wish for, and this too needs to be factored into our analysis. There are lots of reasons for caricatures and simplistic 'constructions' to dominate in this field, and we must seek to unpack and reflect on these if we are to attempt to reach realistic and considered conclusions which might point the way forward, both in terms of further study and policy development in the interests of children.

So, why are we worried about children? And why do we always seem to think the situation is getting worse? 'Moral panics' (Cohen, 1972) may be endemic, although there does seem to have been an intensification of concern in recent years, which has not been offset by year-on-year reports of improvements in children's educational attainments (McNally, 2006), or their other noteworthy achievements and contributions to the common good!

Parallels can also be noted between intensified public concern (at the time of writing, I have just been listening to yet another 'phone-in' on the problems of children getting out of control) and the proliferation of academic texts and research inquires into the subject.

These have also been matched by the emergence of swathes of new educational courses on childhood, both of a practical and theoretical nature. A common theme, however, is a darkening mood of concern and apprehension (Postman, 1994, for instance). Something seems to have gone wrong with our children, or the way we bring them up (parents are as much the focal point for our worries and fears as children, in many ways). For instance, Foley and colleagues (2001) comment that children have been affected by numerous changes in recent years and that they seem to have 'lost' something in the process. This reflects a belief that children are now introduced to the 'adult world' too early and that they are unduly influenced by commercial interests and corrupting forces. Others, too, have referred to a prevailing sense of 'crisis' in childhood (for instance, Scraton, 1997). The idea of crisis is often characterized in terms of a widely held image 'of disintegration, or even disappearance, rather than change' (Foley *et al.*, 2001, p. 1). But even where the presence of negative trends is agreed upon, their origins and consequences may be disputed; Scraton argues, for example that popular images of dissolute and threatening children may have 'masked the structural and material realities which oppress young people' (1997, p. xiii). In other words, they are blamed for their own misfortunes, irrespective of other factors at play.

We should always try to retain a sense of proportion in relation to the rather fevered debates which often surround children and young people, and it will help in considering what is to follow to remember Pearson's (1983) historical analysis which has drawn attention to the periodic heightening of popular concerns about the young and their behaviour (in the same way as Cohen's (1972) account demonstrates some of the mechanisms by which these fears are intensified). Nonetheless, the present era has witnessed a proliferation of doom-laden accounts of the damage which we appear to be doing to children (and their childhoods) as a result of peculiarly modern developments, such as ever-expanding exposure to unsuitable media content (see Byron, 2008). Major strands in these emerging concerns are an imputed erosion of the boundaries between adults and children and the loss of adolescence; a shift in the balance of power between adults and children (although the direction of this is also disputed); and the loss of separate places and experiences for children. One relatively recent book was sub-titled 'Growing up too fast in the world of sex and drugs' (Winn, 1984), while the media are often held to account for over-accelerating children's transitions into adulthood (Buckingham, 2000, for example). Buckingham is ambivalent, though, suggesting that change in the meaning and structure of children's lives as a result of developments in the media and electronic technologies is not always deleterious, and that there are aspects of their experiences and opportunities which are significantly improved (for example, the capacity to communicate more widely, and to ensure personal safety more readily).

However, Postman (1994) has suggested that the consequences of media influence, in terms of homogenization and routinization, will be almost entirely negative for children. Part of the reason to be concerned is believed to be the loss of adult and particularly parental control in the face of the undiluted and unmediated presence of the media (especially television) as an increasingly central feature of most homes (see Byron, 2008).

As other social forces appear to have been destabilizing the family and undermining parental influence in various ways (see, for example, Smart *et al.*, 2001), and parents' own skills and capacities have been increasingly questioned, the moral influence and guidance available to children now appear to have devolved by default to the omnipresent screen in the living room, and increasingly, the bedroom, too. In summary, then, one of the consequences of change in modern societies has been a weakening of the moral framework within which children were brought up in the past, with damaging outcomes, in the view of many commentators.

It's not all bad though, or is it?

On the other hand, it is possible to be positive about some aspects of contemporary change for children (Foley *et al.*, 2001, p. 1). Indeed, the emerging recognition of children as consumers (Gunther and Furnham, 1998) or as citizens in their own right might be seen as liberating by some, who would also question the value (and accuracy) of idealized preoccupations with a historical 'golden age' of childhood innocence. The growth of the children's rights movement might be recognized as a positive manifestation of these trends in some respects (Foley *et al.*, 2001, p. 4). The emphasis on children as a distinct social group and on their individual entitlements inevitably leads to acknowledgement of their independence from and equivalent standing to adults. At the same time, the developing competence of children and young people as educational standards are raised, and as they become the acknowledged 'experts' in using the new media, becomes further legitimation for their claims to be treated as 'competent' and autonomous citizens in their own right. They should therefore be seen as entitled to express an opinion about matters that impact on them and to influence the outcome of such issues, according to some (Franklin, 2002a). Autonomy and empowerment may thus be seen as positive developments resulting, in part, from current changes in the way social structures and networks impact on children's upbringing.

Despite this optimistic take on the recent history of childhood change, there is still a prevailing sense that children are 'out of control', and that they represent a real challenge to the social order in a number of ways. Although a number of sources in the UK have, explicitly or implicitly, attributed the origin of present concerns to the killing of one young child, James Bulger, by two others (aged 10 and 11) in 1993 (Jenks, 1996; Davis and Bourhill, 1997; Goldson, 2001, for example), the persistence and diversity of our worries suggest that there are other driving forces at play here. It has been noted, too, that it is important to try to understand the reasons for differential reactions to pivotal events such as this (the rehabilitative response of Norwegians to another similar child death, for example). There is believed to be something distinctive about the way British society thinks about and problematizes children, and this, indeed, is one of the elements of the contemporary 'crisis' of childhood, which is explicitly 'located' in this social milieu (see Mannheim, 1952).

The search for explanations reveals not just a 'local' dimension to these concerns, but a degree of complexity, too. It cannot simply be taken for granted that 'children lack appropriate discipline, parental control or professional guidance' (Scraton, 1997, p. vii), or that these failings, if they are present, are the root cause of our current difficulties. Buckingham (2000) observes that our anxieties and their origins are actually quite varied and disparate. Thus, children are thought to be less subject to parental influence at the same time as they are also more likely to be the targets of media bombardment and other forms of surveillance and control; they are believed to be threatened, and more acutely 'at risk' (Parton, 2006), while also being more and more 'threatening' and dangerous. The ambiguities of our perceptions appear to reflect generic uncertainties, so that children, actually and symbolically act as 'a focus for broader concerns about social change, "indiscipline" and moral collapse' (Buckingham, 2000, p. 76).

Fears *for* children, as well as about them, appear to have intensified, and thus the 'demonization' of children (Fionda, 2005) proceeds alongside a gnawing insistence that we have continually failed to protect them properly, such as in the high profile cases of Victoria Climbié

(Laming, 2003) and Baby 'P' (or Peter). This is not a new dichotomy (see Chapter 2), but it is a powerful influence in terms of the way in which discussions about the problems of children come to be framed, and indeed, in which preferred forms of intervention in their lives also seem to be based on polarized and contradictory assumptions.

The 'punitive turn'? Contemporary fears about children who offend

Despite the persistent ambiguities about the ways in which children and their problems are characterized, there is no doubt that the current mood is very much one of preoccupation with their behaviour, and the most effective ways to control it. Developments in the UK find clear parallels in other countries and the ways in which they think and act in relation to widely perceived increases in youth crime (Muncie and Goldson, 2006). The backdrop to these trends is framed by an assumption that policy and practice in the past have been too tolerant or 'soft' and that a tougher response is needed. Interestingly, this consensus has bridged political divisions and in recent times both Conservative and Labour governments in the UK have introduced punitive measures for dealing with youthful transgressions. Most recently, indeed, there has been a move to take stronger measures to deal with 'anti-social' as well as criminal behaviour (Squires and Stephen, 2005). Holding young people to account in this way not only represents a shift to a more punitive ethos, but it also incorporates a particular view of childhood and child development, which is significant in the present context. Thus, it has been noted that a progressive separation of systems for dealing with the welfare needs of children and young people from those for responding to their wrongdoings has been accompanied by a process of 'adulteration' (Goldson and Muncie, 2007), whereby young offenders are increasingly assimilated into adult criminal justice processes. Hill *et al.* (2007) observe that this is a common trend across a number of Anglophone developed societies. Examples can be observed in the extension to young people of previously adult-oriented measures such as tagging, and the wider availability of custodial sanctions, following the Crime and Disorder Act 1998. At that time, the rule of '*doli incapax*' was abolished removing the presumption of a lower level of criminal responsibility for children aged 10–14. Thus, significantly, the 'developmental' notion which had informed this earlier position was replaced by a straightforward assumption that children as young as 10 are capable of holding full (adult) responsibility for their actions. International parallels can be found in the proposals recently published to lower the age of criminal responsibility in France, and at the same time to make available a greater range of penal sanctions for children (reported by the International Juvenile Justice Observatory, *Newsletter 53*, Dec. 2008).

Here, interestingly, the policy and legislative ethos actually contribute to the erosion of childhood as a distinctive life stage, a development which is bemoaned elsewhere, and often, ironically, by the same voices. As the argument of this book develops, it will become clear that ambiguity and contradiction are central both to the ways in which children and childhood are thought about, and the ways in which they are provided for. Importantly, though, the increasing emphasis on the status of children as responsible beings in their own right in the criminal justice arena has quite specific consequences in conceptual terms. From a relatively early age, they are to be treated as autonomous and competent citizens, it seems. Again, it is somewhat ironic that this conception is mirrored in the arguments of those who support a rights-based approach, but at the same time, also heavily criticize what they see as excessively punitive forms of intervention (Scraton and Haydon, 2002, for example).

There has been some recognition of children's rights in policy terms, too, with the UK's ratification of the UN Convention on the Rights of the Child in 1991, and some (selective) attempts by government to justify subsequent policy measures in light of the convention (despite repeated claims of systemic failures from children's organizations and the UN Committee on the Rights of the Child).

The 'punitive turn' thus reveals a degree of certainty and specificity about the nature of childhood, and emphasizes the importance of seeing young people as responsible for their actions, while, at the same time, this also (if unintentionally) paves the way for a greater emphasis on their independent rights as autonomous citizens.

The 'child in need': a different form of conceptualization

While there has been a recurrent pattern of concern about the behaviour of the young, and the 'risk' they represent (Sharland, 2006), this has found an echo in a parallel strand of thought which has focused on children as vulnerable and 'in need'. Hendrick (2003) and Ferguson (2004), for example, have both traced the historical path which fears about child abuse have followed. As Corby (1993) has pointed out, 'child abuse' is not a modern invention, and it would be unhistorical to imagine that concerns about the well-being of children have only arisen in the modern era, where 'childhood' has been more explicitly recognized as a distinct life stage. In a way, what can be identified by the pattern of recurrent heightening of concern is a sense of 'newness' about the recognition and response to child harm in each succeeding era, typified most dramatically by the 'discovery' of the 'battered child' in the 1960s (see Kempe and Kempe, 1978).

This pattern is complicated by what appears to be a different kind of cycle, which demonstrates a tendency to alternately conflate and distinguish sharply between children who are 'at risk' of harm and those who pose a risk to the community by virtue of their unacceptable behaviour. While in the 1970s, for example, and to some extent very recently in the UK (DfES, 2003; Smith, 2007), the commonality between children who are harmed and those who misbehave has been emphasized, at other times in the world of policy and practice, these have been viewed as two separate constituencies that should not be dealt with in the same way, or by the same services.

What this represents for us is something of a perennial state of confusion about children's characteristics and the nature of childhood, with resultant uncertainty about how their needs should be met or their behaviour dealt with in the sphere of public policy and welfare practice. Policy shifts appear to be driven by an underlying need among those in authority to achieve clear and unequivocal answers to these persistent challenges, and to apply the lessons consistently and effectively.

Whether or not this degree of clarity and certainty is achievable, it certainly will be productive in the present context to 'unpack' the ideas and arguments lying behind these practical attempts to solve the 'problems' of our children. There can be nothing 'taken for granted' about our understanding of the young, it would seem, despite the regular reappearance of popular stereotypes (of vulnerable children or 'threatening youth'; Davies, 1986).

Social science and childhood

In order to set the scene further, it may be helpful to think briefly about the ways in which academic theorists, especially but not exclusively social scientists, have attempted to analyse and understand childhood. The first point to make is that there has been a tendency to

categorize childhood(s) as highly variable, as between different forms
of social organization and cultures. That is, as Erikson (1965) and
others (Whiting, 1963, for instance) have suggested, different societies organize and construct childhood very differently, usually to
reflect the character of their particular culture, and in a functionalist sense, to ensure that its needs are met. There are therefore many
different 'childhoods', in terms of perceptions, representations and
experiences, and these variations may be identified both between and
within societies (based on class, gender or ethnic divisions, for example). This kind of approach, drawing on sociological and anthropological traditions, tends to highlight the distinctive aspects of being a
child rather than those features which might be held in common, or
consistently observed across other boundaries.

Additionally, influenced by postmodernist interest in diversity and
atomization, recent sociological writings have sought to distinguish
themselves from previous approaches to the subject (for example,
Corsaro, 1997; James *et al.*, 1998; Thomas, 2000; Prout, 2005). The
emergence of this new perspective is captured thus: 'Both the form
of childhood as a social and cultural institution and the process of
'growing up' became seen as dependent on their context rather than
naturally unfolding processes' (Prout, 2005, p. 1). The logic of this
argument has led also to the contention that children should not be
seen in terms of their 'incompleteness' or as adults-in-training, but as
autonomous individuals in their own right. Thus, by extension, the
activities, experiences and characteristics of children should be attributed equal validity to those of adults (see Corsaro, 1997). Theoretical
constructs of childhood have thus begun to try to develop frameworks for understanding not just the direct experiences of children,
but also the ways in which they had previously been defined, or
'constituted sociologically' (James *et al.*, 1998, p. 26). One such model
suggests four ways in which children could be conceptualized ('tribal
child', 'minority child', 'social structural child' and 'socially constructed child'). This framework enables us to recognize that diversity is a central feature of children's lives, both in terms of their own
experience and the ways in which they are categorized: this necessarily leads to a 'deconstruction of childhood's conventional, singular
and reductive form' (James *et al.*, 1998, p. 34).

At the same time, this rejection of standardized, externally imposed
definitions also draws attention to the validity of children's own
perspectives, and their place as social actors, who inevitably play a
part in defining and constructing their own and each other's worlds

(see Smith, 2000a, for example). Children's *agency* becomes an important part of the analytical (and political) mix:

> Children are and must be seen as active in the construction and determination of their own social lives, the lives of those around them and of the societies in which they live. Children are not just the passive subjects of social structures and processes.
>
> (Thomas, 2000, p. 17)

Sociologists of childhood therefore tend to distinguish two areas of inquiry quite sharply: the task of investigating and understanding children's lives (see Moss and Petrie, 2002, for example), on the one hand; and the equally significant project of identifying and analysing the processes by which childhood itself is socially constructed. The relationship between these two areas of inquiry is not straightforward or self-evident, but must be explored, analysed and articulated carefully. This analytical approach is said to represent 'a challenge to the dominant view of childhood in modern Western society' (Thomas, 2000, p. 19).

It is possible to summarize this developing strand of social scientific thought as stressing certain aspects of childhood, such as its diversity, malleability, provisional, contingent and essentially negotiated character. Boundaries between different childhoods and between children's and adult worlds are fluid and indistinct, and children themselves have the capacity to influence the ways in which their lives are shaped and understood.

In setting out a distinctive but variegated view of childhood, this model challenges perspectives which assume fixed and unchanging features of the child, posing difficult questions for deterministic developmental models. However, this challenge does not go unanswered, and there have also been important developments in other disciplines indicating universal features of childhood, which are not simply contingent products of a particular social form.

Not everything is 'social' or 'constructed', surely?

With a longer history and wider acceptance, it may seem that developmental ideas of childhood drawing on psychological and biological understandings are well placed to resist sociological deconstruction. The idea that children's physical growth is accompanied by a range of other enhancements in terms of intellect, emotional and behavioural capacities seems obvious: 'The concept of *development* underlies most psychological theories of childhood. Borrowed from biology, it implies that the

characteristics of an organism change over time according to a pattern'
(Thomas, 2000, p. 21). This process is typically captured in the notion
of developmental 'stages', which may be subject to a degree of variation (see Fahlberg, 1994, for example), but essentially reflect the growing capacity of the brain which 'sets some parameters for the operation
of both cognitive and emotional processes' (Thomas, 2000, p. 22).

A number of key thinkers are associated with theories of child
development, including Erikson (1965), interestingly, given his work
on diversities within childhood, Piaget (1959) and Vygotsky (1986).
However, their common staring point does not imply any great degree
of agreement about developmental processes and trajectories. The idea
of developmental stages has influenced much thinking in the fields of
education and child care (Daniel *et al.*, 1999; Mooney, 2000, for example), and given this influence, it is of course important to try to unpick
some of the significant assumptions underpinning this kind of model.
There appears, for example, to be an implicit assumption of progress
from immaturity to the fully developed adult life stage, across a range
of cognitive, social and emotional dimensions. Piaget had a clear view
of the approximate ages at which children would move from one stage
to another in terms of cognitive ability, for example, being able to carry
out 'concrete operations' at the age of 7, and 'formal' or 'logical' operations from around 11 or 12. Intellectual development is not just a matter
of accumulating knowledge or specific skills, it also reflects enhanced
cognitive abilities which are associated with changes in the way children
perceive the world around them (cf. Corsaro, 1997). Also implied here is
a distinction between the fluid and unfinished nature of childhood, and
by contrast, a fixed and finished state of adulthood. (Whether it is helpful to see adulthood in this way is the subject of a different book).

While it is clear that our understanding of the physiology of the
brain (Blakemore and Frith, 2005) has been substantially increased
since the early proponents of developmental theories were writing,
their ideas remain highly influential. They are not purely deterministic, though; Piaget acknowledges the child's *active* role in making
sense of words and concepts. At the same time, he conveys a clear
sense of growing competence and capacity, as the child moves predictably from a state of immaturity to completion and maturity. The
shift towards 'logical', social and abstract forms of thinking is only
demonstrated through children's linguistic interactions from the age
of 7 upwards, he maintains (Piaget, 1959, p. 126).

Like Piaget, Vygotsky initially identified 'stages' of child development, but he gave much greater emphasis to the 'social' elements of this

process. For him, unlike Piaget (1959, p. 79), cognitive development is much more a product of social processes, and mutual learning, than it is inherent in the individual child. Learning thus occurs in a social setting; knowledge and skills are gained through interaction with others, who may be more experienced, but not necessarily so; the individual makes sense of and internalizes the necessary capacities to act competently in the social sphere, and culture, language and tradition are central to this process (see Erikson, 1965). Importantly, this distinction represents a more fundamental divergence of views about the way in which the individual develops as a *social* being. For Vygotsky and associated thinkers, 'human activity is inherently mediational in that it is carried out through language and other cultural tools' (Corsaro, 1997, p. 16). In this sense, child development cannot legitimately be detached from its social and cultural context, since it is an interactive process.

We have seen this notion applied concretely in areas such as the development and implications of children's early 'attachments' (Aldgate and Jones, 2006). Focusing on emotional rather than cognitive development, this strand of research and theory places considerable emphasis on the social dimension, notably on the place of parents (especially mothers) in the process (Bowlby, 1953). More recent refinements have suggested that attachment needs to be understood in the context of a wider range of relationships (Aldgate and Jones, 2006), and that its meaning and impacts may vary according to social and cultural context (Nakagawa *et al.*, 1992), but its underlying dynamics are still seen as significant for children's emotional and behavioural growth especially where their relationships are disrupted or they experience institutional forms of upbringing (Katsurada, 2007).

While developmental theories are by no means uniform in their assumptions, and have themselves been criticized and revised, there is no doubt that this perspective remains at the centre of our conceptualization of childhood, its processes and its purported trajectory, towards maturity and adulthood. Children's 'unreadiness' is thus believed to be a common feature of their lives, and one which has certain clear implications for the ways in which they ought to be treated.

Biological development and childhood

Increasingly sophisticated scientific study has also offered us a perspective on child development rooted in biology. It is now recognized that the brain develops in complexity and capacity as children grow (Blakemore and Frith, 2005), which gives support to the argument that childhood may be identifiable as a distinct life stage, with its own patterns of physiological change. Thus, it is reported that: 'During development the brain undergoes several waves of reorganization' (Blakemore and Frith, 2005, p. 18). There is both an increase in the number of brain cells in specific areas and in the number of 'connections' between them. In fact, the initial growth in these connections means that young children have substantially more than are found in adults (Blakemore and Choudhury, 2006, p. 297). Part of the process of development therefore includes reducing the number of neural connections ('synaptic density').

As with developmental psychology, neuroscientists believe that they have identified 'sensitive periods' (Blakemore and Choudhury, 2006, p. 26) when the brain is more susceptible to change. However, it also seems clear that the nature of these changes depends substantially on environmental influences, such as the level and types of stimulation to which the brain is subject (Johnson, 2008).

Evolutionary biology offers us some insight into the physical manifestations of developmental processes, in childhood and beyond, and it is suggested that some childhood characteristics 'were selected in evolution to serve an adaptive function at that time in their life history rather than to prepare individuals for later adulthood' (Bjorklund and Pelligrini, 2000, p. 1687). Thus, certain aspects of human evolution are specifically geared to the situated processes of childhood growth and development. This implies that genetic influences may be significant, both in terms of general human development, and in terms of individual features and characteristics beyond the purely physiological. Childhood may be predetermined to some extent by these but 'Genetic programming is not enough for normal brain development to occur' (Blakemore and Frith, 2005, p. 4) though.

It is sometimes believed that proponents of biological models of development are necessarily deterministic in their outlook, but it seems that this is something of a caricature, and the interaction between 'nature and nurture' (Blakemore and Frith, 2005, p. 5) is recognized as being crucially significant.

Opposing views or emerging consensus?

While different scientific traditions have inevitably focused on different aspects of childhood, and have imported their own assumptions, it may be too simplistic to suggest that the oppositions between them are clear-cut, fixed or unbridgeable. It is rather the degree to which different factors are significant, and the nature of the interaction between them which are of particular interest to those seeking to understand the phenomenon of childhood more clearly.

Analysis of children's lives and experience appears understandably to be strongly influenced by the discipline of the investigator. This could be taken as an indication that the differences identified are irreconcilable. However, we should take care to distinguish between different belief systems, alternative modes of inquiry, and the products of these in terms of findings and theoretical observations. One does not necessarily follow straightforwardly from the other. Thus, for example, even the apparent determinism of the biological sciences is tempered by conceptual innovations such as chaos theory (Lorenz, 1993).

We have collectively tended to fall into the trap of exaggerating divisions between disciplines and perspectives, such that ideas about childhood have been attributed to opposing 'camps'. One has been identified with a stance which minimizes the distinction between childhood and adulthood, while also drawing attention to the impact of diversity and varying social conditions on children's lives. There is nothing here which prescribes certain 'essential' or natural characteristics of children. On the other hand, more scientistic models appear to rely on a belief that childhood is a distinct phase of life with its own specific features. Different experiences of childhood may be less important than their commonalities, such as biological transitions (puberty, for example), which signify a clear separation from adulthood.

This disciplinary divide is also sometimes associated with a profound epistemological dissonance between social scientific perspectives which focus on experience and meaning as core features of human life, and natural sciences which concentrate on observable and measurable patterns of behaviour or physiological change. This contrast is associated with dichotomies such as 'nature' versus 'nurture', diversity versus uniformity, essentialist versus experiential explanatory frameworks, or determinism versus human agency.

As already indicated, there is a degree of over-simplification and caricature in this polarized and often politicized representation of debates about children and childhoods. It may, nonetheless, provide a useful basis for detailed analysis, in the manner of Weber's (1957) 'ideal types', providing a methodological (and methodical) grounding for the clarification of debates and distinctions. This, though, is the starting point for an attempt to elaborate and subsequently synthesize disparate positions rather than a precursor to taking sides.

2

Children and Time:

Historical and Contemporary Ideas about Childhood

The value of thinking historically

There is a prevailing tendency to think about our knowledge and understanding of children and childhood as constantly moving in a progressive direction. Looking backwards, it seems as if there was a point at which the modern idea of childhood as a distinctive life stage emerged and began to be a subject of interest in its own right. Much of this attention focuses on the Middle Ages, and their distinct character. This era is assumed widely to represent both a break with earlier times, and an equally distinctive precursor of childhood's modern-day manifestation. Part of the reason for this concentration on medieval times as pivotal is attributable to the work of Ariès (1962), who has been particularly influential in contemporary discussions of the subject.

This chapter will focus on his work, as well as that of others who have sought to provide us with greater insight into children's lives over the course of history (for example, Pollock, 1983; Houlbrooke, 1984; Cunningham, 1995). As well as considering the arguments as to whether childhood, children's lives and their treatment have changed over the course of time, it will also be helpful to consider the extent to which the different positions identified reflect substantive change on the one hand, or merely shifts in contemporary perspectives, on the other.

The problem of understanding the history of childhood is approached in the light of the difficulty of achieving any great degree of certainty about historical evidence, especially as it is viewed from a specific viewpoint in the present. This chapter will seek out, as far as possible, indicators of apparent change over time, as well as those factors which point towards continuity in children's lives, relationships and treatment. This should shed a little more light on the question of whether or not the available evidence supports the argument that some aspects of childhood are, indeed, 'universal'.

Ariès and his influence

It is impossible to conduct an evaluation of histories of childhood without reflecting on the work of Ariès (1962) and its influence. The impact of his findings may seem all the more striking given his warning at the outset that his is: 'not the work of a specialist' (Ariès, 1962, p. 9), although neither was he simply an 'amateur "weekend historian"', as he has been described elsewhere (Heywood, 2001, p. 12). It may be that the timing of his publication was as influential as the content in prompting new interest in childhood as a subject worthy of study. However, it must be accepted now that his work is central to what has followed in this area, despite (or perhaps because of) the waves of criticism his work has encountered (for example, Pollock, 1983; Heywood, 2001; Lavalette and Cunningham, 2002).

At the heart of Ariès' thesis is the claim that childhood was 'discovered' in the Middle Ages. Drawing on the appearance (or rather, *non*-appearance) of children in visual art before that time, he has suggested that this reflected a 'marked indifference ... to the special characteristics of childhood' (Ariès, 1962, p. 50), which was also evidenced in other respects, such as the absence of any distinctive form of dress for children. Ariès also argues that there was little differentiation between children and adults in the forms of recreation in which they engaged. This was partly because: 'games and amusements extended far beyond the furtive moments we allow them' in modern societies dominated by the work ethic (Ariès, 1962, p. 73). These observations led to the categorical conclusion that in 'medieval society the idea of childhood did not exist', although it does seem that 'infants' were placed in a different category (Ariès, 1962, p. 128). However, this did not imply that children were 'neglected, forsaken or despised' (Ariès, 1962, p. 128). In fact, he takes the view that it is rather the 'puerile' nature of 'adult society' which tended to blur the distinction between different life stages, than the oppressive treatment of children or denial of their rights.

It is important, too, that we distinguish between this apparent blurring of the 'social' categories of child and adult, and the chronological demarcation of developmental stages, which Ariès clearly acknowledges as being well established by the Middle Ages (Ariès, 1962, p. 19). In other words, the primary focus of Ariès' assertions about the absence of 'childhood' was the social world in which family and other relationships are organized and played out. The absence of a distinct focus on children in medieval art is interpreted as showing that they were not emotionally important to parents, and that this was possibly associated with a high child mortality rate. Parents would not take the emotional risk of investing in close attachments to children whose long-term survival was far from certain: 'People could not allow themselves to become too attached to something that was regarded as a probable loss' (Ariès, 1962, p. 38). This he contrasts with the growing sentimental attachment to children from the seventeenth century onwards, which by inference has led to the modern-day emphasis on emotional 'attachments' within the family (Bowlby, 1953, for example), particularly the mother–child bond. This is associated with one of two 'concepts of childhood' which Ariès identifies, with families beginning to 'coddle' their young (1962, p. 132), as they became more highly valued and sentimentalized. Children's 'innocence' came to be emphasized (Ariès, 1962, p. 110), as were their 'weakness and ignorance' (1962, p. 122). Interests 'outside the family' had also 'become alive to the formerly neglected phenomenon of childhood, but they were unwilling to regard children as charming toys, for they saw them as fragile creatures of God who needed to be both safeguarded and reformed' (Ariès, 1962, p. 133). The recognition of childhood as a distinct phase of social life appears to have led to a set of characterizations which both assured them of preferential treatment in terms of care and protection, but also highlighted their supposed inadequacies and treated them as incomplete citizens.

Although Ariès makes stark claims at some points, these tend to be modified in the detail of his account. Thus, despite his emphasis on the seventeenth century as a turning point in the representation and treatment of children, he also dates the beginning of this process of 'discovery of childhood' (Ariès, 1962, p. 47) from the thirteenth century. He also draws on evidence of changing patterns of dress from the fifteenth century (Ariès, 1962, p. 55). These inconsistencies are to be expected, and they do not necessarily invalidate the claim that change was taking place, more as a process than a sudden transformation.

However, this does imply a more nuanced conceptualization of historical change, which is of currents and continuities rather than sudden dramatic upheavals. Ariès also distinguishes along the lines of gender and class in his work, suggesting that the recognition of childhood as a distinct life stage affected boys before girls and more affluent classes before those who were less well off, who 'kept up the old way of life which made no distinction between children and adults, in dress or in work or in play' for much longer (Ariès, 1962, p. 61). Nevertheless, it seems to be the definitive character of his claims which has marked Ariès out as a major contributor to the contemporary 're-discovery' of childhood, and as the source of a substantial amount of critical and constructive debate.

Taking Ariès further: criticism and development

As with any major contribution to debate, it is important to avoid over-simplification, although Ariès' work lends itself to this, because of his tendency to make grand claims, even if these are modified in the detail of his argument. Perhaps because of this though, subsequent commentators have been somewhat polarized in their responses (see Heywood, 2001, p. 12). Some have responded 'with enthusiasm', using his analysis to anchor their own work, while others have been 'downright hostile': '[Ariès'] sweeping assertions on childhood may dazzle the intellect, but they also give numerous hostages to fortune' (Heywood, 2001, p. 12).

Criticism takes a number of forms. First, Ariès' use of evidence is questioned, given that he relies largely on limited and partial data, notably early medieval art, from which children were essentially absent. The selective use of material is believed to influence his conclusions.

In addition, the point is made by some that Ariès interprets history in an extremely 'present-centred' way (Heywood, 2001, p. 13). In other words, he is purported to judge past events and social processes from an exclusive and somewhat judgemental modern Western perspective. Childhood and children's treatment are thus interpreted more or less normatively from the idealized standards of today. This is strongly challenged: 'Why should past societies have viewed children in the same way as Western society today? Moreover, even if children were regarded differently in the past, this does not mean they were therefore not regarded as children' (Pollock, 1983, p. 263).

In the third line of criticism identified by Heywood (2001), the suggestion is that Ariès' claims that there was no consciousness of childhood in or before medieval civilization were simply 'over-drawn' (Heywood, 2001, p. 14). Evidence can be produced of much earlier forms of differentiation between adults and children, such as the attempt by the Saxon king, Athelstan, to differentiate between offenders aged less than 12, those aged 12–15 and others.

I will consider these criticisms in turn, in order to shed more light on the potential contribution of historical analyses of child-hood. Pollock (1983), for example, has focused on the problematic nature of the evidence available. Of course, it is difficult in many cases to obtain primary sources, but a reliance on other material, such as 'advice manuals' or artistic works does require that their role and purposes also need to be taken into account. This kind of evidence reflects very specific forms of representation rather than general truths. Even the practice of dressing children over the age of 7 as adults, 'should not be taken to mean that they there-fore entered the adult world' (Pollock, 1983, p. 49). The problem here revolves around two linked but separate problems of historical research. The first is that the material available will almost inev-itably be of a partial nature, reflecting idealized views about the subject in question. Guidance manuals, and indeed law and policy initiatives, should not necessarily be taken as an indicator of the way things *were*, but rather of normative assumptions about the way they *should be*. Indeed, the very need for this kind of material might suggest that the reality of the time was rather different from that evident in 'official' or formal accounts. In contrast to Ariès, Pollock, for example, appears to have been rather less selective in her choice of sources, drawing on diaries, autobiographies and newspaper sources, with the result that her conclusions about the nature of childhood and the timing of changes were also rather different. Parental affection was not, in her view, diminished by the high infant mortality rate, but demonstrated by their efforts to ensure their children's survival even in adverse circumstances: 'Parents liv-ing in cultures where there is every possibility that young children will die, do not "ignore" their children but adapt their methods of child-rearing in such a way as to maximise their offspring's chance of survival' (Pollock, 1983, p. 51). The point is made here that this is not just evident in the histories of Western societies, but also in other contemporary cultures whose developmental trajectories are rather different.

This suggestion that historical evidence has been read selectively is thus linked to the second point of criticism which is that it has also been construed from a specific standpoint, that of modern Western societies, with the associated connotations that past behaviour is being judged according to specific situated contemporary standards. As Heywood (2001, p. 170) points out, for instance, there is a tendency for writers in the present to look back towards an age of depravity and pre-civilization. In keeping with a number of similar ironies which will recur throughout this book, this sits rather oddly with Pearson's (1983) observation that popular opinion tends to see children's behaviour and upbringing as consistently worse than in the immediate past. Nonetheless, the idea that children were born into 'sin' seemed to hold sway at least through the Middle Ages (Heywood, 2001, p. 33), and this may be associated with the belief that they were harshly treated in that era (Houlbrooke, 1984, p. 141). But these assumptions are, in turn, questioned by others, to some extent including Ariès (1962, p. 128), who see things through a different lens. Cunningham (2006, p. 29), for example, notes that the tension between punishment and nurture was already evident in debates about the best way to bring up children in the twelfth century.

Ariès on this point is consistent, judging the whole of medieval society as 'puerile' and in this way sustaining the view that children could not be distinguished from adults in their characteristics or behaviour. This was manifestly an 'immature' era, in his view, but this was a common affliction across the generations.

This leads to the third form of criticism to which Ariès (and others who make grand claims) could be subject, which is the tendency to extrapolate too strongly from the available evidence, and to draw monolithic conclusions. Thus, Cunningham's observations about the persistence of live debates about discipline and care suggest that there may always have been considerable variations in perceptions and experiences of childhood, with factors such as class, ethnicity, culture and gender playing a part. Despite the relative absence of concrete evidence, he notes the early emergence of familiar concerns about children's lack of discipline, over-indulgent parents, and wistful reference to a 'golden age' of childhood honesty and innocence (2006, p. 36). Pollock likewise has suggested that the idea of parental indifference to children and enthusiasm for harsh discipline has to be modified in light of historical accounts, including diaries and autobiographies (1983, p. 23), which do not offer widespread evidence of cruelty.

Equally, generalizing from other historical observations, such as the absence of distinct forms of dress for children before the sixteenth century (Ariès, 1962, p. 129) is not sustainable, given that other factors, such as the availability of materials or poverty might have imposed their own constraints in this respect. Indeed, in modern times, children often seem to aspire to adult forms of dress, too. Of course, the tendency to generalize also subsumes other kinds of 'difference' which should not be overlooked, such as gender. Indeed, it is Ariès himself (1962, p. 129) who notes divergences between boys and girls, at the point where 'specialization' of dress began to emerge. Cunningham (2006, p. 55) observes that this kind of distinction could be traced back further, with girls being 'excluded' from most forms of education in the Middle Ages. Similarly, there was clearly a difference between rich and poor in terms of access to and affordability of schooling (Cunningham, 2006, p. 56).

From a present-day standpoint, Ariès could also be criticized for overlooking the perspective of children themselves. Of course, the available sources of evidence are likely to have been extremely limited, but as Heywood observes: 'children were by no means passive victims . . .: they had some capacity to select, manipulate, resist and above all escape with their friends' (2001, p. 171). Children's role in constructing their own childhoods can thus be seen to have a historical as well as a contemporary dimension, and their capacity for resistance and challenge can be traced back some way (Cunningham, 2006, p. 82).

The nature of these criticisms raises some important points for our efforts to understand and account for childhood as a distinctive phenomenon. First, the question arises of whether it is simply a modern invention, emerging from a pre-history when the concept had no value or meaning; this is an 'absurdity' according to Heywood (2001, p. 171). Pollock is also dismissive of this assumption: 'Many historians have subscribed to the mistaken belief that, if a past society did not possess the contemporary Western concept of childhood, then that society had no such concept. This is a totally indefensible viewpoint' (1983, p. 263).

However, even if we accept that the idea of a radical break at some point in early modernity is implausible, this still leaves us with a second and more complex question about the nature and dynamics of change. Evidence in support of continuity between eras is similarly capable of being obtained and applied selectively, as Pollock observes: 'Some writers feel that the sources which are available for the history

of childhood are so problematic that the subject cannot be studied' (1983, p. 65). Nonetheless, she and others would claim to have
identified some features of childhood which are so deeply embedded
as to represent constant factors. There was, for example: 'no significant change in the quality of parental care given to or the amount
of parental affection felt for infants' during the period 1500–1900,
she states (1983, p. 235). While this might be taken as an indicator
of consistency in the treatment of children, and not necessarily in
their experience or characteristics: 'It does appear as if childhood and
play are two inseparable entities' (1983, p. 239). Childhood therefore
appears to have certain inherent qualities or aspects which are timeless
and constant.

Likewise, some others in responding to Ariès have tended to make
equally grand assertions about the permanence of childhood as a feature of social life. 'The thesis of this book is simple. The Middle Ages
did recognize stages of life that correspond to childhood and adolescence', states one such source (Hanawalt, 1993, p. 5). According to
this view, certain features of children's lives are bound to recur across
time , such as biological differences, care practices and developmental processes. Children were seen in medieval times as different from
adults, with distinct needs and developmental stages, and they were
also likely to be treated as a distinct group, being encouraged to play,
and provided with formal mechanisms for care and protection. Thus,
both their internal lives and their treatment by the external world
could be seen to have persistent features which have always distinguished them from adults.

However, whether we think in terms of ruptures or continuity, the
problem of over-generalization may still be an issue. As a number of
critics have observed, reliance on available sources tends to exclude
those who do not have 'voices', notably women, and children themselves; at the same time, it is important to avoid applying terms such
as 'play' in ways which are too culturally specific. Returning to Ariès,
indeed, it was the prevalence of 'play' as a social form which indicated that children were integrated into the wider medieval society
(1962, p. 129), rather than separated from adult arenas such as politics,
work and commerce.

Ariès and after: the birth and 'death' of childhood?

Whatever we think of his work, and it has clearly been the subject
of some criticism, Ariès' contribution to the study of childhood is

significant in a number of ways. It was of major importance, for instance, in generating interest in this area of social investigation. At the same time, it prompted an appreciation of the changing nature of childhood and our understanding of it. Whether the idea of the 'discovery' of childhood in the late Middle Ages is accepted or not, the evidence did suggest that children's lives and their treatment could be seen to change over time, and not always for the better (Cunningham, 2006, p. 13).

Subsequent inquiry into the social world of childhood and its negotiated and contingent aspects was substantially inspired by Ariès' initial work, although critics have often been rather dismissive of his achievements; as Heywood (2001, p. 12) puts it: 'Sniping is all too easy.'

Nonetheless, Ariès' work has also served to underpin a contemporary emphasis on the 'social construction' of childhood (James *et al.*, 1998; James and James, 2004). There may, though, be a tendency to draw on Ariès somewhat opportunistically to support the contention that childhood only exists as a social convention, and has no substance or meaning beyond that. Childhood is reputedly the subject of definition and redefinition purely according to the temporal and social context. Interestingly, this contention also offers implicit support to contemporary proponents of children's rights who argue that it is unhelpful, and indeed discriminatory, to treat children as lesser citizens than adults based on a set of arbitrary and changeable assumptions or norms (see Franklin, 2002a, p. 3).

Irrespective of the instrumental value of Ariès' work, there is no doubt that it has generated a substantial amount of subsequent interest and controversy. This has been immensely helpful in developing the study of childhood and children's lives, both historically and in contemporary settings. The tension between those who seek out continuities in childhood and those who are more inclined to think in terms of abrupt and dramatic change is still apparent, though. Pollock (1983), as we have seen, inclines strongly towards the idea of continuity, suggesting that: 'scholars have looked for *changes* in perceptions of children, but they have not kept a sense of proportion. They have not related the amount of change they have found to the amount which has remained unchanged' (1983, p. 64).

She cites 'play' as one aspect of this continuity; another is the place and nurturing role of parents: 'Instead of trying to explain the supposed changes in the parent–child relationship, historians would do well to ponder just why parental care is a variable so resistant to change' (1983, p. 271). But even Pollock admits to some degree of change, although she maintains that this is not especially significant (1983, p. 269).

The conclusion we are invited to draw here is that changes in childhood are largely superficial and essentially meaningless, while deeper continuities and stable patterns of behaviour suggest that it has key core features which are immutable. Thus, variations in parenting practices can be observed in any era (Pollock, 1983, p. 65), but these are limited and not fundamentally important (1983, p. 271), apparently.

Others, though, have been more inclined to highlight change as a defining principle, reflecting in dramatic (and often depressing) terms on the 'disappearance' (Postman, 1983) or alleged 'death' of childhood itself (Buckingham, 2000). Of course, proponents of the dynamic view of childhood are also to be found in the optimistic camp, with the language of progress and continual improvement in children's health, welfare and abilities to be found in many accounts, contrasted to their 'barbaric' treatment in the past (Corby, 1993, p. 12). As Corby observes, the progressive view of history focuses on issues such as child abuse and neglect, arguing that the absence of any form of 'protected status' (Corby, 1993, p. 11) before modern times exposed children to gross mistreatment. He suggests that this is an over-simplification, however, and that it partly reflects the inclination to judge historical practices through the moral lens of the present day. Despite improvements over time in health and material circumstances: 'There is evidence that children in every era have been valued, cared for, nurtured and not ill-treated ... [M]any historians ... have underestimated the degree of concern that parents of previous generations have shown for their children' (Corby, 1993, p. 14).

A contrast is therefore drawn between improvements in living standards and welfare, and rather more ambiguous evidence about the quality of care afforded to children. One comprehensive review of children's welfare in the UK is thus reported to have identified improvements in a 'majority of respects' (Bradshaw, 2002, p. 367), but at the same time a deterioration in some aspects of their lives, including growing income inequality, increasing levels of obesity and certain diseases, and a reduction in opportunities to play (Bradshaw, 2002, p. 368). These disparate shifts affecting the lives of modern-day children suggest that we should be cautious about over-generalization about either the nature or direction of change.

The end of childhood?

Despite these observations, some sources have suggested that recent and contemporary social developments have been so dramatic that we must once again think in terms of major transitions in the very nature of childhood. To some eyes, it has 'disappeared' (Postman, 1994), and we have come full circle. What emerged in the Middle Ages, as part of the process of 'modernization' of family life (Ariès, 1962, p. 406), is now under threat in the face of the increasingly rapid and intensive dynamics of the present era. Indeed, tidal analogies are used to suggest a cyclical rather than linear process: 'The period between 1850 and 1950 represents the high-watermark of childhood' (Postman, 1994, p. 67). By the beginning of the twentieth century, childhood had become idealized, if not 'idyllic':

> Like all stages of life, it was, and is, filled with pain and confusion. But by the turn of the century childhood had come to be regarded as every person's birthright, an ideal that transcended social and economic class. Inevitably, childhood came to be defined as a biological category, not a product of culture.
>
> (Postman, 1994, p. 67)

According to this analysis, changes in the forms and substance of communication have played a crucial part in defining and redefining childhood. In its time, the impact of printing on the shape and substance of social life was dramatic and fundamental. Literacy became a necessary requirement of adult competence, and this in turn prompted the establishment of formal educational systems. This led to a new conceptualization of 'the young' in Postman's view: 'not as miniature adults, but as something quite different altogether – unformed adults' (1994, p. 41). In accordance with others, such as Ariès (1962) and Pinchbeck and Hewitt (1969), he argues that childhood came to be defined according to the institutional setting and the formative 'stage' associated with it. This social arrangement remained largely undisturbed by other developments until the emergence of mass broadcast media, especially television, in the mid-twentieth century. The consequences for accepted notions of childhood and social development are reported to have been cataclysmic: 'The new media environment that is emerging provides everyone, simultaneously, with the same information ... [E]lectronic media find it impossible to withhold any secrets. Without secrets, of course, there can be no such thing as childhood' (Postman, 1994, p. 80).

What happens, in effect, is that the forms and substance of social discourse are no longer differentiated. As in the Middle Ages, the 'adult–child' is a 'normal condition' (Postman, 1994, p. 99). Evidence in support of this proposition is garnered from children's literature, films, fashion, behaviour and the 'disappearance' of childhood games. Postman makes it clear that in his view these are mostly undesirable trends, epitomized by the 'Children's Rights Movement' (1994, p. 139) which is described as a 'reactionary' tendency purporting to be radical.

Others are certainly less pessimistic (Zelizer, 1994; 2005, for example), but also use the language of change and restructuring of social life to suggest that the place and role of children may now be changing dramatically. The construction of childhood as a separate, but highly valued, status between 1870 and the 1930s in the United States (1994, p. x) is contrasted to more recent and comparative international contexts where children as economic actors are recognized much more centrally (Zelizer, 1994, p. 227). 'The world is changing' and so is the child's place and role within the family, but this is not necessarily a bad thing as the child also takes on broader but socially cohesive responsibilities within the family.

As we have seen before, though, there are a number of facets to the argument about childhood change. Put simply, these hinge on the answers to two central, but independent, questions. First, what is the evidence for change in children's lives; and, second, is this a good or bad thing?

Buckingham (2000) takes issue with those such as Postman who view recent media developments as entirely negative, but he does not deny the scale or 'complexity' (Buckingham, 2000, p. 191) of contemporary change. At the same time, he makes an important point about the relationship between appearance, or 'representations' of childhood (Buckingham, 2000, p. 34) and the substantive experiences of children themselves. Thus, for instance, 'the fear that children will become prematurely adult' has a well-established pedigree. Indeed, the persistence of 'fantasies' about a golden age of childhood:

> should in itself give us cause to question contemporary assertions about the 'death of childhood'. A particular *idea* of childhood may well be disappearing; but it is much harder to identify the consequence of this in terms of the realities of children's lives.
>
> (Buckingham, 2000, p. 35)

At the same time, Buckingham makes the distinction between 'superficial' and 'fundamental' changes, questioning the significance attributed to some evidence, such as the convergence of adults' and children's forms of dress, 'eating habits or tastes in music'

(Buckingham, 2000, p. 35). This is an important point, particularly in light of other concerns already discussed about the selective use of evidence in some histories of childhood.

Thus, say, a different perspective and a different choice of sources might offer us a contrasting view of childhood and change, with the suggestion being made by some that there has actually been an intensification in recent years of processes of differentiation and classification between the generations (Mannheim, 1952; Alanen, 2001). The emphasis on children's distinctive educational needs does not seem to have declined, for example, and this has been paralleled by growing expectations of parents to understand child development and provide support, care and encouragement accordingly. According to Beck-Gernsheim (2002, p. 90) 'the cultural pressure on parents has grown more intense'. Children cannot be accepted just as they are, but they have to be the objects of 'all kinds of efforts', to correct faults or inadequacies, strengthen abilities and promote good behaviour. Assessment, measurement and intervention are routine tasks, not just of formal systems of education and care but also of parents, as a result of the 'modern discovery of childhood' (2002, p. 90).

This particular 'representation' of childhood as a kind of project whose purpose is to produce the next generation of perfectly adjusted and high-performing adults leads to another important observation; there is a necessary relationship between representation, that is, how children are thought of, and substance, how they are treated and how they live their lives. The ways in which children are portrayed may be idealized, and these may be drawn on selectively, but they are also indicative of underlying attitudes and forms of social organization which must have an impact on the quality and experience of childhood itself. To the extent that they also throw up recurrent motifs, such as the 'parent–child relationship' (Pollock, 1983), they may also be indicative of certain constant features of childhood which are not merely a matter of contemporary social construction.

Childhood and history: change or continuity?

It is worth reflecting again on discourses of continuity and recurrent features, on the one hand, and of repeated and often dramatic change, on the other, in order to draw out the implications of the available evidence and attempt to synthesize theoretical debates on the subject.

In short, historical accounts of childhood pose a fundamental question, namely whether it is fixed and exhibits consistent features over time; or, whether it is contingent and constantly changing depending on the context. This is not simply reducible to the linked question of whether childhood is a 'social construction' or a discrete biological state, since there is also the possibility of interaction between determinate and changeable characteristics, and between the physiological and the social. What are the social consequences of changes in the age of puberty, for example (Laslett, 1977, p. 214)?

Indeed, it seems that we must be very wary of giving way to the desire to achieve certainty. The first reason for this is the partial and necessarily provisional nature of much historical evidence. The possibility of class differentials being under-emphasized is clear, given variations in the means by which records are gathered and documented. Similarly, there may be a tendency to focus on extraordinary events and behaviour at the expense of the mundane features of daily life: 'Ordinary (sic), modest, conscientious men and women did not spend much of their time describing for the benefit of posterity the ordinary conventions which they lived by and their everyday relationships with their children or their servants' (Laslett, 1977, p. 102).

Equally, given the type and nature of evidence available, it is likely that historical accounts of children's lives will focus on representation and forms of social organization at the expense of personal, psychological or physiological dimensions. In other words, we are drawn by much of what is written to *social constructions* rather than what might be seen as underlying changes in the nature of what it is to be a child. Historical sources are often normative too, giving us idealized views of children and their behaviour, often polarized between 'good' and 'evil', as Jenks (1996) observes. Cunningham (2005) extends this argument, suggesting that it is all too easy to generalize from striking sources of evidence, such as a child's sarcophagus from ancient Rome. He cautions that 'it is impossible to be certain that the actuality of the dead child's life was similar in spirit to its representation in sculpture' (Cunningham (2005, p. 21).

Despite such caveats, it will be helpful to summarize what we can infer from histories of childhood. Which features, if any, are constant, and which seem to be subject to change? And what can we conclude about contrasting accounts which emphasize one or the other of these perspectives?

It seems, for example, that there is more or less universal agreement that childhood has always been divided into distinct stages. Even Ariès acknowledges that this idea can be traced back before medieval times, and Jenks (1996, p. 2) refers to the ancient 'Hellenic desire' to understand childhood as a separate phase of human existence. While there is some disagreement over the precise points at which transitions have taken place between these life stages over time, a consistent view that these distinctions are justifiable is apparent.

Following this underlying assumption, there is also broad agreement about the 'developmental' nature of childhood, with a sense of progression across a number of dimensions, usually towards a 'finished' adult status. So, childhood is a time of learning, of psychological and social development, and, of course, of biological growth and change. At the same time, however, there is much less agreement about the extent to which these phases are fixed, either chronologically or substantively, and whether developmental processes themselves have shown any degree of constancy. Laslett (1977), for example, has drawn attention to the likelihood that even biological changes (such as puberty) have been subject to historical variation, and we can be fairly certain that the chances of surviving the early years of one's life have been subject to wide variations in different epochs.

Equally, age divisions which have distinguished children or 'infants' as a specific social category also seem to have varied over time. While it is the modern trend towards institutional education that is associated with a more or less precise grading of children according to their level of attainment (Cunningham, 2005, p. 32), this is not to suggest that this type of understanding only emerged in the post-medieval era. Although the evidence is inevitably less clear, there are linguistic and cultural signs that childhood was seen as a separate life stage much earlier, albeit one that was deficient, and simply 'part of a process towards producing a good citizen' (Cunningham, 2005, p. 23).

Thus, we may also identify another persistent theme, which is a 'deficit model' of children (Jenks, 1996), whether they have been seen either as 'savages' or 'innocents' (Jenks, 1996, p. 73). Childhood has almost always been seen as an incomplete state of being, and as a prelude and preparation stage for the fully realized human state of adulthood. Hence, too, there has been a persistent belief in the family, and the centrality of parents in the nurturing process, a historical depiction with which Pollock (1983) is perhaps most strongly associated, but which is supported to some extent by other earlier material, as Cunningham indicates (2005, p. 24).

We can also infer that the relationship between adults and children has always been unequal, with the patriarchal power associated with the ancient Romans (Cunningham, 2005, p. 22) reflected in similar forms of asymmetrical relationships down the ages, at least until the late twentieth century, when children 'began . . . to acquire rights which placed them more nearly on a par with adults' (Cunningham, 2005, p. 193). At the same point, there appeared to be a 'collapse of adult authority' (Cunningham, 2005, p. 190) reflected in a greater readiness of parents to 'give in' to their children's demands and to be less disciplinarian than their forebears.

Others, though, hold the view that 'generational' fault-lines continue to be significant, both materially and analytically, representing very real and pivotal foci for inequality and structural differences between children and adults (Alancn, 2001, for example).

Nonetheless, as well as being able to identify a number of fairly constant themes in the history of children's lives, there may also be support for those who point rather to the centrality of change, although the extent to which such change is gradual or dramatic is a matter of debate. Those such as Postman (1994) and Ariès (1962), and even Cunningham (2005), who seem to suggest that there are critical turning points may be contrasted to others (Heywood, 2001, for instance) who sketch out a steadier form of evolutionary progress. These sources disagree, too, over whether the state of children's lives is getting better or worse, partly depending on their point of focus. Thus, undoubted improvements in health, education and the physical conditions of many children's lives may be contrasted to the 'loss' of childhood innocence, greater risks of exploitation, abuse and other forms of harm, the McDonaldization (Ritzer, 2004) of childhood, and the reduction in opportunities to play and just to 'be' children.

There is some measure of agreement that certain features of children's lives have been subject to change, such as the points at which they make transitions between one stage and another, the precise nature of parent–child relationships (even Pollock agrees on this), the place and content of education, and the process of physical and personal growth. There is, however, no agreement about the direction or significance of such developments. They are not uniformly seen as beneficial or progressive, as some (de Mause, 1976) appear to believe, and there are considerable differences of opinion about which aspects of change are most important. For some, too, the very direction of change is called into question. Cunningham (2005, p. 204) suggests, for example, that the trend towards differentiation between adults and children 'traced over centuries' by Ariès and others 'has gone into reverse'. As a result, we are beset by a modern-day paradox between the idea of children as 'autonomous' rights-bearing individuals and as a distinct social category whose most important 'right' is 'to be a child' (Cunningham, 2005, p. 205).

The history of childhood offers us some important insights, but also leaves room for a great deal of uncertainty. We can see that there are continuities in the ways in which children's lives are lived and understood but there is also considerable evidence of change over the course of time. The evidence is necessarily incomplete, and sometimes seems to be more suggestive of the history of *ideas about* children, rather than their concrete experiences. Thus, it is important to attempt to integrate knowledge, insights and understanding gleaned from other sources and other disciplines. More light will be shed on the subject when we turn next to consider comparative accounts of childhood 'in space'.

3

Children and Place:

An Inevitable Source of 'Difference'?

What is the effect of 'location' on children's experiences?

Like the previous chapter, this one will consider the question of *difference*, and the extent to which children's lives can (or cannot) be characterized by patterns of diversity. On this occasion, however, I will be addressing this issue across geographical, social and cultural divides, rather than through time. The 'place' of children, in their communities, in the class structure, in their economic roles and in the world is inevitably an important dimension of our wider discussion of identity and difference between them. 'Location', in this sense, is not simply a geographical form of representation, but also tries to capture the various ways in which children as a group may be positioned socially:

> The fact of belonging to the same class, and that of belonging to the same generation or age group, have this in common, that both endow the individuals sharing in them with a common location in the social and historical process, and thereby limit them to a specific range of potential experience.
> (Mannheim, 1952, p. 291)

At first glance, the array of cultures, contexts and forms of social organization known to us favours the thesis that childhood is predominantly determined by local circumstances, relationships and social structures. Although variations between children's lives, treatment and behaviour are not necessarily grounded in social or cultural diversity – since aspects of these could equally be attributable to genetic or environmental differences – the sheer range and variety of social and cultural forms might be taken as offering *prima facie* support for the view that childhood is essentially a constructed and socially specific phenomenon (for example, James *et al.*, 1998, p. 26).

There is a mass of anthropological, geographical and archaeological material available to us, reflecting different aspects of childhood, such as their forms of play, art, processes of education and development and the ways in which children themselves are represented in art and other forms of cultural expression. However, the very richness of the material available generates its own challenges. Unlike historical inquiry, contemporary comparative studies of childhood have a much wider range of material on which to draw, and there are additional means available to gather this, such as direct observation and children's accounts of their own lives. While Ariès (1962) seems to present an obvious starting point for a discussion of the relative merits of childhood histories, in relation to the 'spaces' of childhood, the choice of starting point is much less clear-cut. There are an increasing number of studies relating to individual countries or sometimes comparison groups of relatively small numbers, but relatively few larger 'meta' studies of this kind (eg, Whiting, 1963). As James *et al.* observe, there is a shortage of such material, perhaps understandably in view of the inherent problems in generating compatible data, and translating accurately linguistic and cultural 'meanings' (1998, p. 124).

Even for those anthropologists 'who have perhaps the longest tradition of comparative research in the cross-cultural study of childhood and child-rearing . . . attempts at large-scale cultural comparison are viewed with scepticism or rejected altogether' (1998, p. 124), on methodological grounds. Equally, of course, there are inherent problems in bringing together material from alternative disciplines, and this is an area in which a number of these can claim a legitimate interest, including anthropology, sociology, geography, cultural studies, and even archaeology (Baxter, 2005). All of these, in turn, are open to the criticism of displaying ethnocentric characteristics, something which has been levelled at Western anthropologies, in particular. This raises both methodological and normative questions, for instance, when we come to consider the meanings and interpretations applied to global projects, such as the United Nations Convention on the Rights of the Child, to which virtually all independent states are committed. Nonetheless, collective agreements such as this stand as a valid starting point for evaluating different interpretations and applications of its principles across national boundaries. The ways in which we understand and apply terms such as 'child labour' may well offer instructive comparative lessons, when seeking to relate disparate practices in 'developed' and 'developing' countries, or between 'north', 'south', 'east' and 'west'.

But the challenge of establishing an effective baseline for comparative analysis is further compounded by the possibility of inequalities and diversity *within* nations, between regions, classes, ethnic groups and genders, for instance. Generalizations at country level may be based more on statements of policy, or aggregated statistics, than on a finer understanding of internal divisions. Detailed policy analysis (Bradshaw, 2002, for example) opens up the issue of children's relative poverty and social inequality for individual societies, which again poses challenges for those investigators seeking to identify possible commonalities or universal features of children's lives. Rapid social change within societies also has an impact on our capacity to make effective comparisons, as recent histories and contemporary studies seem to demonstrate. For instance, children's differential access to and use of 'space' are subject to significant influences in the here and now (Moss and Petrie, 2002).

So, we must approach the question of comparative analysis of childhood on spatial or geographical grounds somewhat cautiously. This exploration will begin with a discussion of anthropological sources which have indicated striking differences in children's life experiences across geographical and cultural divides, as well as some possible areas of continuity between these. The chapter will move on to discuss important dimensions of difference, based on the 'location' of children in the various senses of the word, particularly as between communities and societies which can be contrasted according to factors such as their level of development or their cultural and religious practices; and following this, similar questions will be posed in terms of divisions within societies, based on geographical and social variations, such as access to resources and material inequality. Poverty and other forms of inequality are important, and sometimes overlooked, barometers of 'difference' as between childhoods.

Drawing on these observations, the chapter will then go on to discuss the idea of 'work' and the social and economic contributions made by children – activities such as schooling, caring, and undertaking domestic 'labour'. The contrasting conceptual category of children's play will also be considered as a counterpoint to this discussion. To what extent, might the languages and content of children's unsupervised, imaginative and creative activities offer important understandings of their inherent common characteristics? How far, too, do these sites of inquiry confirm or call into question specific differences, such as those determined by gender (see Thorne, 1993, for example)?

Anthropology and the significance of 'culture'

In recent times, there have been a number of important studies of childhood in different cultures, based on attempts to investigate and understand the practices and behaviours of peoples who are seen as less 'developed' (Benedict, 1961, p. 13). This, suggests a kind of ethnocentrism which is highly problematic, and may indicate a tendency to impose externally generated models on 'other' childhoods more generally. Nonetheless, these are important sources, and their insights are telling (see, for example, Whiting and Child, 1953; Benedict, 1961; Whiting, 1963; Erikson, 1965).

Mead (1973) is seen as a seminal contributor to this field of study, notably through her work on aspects of childhood and adolescence in Samoa in the early part of the twentieth century. This, as she later observed, is now a historical as well as an anthropological record of the ways in which children's lives were shaped in a particular society. The approach taken in this and other studies of its kind was to spend time with a village community, to participate in, observe and record the detailed patterns of daily life. Thus, the belief systems, norms, customs and experiences of the members of the community could be described, articulated and analysed. This type of approach also offered the opportunity to make comparisons between societies. Mead somewhat untypically spent some time comparing child-rearing and educational practices in the United States with those in Samoa, often unfavourably. The Samoan way of life, as observed in the 1920s, produced 'stable, well-adjusted, robust individuals' (Mead, 1973, p. 154), while America had 'developed a form of family organization which often cripples the emotional life' (Mead, 1973, p. 148).

The contrasting ways in which play and learning are organized in the two societies are one possible reason for such apparent differences in the experiences and consequences of childhood. Echoing Ariès, Mead (1973, p. 156) found that there was little distinction in Samoa between children's and adults' 'responsibilities' for carrying out household and other tasks. Children appear to have been given age-appropriate responsibilities which would earn them respect and a sense of place in the communal order. By contrast, 'American children [and adults] make a false set of categories, work, play and school; work for adults, play for children's pleasure' (Mead, 1973, p. 157). The analytical (and wider) dangers here are self-evident; children's 'play' is at risk of being imbued with less significance and under-valued compared with adult 'work', or practices geared towards this such as the delivery of children's formal education.

Of course, Samoa is not the only source of comparative evidence of this kind, and other societies, and other investigators have suggested different conclusions. Some, for example, seek evidence of similarity rather than difference: 'child training the world over is in certain important respects identical . . . in that it is found always to be concerned with certain universal problems of behaviour' (Whiting and Child, 1953, p. 63). For these authors, influenced by functionalism, the common features of 'the human infant' and the common challenges of 'enforcing conformity' outweigh the observable differences in approaches to achieve these ends, even though these differences may be quite wide, such as variations in the age of weaning (Whiting and Child, 1953, p. 70).

Benedict, on the other hand, is inclined to minimize the significance of biologically determined 'universal traits' (1961, p. 13), which are 'few'. In this sense, the varying forms of social and cultural organization are more important factors than the supposedly common underlying drivers of 'maintenance' and conformity (Whiting and Child, 1953, p. 310).

Erikson (1965, p. 163) likewise observed substantial contrasts between the 'worlds' of the Yurok and Sioux peoples. The former society was found to be essentially self-contained and passive, while the latter was more aggressive and 'vigorously centrifugal'. Erikson argues that these contrasting societal characteristics find their parallels in differing approaches to child-rearing and education. From the very early days of a child's life, differential patterns of breast-feeding and weaning could be identified which were believed to reflect the expectations and roles to be fulfilled in each culture, with Sioux mothers arousing a 'hunter's ferocity' in their young (Erikson, 1965, p. 124), while self-control and restraint were promoted through the disciplines imposed at mealtimes (Erikson, 1965, p. 160) among the Yurok.

There is a tendency within much anthropological writing to apply deterministic psychological concepts to the processes and outcomes of child-rearing practices, with the implication that much of the child's character and temperament is shaped by the predominant influences and patterns of behaviour associated with a particular form of social organization. The greater 'simplicity' of traditional societies (Benedict, 1961, p. 13) might account in part for the relative ease with which they appear to have been able to socialize children into established patterns of behaviour, in contrast to the more individualized (Erikson, 1965, p. 293), complex and challenging (Mead, 1973, p. 168) forms of modern (and post-modern?) Western society. This hypothesis echoes Durkheim's (1947) distinction between 'mechanistic' and 'organic' societies.

Although the cultures which are represented in much anthropological study may be consistently 'simple' in this analytical sense, they, and by implication their 'childhoods', are by no means uniform, as Benedict notes (1961, p. 171). In the same way as historical distinctions have been made between 'Apollonian' and 'Dionysian' representations of children (Jenks, 1996), she contrasts entire cultures. Indeed, difference is the prevailing motif:

> The cultural pattern of any civilization makes use of a certain segment of the great arc of potential human purposes and motivations . . . The great arc along which all the possible human behaviours are distributed is far too immense and too full of contradictions for any one culture to utilize even any considerable portion of it. Selection is the first requirement.
>
> (Benedict, 1961, p. 171)

In one sense, then, anthropology steers us towards a view of societies and their constituent members as highly diverse, in which children's lives and experiences can be shown to differ widely, and which lead to measurable differences of personality and attitude (Whiting and Child, 1953). On the other hand, the very fact that these differences reflect reputed uniformities *within* societies might suggest that there are certain predictable underlying human qualities and processes which give rise to a degree of commonality. In other words, contextual differences and variable social forms are overlaid on, and interact with, patterns of growth and development which demonstrate certain regularities irrespective of the context. Divergent outcomes do not necessarily reflect huge variations in the raw material of childhood, but rather its 'plasticity' and susceptibility to external influences and constraints. Benedict, for example, describes the varying forms of behaviour manifested by different communities which might be taken to indicate the presence of mental health problems according to certain contemporary individualized and pathological behavioural models; however, these 'idiosyncrasies' are generalized in some societies, and reflect the 'behaviour dictated' by specific social norms, which is then manifested in light of these normative expectations (1961, p. 183). Underlying their situated conformity, then, it appears that: 'Most people are shaped to the form of the culture because of the enormous malleability of their original endowment. They are plastic to the moulding force of the society into which they are born' (Benedict, 1961, p. 183).

Does this suggest some *essential* quality present (or indeed, absent) in all children? It does seem to imply a *tabula rasa* conceptualization of children, who are seen as infinitely susceptible to adult influence and shaping, an assumption which has increasingly been questioned by those who see children as active participants in constructing their own childhoods (Punch, 2000, for example). This rather passive and pliable view of children is not straightforwardly reflected in the anthropological work of Mead (1973) or Erikson (1995) who, in different ways, draw attention to children's distinctive characteristics and active role in making sense of and shaping their own lives. Erikson views this kind of development as culturally specific, but nonetheless does identify a constructive role for children: 'In our country [the USA], probably more than in any other large country, the child is the adult's partner . . . wherever childhood provides a status of its own, a sense of identity, fraternal conscience, and tolerance results' (1965, p. 377). This again parallels the Durkheimian distinction between relatively simple and mechanistic cultural forms and those found in modern, complex societies, although it also appears to be based on a politically founded distinction between the USA of the 1950s/1960s and the 'inhumanity of colossal machine organization' associated with the Communist bloc. For Durkheim (1947), of course, the transition from 'mechanical' to 'organic' forms of social solidarity represented a form of evolutionary progress, which has precipitated the emergence of more complex and flexible relationships and structures. In the latter, childhood may be expected to be less predictable and rigidly organized, and more a matter of negotiation, in the way that Erikson (but not Mead, 1973) suggests. Once again, the notion of progress and radical distinctions between social forms echoes those historical accounts which tend to distinguish modern childhood from previous eras. While these distinctions can sometimes be pejorative, they also seem to suggest that 'childhoods' are highly specific, and that their common features are of less significance than those cultural and contextual factors which set them apart.

Ironically, this perception has been further strengthened as anthropological accounts themselves have sought to correct earlier ethnocentric tendencies and focus more closely on children's lives in context, where 'children devise ways to counteract adults' power and control over their lives' (Punch, 2000, p. 48). Based on these analytical developments, we could begin to hypothesize a historical trajectory which links the emergence of childhood to a specific (modern) era (and Westernized) social form, and which has also begun to prefigure the 'end' of childhood as post-modern developments start to erode inter-generational distinctions (see Chapter 2).

Cultures and contexts: the importance of 'place'

While anthropology has largely concentrated on differences between rather than within societies, more recently attention has turned to other potential cross-cutting dividing lines, such as those of geography, class, culture and religion. Interest, too, has shifted to a different set of dynamics, with the focus not being so much on how entire societies organize themselves, but on the ways in which broad global influences and changes interact with children's lives in their localities (Hengst, 2005, for example). In this sense, the 'spaces' occupied by children are necessarily permeated and circumscribed by external influences, which have consequences for the particular experiences of children individually and collectively. Hengst argues, following Erikson, that contemporary influences such as markets and the media transcend boundaries and geographical distance, and that: 'The predominant experience of everyday life in the modern global world is that locally situated life worlds are penetrated by remote events, relationships and processes' (2005, p. 24). In this sense, childhood in the present day can be said to be qualitatively different from its historical and distant forms. Children's worlds appear to be much less 'closed', too, in the sense that the influences which impact on them are less likely to be controlled or limited by those around them. Families and communities may act as mediators, but they are increasingly unable to act as censors of messages from outside: 'Children are confronted with processes of socio-cultural change . . . that are not filtered in any decisive way by' parental or other adult controls (Hengst, 2005, p. 25).

Despite the globalization of childhood in this way, local contexts, the people around them and the ways in which external influences are mediated remain important, especially in determining the extent

to which children and those around them deal with conflict and
'mixed messages'. This is made clear for us in concrete form through
the experience of Asian children in Britain, for example (Bhatti,
1999). This detailed account of schoolchildren negotiating competing influences and expectations helps to illustrate the tensions
inherent in establishing a distinctive identity in a very specific set of
circumstances. The children in the study 'could remember not being
able to speak English fluently' (Bhatti, 1999, p. 104), for example,
but also recognized that they would need to learn the language to
be able to do their school work. As they became competent, they
began to speak English at home when conversing with brothers and
sisters. But their parents objected to this because they felt it threatened to 'take them away from their cultural and linguistic heritage'
(Bhatti, 1999, p. 105). As a result, the children learned to compromise
'by speaking to their parents in Hindi, Punjabi, Urdu or Malayalam
but to their brothers and sisters in English' (Bhatti, 1999, p. 105). In
fact, the children's sense of identity did not appear to be significantly
disrupted by this process, because in other respects they remained
clearly committed to their distinctive religious and cultural heritages.
Thus, they reported feeling uncomfortable in Christian religious
assemblies in school: 'I closed my eyes and said my own prayer words'
(Qasim, quoted in Bhatti, 1999, p. 113). The teachings offered by
their own religious authorities outside school were thus more, rather
than less, significant to them.

Nonetheless, there were tensions associated with children's task of
finding a place in a world which was clearly different from that of
their parents and their traditions. Parents were uncomfortable with
their children creating links with peers from other religious or cultural backgrounds (Bhatti, 1999, p. 118). In effect, these children
were increasingly finding themselves negotiating a complex array
of expectations and identities at a number of 'levels' (Bhatti, 1999,
p. 119). For some these complexities reverberated in a sense of being
'out of place': 'Don't help does it, being Paki around here' (Nazim,
quoted in Bhatti, 1999, p. 118). Thus, as the author observes, for this
boy and his peers, 'being Pakistani got mixed up with being Muslim
which was mixed up with racism' (Bhatti, 1999, p. 118). This sense of
discontinuity was illustrated graphically in young people's reflections
on visits 'back home', where their own sense of disadvantage in relation to their white peers was entirely at odds with family members'
pride in their and their parents' achievements (Bhatti, 1999, p. 123).

A rather different illustration of the interaction between children
in their localities and external (global?) influences is provided by

Kong (2000), in her account of children's attitudes to and experience of the increasingly urbanized environment of Singapore. The rapid growth of a city landscape, associated with other social changes, appears to have resulted in a paradoxical destruction of green areas alongside the construction of 'managed' recreational spaces in the city, and this in turn is reflected in children's perceptions and experiences (Kong, 2000, p. 262). For some, the de-naturing of their environment was mirrored in their own words, with expressions of 'dislike for the heat of the sun and fear of water' or a dismissive response to the sensory possibilities of flowers: 'I can't smell anything. I go to the gardens or whatever, but I can't smell anything' ('Robert', quoted in Kong, 2000, p. 262).

For some of these children, though, the loss of their connections with the natural world was resisted. Despite their wishes, though, some parents were also reluctant to let them loose in unknown territory, where risk and danger might lurk. These fears appeared to transmit themselves in various ways to children, so that their experiences and attitudes came into alignment. Children living in high-rise settings 'not only did not express care and love for nature, but feared touching or going near even domestic animals' (Kong, 2000, p. 266). Despite some contrary views, apparently expressed by those whose backgrounds were not so strongly urbanized, the fear expressed in this case is that socialization works only too well, and 'that children become predisposed in their older years to adopt the rationality of the state when confronted with situations in which a development priority conflicts with the needs of wildlife and greenery' (Kong, 2000, p. 268).

The highly specific nature of the relationship between children, their communities and their 'places' is also noted elsewhere (for example, Valentine, 2004). Differences across generations, between classes and in environmental settings are all noted as significant in shaping children's experiences of the spaces around them, with consequent implications for the way in which 'children develop physically, mentally and socially' (Valentine, 2004, p. 80). Class, for example, has implications not only for the quantity of opportunities to participate in a range of activities, but also the *quality* of the experiences gained, although this may not always operate in predictable fashion:

> It is the children from lone parent households whose play is more independent and 'public' focused, and who therefore may well have the richest environmental experiences ... creating their own rich microcultures and geographies out of stark and harsh landscapes.
>
> (Valentine, 2004, p. 80)

Not only do these differences produce variations in childhoods as they are lived, but they may also have more substantial consequences for the future and for their life trajectories, as the positive benefits of more varied environmental encounters for (lower-income) lone parent families are offset by the 'enhanced "cultural capital" acquired by "middle class" children when they participate in institutional activities' (Valentine, 2004, p. 81).

Here we see evidence of the interactive nature of children's relationship with the world around them; the impact of external influences on them is mirrored by their active role in making sense of these influences and drawing on them to reinvent their worlds, and at the same time to develop their self–perceptions and sense of place within the social order.

The place of work in shaping children's lives

The issues of children's 'social location' (Mannheim, 1952) are significant, too, when we move on to consider the relationship of children to paid and unpaid work, and how this is played out in different contexts. This is an area of investigation which has received substantial recent attention, often focusing on the exploitation of children (Qvortrup, 2005). Just as Mead (1973) identified productive work as being a communal expectation of children from a very early age, so Zelizer (2005) notes that their productive contributions to households, communities and the economic sphere have been and remain substantial. Importantly, Zelizer questions some of the implicit (common sense?) assumptions which are sometimes made to distinguish between 'work' and other productive activities carries out by children (such as: 'Housework, barter, volunteering, *pro bono* service, unpaid caring, family enterprises', 2005, p. 186). As a consequence of the variations observed in practice; 'children's work . . . varies systematically and dramatically from one setting to another' (2005, p. 187). Indeed, their contribution might vary significantly *within* settings, incorporating 'care work' and translation on behalf of their parents as well as assisting with the family business in immigrant communities. Although distinctions may be made between paid and unpaid work from other perspectives, Zelizer (2005, p. 194) notes that the children she observed 'did not remember their business involvement as distinctive training, but rather as a "natural" part of growing up . . . they treated the payments they received from their parents not as standard wages but as a perk', although some also 'resisted' some of their families' demands.

In this way, children's 'work' appears to have represented (for them) an extension of their 'natural' roles and responsibilities within the family. Developing this theme further, Zelizer also suggests that recognizing the 'variety' of such activities should also 'alert us' to the differences in the ways in which children's work is understood and experienced, depending rather on the context than the content:

> The very same child effort ... qualifies as acceptable or unacceptable depending on whether it produces benefits for participants in the social interactions the effort involves, who it produces those benefits for, and with what consequences for the children themselves.
>
> (Zelizer, 2005, p. 195)

So, the relationship of the 'child' to 'labour' does vary depending on the time and place (see Chapter 6). As market forces take an increasing hold over social life in developed countries, the relationship between children and the economic sphere is changing (Lavalette, 2005), and exploitative and dangerous paid work outside the family is reported to be an increasingly common experience for them (p. 157). In fact, it is part of the rationale for employing children that they should be 'cheap' and willing to work in difficult and demanding conditions. While some might argue that there is an offsetting benefit to young people in gaining an adult perspective, a degree of financial autonomy and a sense of responsibility, this does not compensate for the negative consequences of being exploited by 'unscrupulous employers' and exposed to the risks arising from 'inadequate regulation' (Lavalette, 2005, p. 162). Thus: 'Working children in Britain ... are overwhelmingly the victims of these processes, not their beneficiaries . Work is not an example of 'liberation' but of 'adulterization' (Lavalette, 2005, p. 163).

However, the relationship between children and the economy is subject to substantial geographical variations, and that those who view this simply from a Western perspective may be 'naïve about the role of work in some children's lives' (John, 2003, p. 176). Children's relationship to paid work in poorer countries, for example, is likely to be complex (Nieuwenhuys, 2005, p. 168), with 'non-wage labour' often being the norm in the South. Whether this is exploitative or not, and how it affects children themselves, is not simply a matter of whether or not this is paid work, but depends on an important distinction 'between what children do (children's work) and the subjects of' economic exchange '(working children)' (Nieuwenhuys, 2005, p. 169). Children are undoubtedly exploited and exposed to harm in the paid work that they do, but 'they are also active participants if not social agents in their own right'. Listening to their own accounts helps to illustrate how they make sense of and negotiate their own roles and relationships within complex patterns of social responsibilities and economic imperatives: 'To work is a natural thing to do. Our friends do it. My parents work. My brothers work so why shouldn't I work? Even schooling is not an excuse not to work' (Working child in the Philippines, quoted in Woodhead and Faulkner, 2008, p. 33).

Young people 'stressed the importance of finding ways of earning a living' (John, 2003, p. 177), while children working in the 'sex industry' and thereby being exploited and abused in Thailand also account for this in terms of meeting their family obligations (Nieuwenhuys, 2005, p. 168).

In these examples, and in others, it seems that a contradictory process is taking place. According to Nieuwenhuys, children have limited capacity to exercise choice and control, not necessarily on purely economic grounds, but also because 'exchange between generations is rarely symmetrical' (Nieuwenhuys, 2005, p. 170). This is especially the case for children in poorer settings, whether in the North or South, which leads to another distinction between 'nurtured' and 'nurturing' childhoods – that is, between those which create economic goods and those which benefit from this output. As already acknowledged, though, unequal relationships and oppressive demands may be experienced across social divisions and in a wider range of settings – young carers, for example, may face huge demands to take adult responsibilities while also 'being children' (Becker *et al.*, 1998).

At the same time, children in exploitative circumstances will also be taking an active role, making sense of and attempting to transform their activities, within the network of existing relationships and social structures around them. The notion of intergenerational power imbalances suggests a greater degree of commonality in children's lives than might be expected, given the great range of contexts and pressures which they will experience. Perhaps we should pay closer attention to and recognize the value of their own engagement with challenging circumstances:

> Rather than seeing in them either broken lives or virtuous sons and daughters, working children who have experienced prostitution, drug trafficking, war and violence should be acknowledged for having precious real-life knowledge that will help them face whatever new difficulties come their way later in life.
>
> (Nieuwenhuys, 2005, p. 181)

At the risk of idealizing damaging experiences for children and young people, this observation draws attention to an important theme which we should remain aware of, and this is their capacity to assimilate, make sense of and respond to external influences and demands.

For some (John, 2003, p. 190), it is the very diversity of children's 'present forces' which means that this active, productive process will in turn lead to such diverse outcomes 'that a universal view of what childhood and children are about is inappropriate'. It might, of course, be suggested on the contrary that it is the very commonality of children's capacity for resistance, their sense-making and constructive engagement with their varying circumstances which suggest a degree of uniformity in their social and psychological functioning. How else, for instance would they 'in troubled times ... develop a sense of morality and some sense of moral order?' (John, 2003, p. 191)

Play and creativity: making the world

Children's play has offered another lens through which differences (and similarities) have been observed, not least because their opportunities for self-determination and independent expression are believed to be captured most effectively through analysing the ways in which they occupy their unstructured time and 'free' spaces. This is particularly helpful in light of the preceding discussion because it enables us to reflect on those aspects of childhood which are not shaped by others explicitly or directly, but where children themselves organize and construct their own activities, rules, norms, social structures and realities. Play is sometimes viewed disparagingly, and as somehow less significant than 'work', which may include meeting family and household responsibilities, or formal education. The apparent lack of structure and purpose associated with play may lead to a tendency to devalue it from an adult perspective, and to overlook what it represents in children's lives, of value in its own right, but also a significant site of learning and social development. In Western cultures, this may be reflected in the kind of distinctions sometimes made between children's 'care' in the early years and education which is expected to take place subsequently in structured settings (schools) and according to prescribed learning pathways (curricula). On one level, this may be about socialization and state control, primarily exerted 'through schools' (Moss and Petrie, 2002, p. 98), but it also reflects a distinction between aspects of childhood which misrepresents the currents of lived experience: 'we hope we have suggested the inadequacy of our current conceptualization of work with children as either education or care' (Moss and Petrie, 2002, p. 99). Children's lives are, according to this analysis, about much more than the contexts and modes by which adults choose to interact with them. Children's 'play' is very often the medium for an active process of exploration, learning and achievement. It is something which they control, and where they determine the rules and content of activities away from adult oversight or interference. As Corsaro has observed, children themselves distinguish very clearly between 'play' and 'planned activities like soccer and piano practice' (1997, p. 38), which are structured for them and leave little space for them to take the initiative or be independently creative.

In fact, there appear to be some important processes taking place in those settings where children organize and carry out their own 'play' activities. For instance, Corsaro contrasts the formal school settings where 'cross-gender interaction' is promoted, and the informal 'peer-dominated' places where gender difference is negotiated and addressed. In these peer-initiated 'activities and routines, girls and boys try to make sense of and deal with ambiguities and concerns related to gender differences and relations. Many of these activities involve conflict, disputes, and teasing' (1997, p. 182). Chasing games epitomize this kind of process, and also illustrate the importance of children's ability to control and use their own 'space':

> Safety zones are more than geographical spaces to which children flee to escape threatening agents. For preadolescents, the areas serve as both physical and psychological havens where the children reflect on and talk about the meaning of their experiences. In this way, the preadolescents have more direct control over the meaning of play and collectively create shared histories of events.
>
> (1997, p. 183)

Some important observations can be made here about children's use of their own autonomous environments to carry out some significant 'work' of their own. They appear to have been engaged in processes of socialization, relationship-building, gender definition and identity creation, in their own right, through what sometimes might be belittled as mere 'play'.

Thorne (1993) has identified patterns to such behaviour, whereby gender stereotypes are often developed and supported. 'Borderwork' is her term for the sort of activity where girls and boys negotiate

and develop understandings and identities in a context of acknowledged 'gender difference' (Corsaro, 1997, p. 184). However, these differences are not uniform, and both girls and boys act in ways which
are contrary to established stereotypical assumptions. Girls would
sometimes invade boys' space, contrary to the norm, and some boys
would be less inclined to act provocatively towards girls than others.
In this instance, then, children are not simply seen to be reproducing
established norms of behaviour and mutual interaction, but they are
actively negotiating and renegotiating these, through the medium of
unstructured play. It seems as if there is something significant about
the opportunity to interact autonomously with peers in unsupervised settings, which leads to different outcomes than when adults
are around and, in all likelihood, setting the rules. Children have
been recognized as 'inventive' (Bruner *et al.*, 1976), perhaps more so
than adults, so having the chance to exercise their own creativity is
important to them.

It is unfortunate, then, in Valentine's view that the opportunities
children have for unstructured activities are declining, in what she
terms a 'Retreat from the Street' (2004, p. 69). Increasing parental
concern and changing contemporary patterns of behaviour (such as
greater car use) appear to have resulted in a more restrictive approach
to 'children's independent use of outdoor space'. The place of disorganized and 'free' play has been taken up by a greater reliance on
planned and managed 'adult-led activities' (2004, p. 70). This restructuring of 'generational' relationships might be seen in one sense as a
reassertion of adult authority and control, while, at the same time, it
is also arguable that it is no more than a legitimate and considered
response to new forms of 'vulnerability' to which children are now
believed to be exposed.

The 'privatization' of play also has implications for the use and
distribution of public play spaces, and the social distribution of different forms of play among children, echoing our earlier observations on changing patterns of activity among children in Singapore
(Kong, 2000).

This loss of independent play opportunities is a particular feature of 'contemporary western society' as epitomized by New York
(Valentine, 2004, p. 73) and this is believed to run counter both to
children's best interests and their aspirations (Valentine, 2004, p. 75).
It is the very 'flexibility' of unpredictable and unmanaged environments, for example, that ensures that 'meanings are open to manipulation, as key qualities of play that shape how the self develops'

(Valentine, 2004, p. 76). Mapping this sort of trend can lead to the sort of polarized view discussed in the previous chapter, whereby it is possible to hark back to a 'golden age' of childhood (Poster, 1979) before modernity took hold. But we must be cautious about over-generalizing. We should, too, be careful about idealizing children's independent play as always being collaborative and constructive, when it may also be the context for bullying, hurt and distress.

What this analysis does suggest is that there is a qualitative difference between children's experience and use of unstructured space (and time) and that which is organized for them, in or outside the home and at school. Interestingly, Corsaro (1997) associates this with developmental discourses, suggesting that the opportunity to interact in this sort of way is particularly significant for 'preadolescent children' (1997, p. 186), precisely because it is a time of 'struggle' when identities are emerging and becoming stabilized, and where they need an 'arena for dealing with uncertainties of an increasingly complex world' (1997, p. 188). Even though clear differences may be identified across class (Valentine, 2004) and ethnic groups, these experiences still appear to be offering the same sort of facility to children at this age, to test out mutual relationships and perceptions and to establish their own rules of behaviour and interaction. At the same time, of course, these activities cannot be seen as entirely independent or free of adult influence, and, as in the case of gender roles, children are also likely to be responding to and mediating pre-existing patterns of belief and social organization through their play 'work'.

Children's contexts: different places but common experiences?

This chapter has highlighted differences in the lives of children's, dependent on geographical and social 'location', including variations of 'place' and other differentiating factors, such as class, ethnicity, culture and gender. However, there are a number of other significant issues raised by this brief excursion across a number of disciplinary terrains. Anthropology, for instance, illustrates demonstrable differences in societies' attitudes and practices towards children; but at the same time, it has tended to imply a degree of uniformity in the ways in which children are socialized in each setting. Implicit in this perspective is embedded an assumption that there are discernible material differences in culture, social structure and environment, but that in essentially 'mechanistic' societies (Durkheim, 1947) children are

socialized into the appropriate norms and roles to be able to participate and contribute effectively in the specific context in which they
find themselves.

While anthropologists have more recently adopted a more critical
and child-centred tone, this changing mood is also apparent in other
disciplinary accounts of changes in 'modern' societies, and the ways
in which socialization processes have become more fragmented and
contradictory (Valentine, 2004, for example). As attention has turned
to the ways in which children make sense of their contexts and the
expectations of them, it has also become clear that they are engaged
in an active process of interpretation and construction of their own
social worlds and sets of meanings (Corsaro, 1997; Moss and Petrie,
2002), epitomized in the lives of street children, who are 'invisible' to
mainstream society (Ennew, 2002, p. 389).

As I have suggested elsewhere (Smith, 2000a), these observations
suggest that we need a processual frame of reference for understanding the processes by which children's lives take the forms that they
do. They must be seen as simultaneously (and interactively) 'consumers', or recipients of external influences; interpreters, who analyse and
make sense of these messages; and, creative actors who draw on these
understandings to construct and engage with their own 'childhoods'.
In this way, something of the dynamic relationship between concrete
external influences and individual characteristics, perceptions and
circumstances can be captured. It helps, in turn, to explain the differences observed by Mead (1973) in the lives and relationships of
girls and young women in Samoa. Rather than following predictable, functionalist, life trajectories, they were observed to demonstrate
independently the capacity to make sense of their cultural norms and
roles and, indeed, to renegotiate and adapt these to their own ends
and aspirations.

4

The Search for Common Ground in Accounts of Childhood

The possibility of developmental explanations

In the previous chapters, the focus was very much on aspects of the contextual circumstances which have shaped children's lives across different times and places. These reflections point towards the conclusion that childhood is a very diverse phenomenon, which is defined and experienced according to a range of contingent influences. These influences appear to operate externally to the child, almost irrespective of the internal processes and mechanisms which may shape her/ his growth and development. This chapter, by contrast, will shift the focus from wide-ranging studies of children's experiences in a variety of settings to the more restricted terrain of the processes and characteristics operating *within* and between children individually and interpersonally. It is here that attempts have been made to explore and account for physical, biological, psychological and micro-social change as it impacts on children and is reflected in changing personal attributes and behavioural characteristics. Work based on this kind of disciplinary perspective has tended to seek out evidence of uniformity and regularity in the patterns of children's lives, and to seek explanations in terms of internal processes which are measurable and predictable (Turmel, 2008), but this is not always the case, as recent neurological research indicates.

Approaches of this kind are seen as the antithesis of those which characterize childhood as a fluid, multi-faceted and historicized entity. Their proponents have been criticized for their deterministic and relatively restricted view of childhood, which does not recognize the importance of social interaction, or children's own agency. Recent sociologies (and psychologies; Morss, 1995) of childhood have emphasized its socially constructed character, and the place of children as deliberative contributors to this process. While the articulation of these polarized positions is problematic, it is at the same time helpful, to the extent that it opens up new areas of investigation, and raises specific possibilities of developing new and productive syntheses.

This chapter will proceed by exploring the opposing strands of inquiry and analysis identified here which can be categorized, if rather simplistically, under two headings:

> *Developmental approaches* (usually, but not always associated with biological and psychological perspectives) which emphasize the programmed and sequential qualities of cognitive, emotional and behavioural development through childhood. These approaches see these processes as susceptible to explanation in terms of the maturation of the brain and the body, and concomitant patterns of growth in capacity for social learning (for example, Smith *et al.*, 2003; Blakemore and Frith, 2005). Here general differences between individuals of different ages (or 'stages') are emphasized, as well as features which are consistent among children (such as their heightened aptitude for learning). These arguments point towards the conclusion that there are certain physiological and psychological factors which distinguish childhood as a life stage.

> *Constructionist perspectives* which tend, on the other hand, to conceptualize and explain children's experiences and actions as the product of complex interactive (and primarily social) processes which give rise to enormous variations in the ways in which 'childhoods' are lived and experienced (see, for example, James *et al.*, 1998; Robinson, 2007). This way of approaching the subject sees childhood more as a kind of creative project, in which adults (parents and teachers, for instance) and children themselves are engaged in an active process of defining mutual expectations and shaping patterns of behaviour interactively. Children's perceptions

of what is 'real' are accorded as much validity as any other's. Differences between children are emphasized, as are their distinct generational interests and modes of expression. Commonalities in child development become less significant than diverse and situated experiences according to this frame of reference.

In seeking to elaborate and explore these positions, the aim will be to create a basis for identifying common ground as well as points of divergence. The appearance of irreconcilability may conceal opportunities for dialogue. It will be argued that, rather than being mutually exclusive, these positions may instead be complementary and, to some extent, interdependent – they actually 'need' each other if a fuller understanding of childhood is to be achieved. This is not just a debating point in the sense that an argument needs an opposing position to acquire substance and meaning; it is also of significance to the extent that it begins to sketch out an iterative model of childhood, which depends on a close and continuous interaction between uniform features of growth and change and the very diverse individuals in very diverse settings where these are played out.

The biology of child development

In the present era, it appears that we are gaining powerful and persuasive insights into the ways in which humans grow and develop through the application of increasingly sophisticated natural scientific techniques, such as brain imaging (Tracey, 2005). However, we should be careful not to over-estimate the scale of these achievements, partly because they have only succeeded so far in demonstrating just how complex the subject is. The sheer number of genes we share and the potential for interaction between them suggest that definitive explanations will be difficult to obtain (Smith *et al.*, 2003, p. 26). The argument that genetic influences shape children's development tends to be supported by evidence from specific types of studies, such as those focusing on twins, or on 'chromosomal abnormalities' (Smithe *et al.*, 2003, p. 31). Thus, genetic similarities have an obvious influence on appearance and physical likeness. Equally, genetic changes are associated with specific 'conditions' such as Down's syndrome (Smith *et al.*, 2003, p. 31). Because genes 'determine the first stages in cell growth and differentiation in the body and in the brain' (Smith *et al.*, 2003, p. 33), it may be assumed that they provide a fundamental basis not just to physiological characteristics but also to behaviour. Genetic 'instructions' of this kind are believed to take two separate forms; they prescribe 'instinctive' behaviour which is inbuilt in all animal species, while at the same time they also determine the course of behavioural 'maturation' (Smith *et al.*, 2003, p. 34), whereby physical development is matched by the emergence of distinct patterns of behaviour.

It might be thought that just as biological and genetic factors determine both the physical form and development of human infants, these are paralleled by the developing shape and structure of the brain. In other words, it is simply another element of the physical whole, which is formed and grows in the same way as any other part of the anatomy. Nonetheless, the brain is an incredibly complex organ, comprising about 100 billion cells, and the relationship between its composition and characteristics and mental processes is similarly difficult to specify with any degree of certainty.

Recent scientific activity has focused on the use of techniques to identify what is going on within the brain which are necessarily constrained by the need to avoid invasive methods (Blakemore and Frith, 2005). These techniques are capable of measuring electrical and magnetic activity and 'imaging' what is going on in different regions of the brain (Blakemore and Frith, 2005, p. 14). It has thus become possible to identify processes of change and development within the brain from the point of birth (and even before that).

In the early stages of a child's life, there is a period of 'dramatic' change in the structure and organization of the brain. Significantly, the number of cells in certain regions of the brain increases rapidly following birth, as does the number of 'connections' between cells. In fact:

> the number of connections in a baby's brain greatly exceeds adult levels. Many of these excess connections have to be cut back and this cutting back, or *pruning*, is just as important a part of development as is the initial growth of connections.
>
> (Blakemore and Frith, 2005, p. 18)

Interestingly, then, the process of 'development' in the early stages of human life is not simply one of linear changes or generalized increases in capacity, but also a reduction in the range and complexity of the connections in the 'wiring' of the brain.

Much of the research in this area up to now has been carried out on animals, and thus ideas about the exact nature of neurological changes in children are based on a degree of assumption and inference. Nonetheless, in relation to the extent and timing of what are termed 'sensitive periods', which determine and shape development (Blakemore and Frith, 2005, p. 26), there is some evidence that there are a number of commonalities between children. For instance, the capacity to recognize and distinguish between faces and voices occurs very early for most babies, within days of birth. Subsequently, however, the ability to distinguish between faces becomes more specialized, and 'fine tuned' (Blakemore and Frith, 2005, p. 28), so that, for example, after the age of six months babies actually lose some of their ability to tell the difference between animal faces, while their capacity to identify human faces improves. Blakemore and Frith argue that this process of refinement of shills and aptitudes is part of a specialization process, which concentrates abilities in areas where they will be needed, albeit at the expense of certain other, less functional, competencies, such as the ability to distinguish between monkeys' faces. Children who do not undergo these 'standard' processes of development may experience certain longer-term consequences, they suggest, as in the case of those who have cataracts removed, whose subsequent visual perception is 'not quite normal' (Blakemore and Frith, 2005, p. 29).

The emergence of techniques such as 'brain imaging' has enabled scientists to gain a much clearer understanding of changes in structure and functioning of the brain in recent years (Casey *et al.*, 2005), leading to a greater degree of certainty about the timing and sequencing of neurological 'maturation'. Parts of the brain associated with different functional processes can be observed to change at variable rates and at different points in the life cycle, extending beyond adolescence well into adulthood. There is a definite order about these processes with regions of the brain associated with 'motor and sensory' systems maturing earliest, followed by those linked with 'basic language' and 'spatial attention' skills. Higher-order functions which integrate and develop these specific aptitudes are acquired subsequently.

Differential explanations for these changes may be offered, however: 'The [brain] region-specific differences in activation with age that have been reported could reflect maturation, but might also reflect simple performance differences' (Casey *et al.*, 2005, p. 107). Thus, it may be experience rather than any specific physiological difference which accounts for variations in behaviour and aptitude between children and adults when carrying out similar tasks. On the other hand, fMRI (functional magnetic resonance imaging) techniques have been able to demonstrate distinct patterns of brain activity suggesting both maturational and performance components to changing response patterns in experimental settings

(Casey *et al.*, 2005, p. 107). There do seem, therefore, to be structural and functional differences between children's and adults' brains, which are indicative of physical maturational processes as well as those deriving from experience and environmental influences.

This observation is supported by other evidence of change in the size and composition of the brain with age (Lenroot and Giedd, 2006). As the brain grows, so variations can be observed in the relative volume of specific elements, such as grey and white matter. Further complexity is generated by the differences observed between males and females, both in size and development of specific areas of the brain (Lenroot and Giedd, 2006, p. 723). Additionally, areas associated with specific functions, 'mature' at different rates:

> Notably, late to reach adult levels of cortical thickness is the dorosolateral prefrontal cortex, involved in circuitry subserving control of impulses, judgement, and decision-making. The implications of late maturation of this area have entered educational, social, political and judicial discourse in matters ranging from whether minors are cognitively mature enough to qualify for the death penalty to the age at which teenagers should be allowed to drive.
>
> (Lenroot and Giedd, 2006, p. 723)

In light of this, it is interesting that those who argue for the recognition of children as autonomous rights-bearing citizens also tend to advance the argument that these rights should be realized in the form of special treatment, and non-application of the full force of adult criminal law in the event of any wrongdoing. Such arguments can only achieve internal consistency if they are based on the proposition that children and young people are a special case, by virtue of their limited experience and physical incompleteness.

Notwithstanding the risks that a 'deficit' model of childhood may be inferred from some interpretations of the evidence, empirical observations increasingly do seem to suggest that there may be some physiological substance to the notion that childhood is a distinctive state, and should be treated as such. The point is also made, though, that changes over time in the structure and functioning of the brain are not 'linear', and that therefore straightforward conceptualizations of child development are too simplistic.

While there appear to be predictable paths of change in the structure and functioning of the brain with age, there are also discernible differences which must be accounted for in the attempt to identify potential causal factors associated with the specific forms that 'maturation' takes. A number of studies have suggested that there is a connection between genetic heritage, brain structure and other characteristics, such as intelligence (Thompson *et al.*, 2001; Peper *et al.*, 2007); and certain specific genes have been reported as being associated with particular behavioural outcomes, such as 'disorganized attachment' (Smith *et al.*, 2003, p. 31).

The biological sciences are able to identify specific patterns of maturation and development which can be associated with 'sensitive periods' (Blakemore and Frith, 2005, p. 27), while at the same time, differences in brain characteristics and consequently behaviour are believed to be associated with genetic variations. Scientists have been careful, though, to distinguish between genetic and environmental influences (Peper *et al.*, 2007, p. 469), to the extent that these are reported to have more or less dominant influences on different areas of the brain. However, the inherent limitations of this kind of study are acknowledged, such as the small and specialized (mainly twin studies) nature of the samples, and 'the lack of power to test for the influence of common environment' (Peper *et al.*, 2007, p. 470). Dowker (2006), too, is cautious about the explanatory capacity of brain imaging, arguing that there remain strong similarities between children and adults, and that experience affects brain functioning as well as the reverse. This assumption is supported by studies which associate certain types of media with particular patterns of behaviour. One study, for example, concludes that 'chronic exposure to violent video games specifically – and not just frequent playing of any video games – has lasting deleterious effects on brain function and behaviour' (Bartholow *et al.*, 2006, p. 538).

Biological accounts of child development add considerably to our understanding, although not through the provision of conclusive answers.

It's all in the mind – psychology and children

For a number of reasons, psychology is probably the dominant disciplinary frame through which children and childhood are studied and conceptualized. This is partly associated with the influence of the discipline on thinking and practice in a range of spheres, including children's education, care and behaviour (as consumers, for example). It offers a 'common-sense' basis for understanding: 'In an important sense, we are all psychologists. We are all interested in understanding behaviour, both our own and that of our parents, children, family and friends' (Smith *et al.*, 2003, p. 3).

The root of our understanding of the human mind is to be found in our unique 'self-consciousness', and this is what generates interest in what makes ourselves and others 'tick'. This seems to be a natural starting point for attempts to categorize and theorize aspects of human growth and change, specifically child 'development' (Smith *et al.*, 2003, p. 4).

Early attempts to identify the acquisition of psychological attributes are associated with Darwin (1877) and Taine (1877). Thus, both 'practical reasoning' and emotional states are held to develop over time, based on close observations of young children (his own, in Darwin's case). Similarly, Freud (1977) held a tightly structured view of the ways in which children could be observed to develop, especially in terms of their sexuality.

Subsequent developments in psychology have tried to elaborate the nature and timing of these changes, as well as seeking to account for and explain underlying processes, such as the emergence of self-consciousness – the point at which young people start 'thinking ... about themselves' (Darwin, 1877, p. 292) The discipline has thus tended to incorporate a number of assumptions about the nature and trajectory of 'development' through childhood and beyond, notably associated with the work of Piaget (1959), who describes a number of 'stages' in children's use of language, which represent increasing levels of sophistication and 'a progressive socialization of thought' (1959, p. 55). Children are thereby held to move from an initial 'ego-centric and concrete form of thought reflected in their use of language, towards forms of 'abstract collaboration' which are able to attribute underlying meaning to events, and take account of others' perspectives. The consequences of this kind of representation are far-reaching, and can be found in the rather prescriptive accounts of child development offered in some quarters (for instance, in relation to children in care: Fahlberg, 1994).

As with biological explanations, however, it is important to avoid over-simplification of psychological approaches, and it is clear that both Piaget and others since have offered more nuanced accounts than might at first appear to be the case. Changing perceptions on the part of the child are not simply part of a mechanical and predetermined process, with the transition from 'ego-centrism' to socialized interactions being determined at least partly by the 'social environment' (Piaget, 1959, p. 271). The nature and outcomes of children's exchanges also vary according to context:

> The child ... becomes socialized with his (sic) contemporaries in quite another way than as with the adult. He fluctuates between two poles: the

monologue … and discussion or genuine exchange of ideas, and that is why the child's socialization with his fellows is greater than, or at least different to, his socialization with the adult alone.

(Piaget, 1959, p. 262)

In some respects, Piaget's conclusions are not as dissimilar to those of Vygotsky as is sometimes thought (Smith *et al.*, 2003, p. 497); although they may not be as fully elaborated. Vygotsky (1986) clearly shared a progressive view of children's development, even if he characterized their learning processes somewhat differently, introducing a more explicit social and interactive dimension. The distinction between the two appears to be that, for him, 'all human functioning is by its nature sociocultural' (Smith *et al.*, 2003, p. 499); whereas, for Piaget, the origins of understanding and psychological growth lie within the individual.

Thus, while the notion of 'development' does not seem contentious in general terms, there does seem to be plenty of scope for disagreement about the drivers and mechanisms by which this progressive process is actually realized.

This tension within psychology has led to a sustained but disputed attempt to conceptualize and then demonstrate the ways in which children acquire and apply 'theoretical' constructs about the world around them and other people (Carpendale and Lewis, 2006). It is plausible, on the one hand, to advance the view that 'babies are born with a range of skills that are "hard-wired" into their psychological make-up' (Carpendale and Lewis, 2006, p. 37). Even children's understanding of others' mental states may be dependent on a 'special brain mechanism' with which they are born. Impairment or absence of this mechanism might account for certain specific variations in children's ability to attribute mental states to other people (p. 39). Some studies, for example, have conjectured that conditions such as autism which demonstrate 'deficits' in children's ability to pass 'false belief tests'[1] (Baron-Cohen, 2001) are attributable to 'neurobiological' peculiarities (Baron-Cohen, 2004).

On the other hand, though, this is just one position in a complex and fast-moving debate (Carpendale and Lewis, 2006); alongside 'innate' modular accounts can also be posed 'simulation' and 'theory' perspectives, which all offer markedly different accounts of how children come to develop 'social understanding', that is a way of making sense of other people's thoughts and feelings (Carpendale and Lewis, 2006, p. 29). Simulation accounts, for example, suggest that

'people ground their capacity to mindread in the introspective awareness that they have of their own mental states' (Tirassa *et al.*, 2006,
p. 199). Increasingly sophisticated self-awareness might thus be associated with an equivalent capacity to have insight into what others are
thinking and feeling. 'Theory-theory' accounts are more elaborate in
that they attribute children's capacity to understand others' thoughts
and feelings to the 'theoretical constructs' which they develop and
apply 'in the prediction and explanation of behaviour' (Tirassa *et al.*,
2006, p. 199). Tirassa and colleagues opt though for a 'mentalistic and
nativist view' (2006, p. 197), which holds that children have an innate
capacity to attribute 'mental states' to themselves and others:

> This provides the necessary background against which [the child] can
> interact with her caregivers, communicating with them, trying to make
> sense of what they do and of their attempts to communicate with her,
> acquiring the first elements of the cultural environment in which she
> happens to live, and so on.
>
> (Tirassa *et al.*, 2006, p. 213)

This is not to deny the impact of social and environmental influences, but rather to suggest that these can only take effect given certain (innate) preconditions and a specific process of 'maturation' of
this 'biological faculty' (p. 206).

While not necessarily disagreeing totally, others have certainly
demonstrated a different order of priorities (Carpendale and Lewis,
2006, p. 45). Notably, it has been argued that children's 'social development has to be understood within the study of social interaction'.
This, in turn, has led some to question the very starting point for
psychology: the individual mind: 'Some take a radically perspective and claim that the issue of mental state understanding must be
understood as a social enterprise in which people collectively construct the mind' (Carpendale and Lewis, 2006, p. 46).

It is suggested that it is essentially through interaction by means
of language or other forms of communication that 'children learn
about other people's experience and so develop a more complete
set of criteria' (Carpendale and Lewis, 2006, p. 50) for making sense
of what they observe. Evidence to support this contention is drawn
from observations which suggest that 'mental state understanding is
significantly correlated with factors in the child's social environment'
(Carpendale and Lewis, 2004, p. 92), including attachment experiences, parenting behaviour and presence of siblings (see Chapter 3 on

the impact of geographical factors, too). Thus, the extensive literature on 'attachment' (Bowlby, 1953; Ainsworth, 1962; Rutter, 1981, for example) associates the quality of 'caring' behaviour in early childhood with subsequent 'coping' and relationship strategies, as well as possible 'long-term effects' (Rutter, 1981, p. 197) which may be manifested in the form of changes in 'brain structure or chemistry' deriving from 'adverse social experiences' (Rutter, 1981, p. 196).

While it is recognized that this argument is incomplete and warrants further investigation (Carpendale and Lewis, 2004, p. 94), it does point towards very different conclusions about processes of learning and development in children than, say, those which suggest that there is a uniform predictability about progress and transitions between 'stages'. Changes are more likely to occur gradually and unevenly, it would seem, and certainly not in a linear or routinely predictable fashion.

However, problems arise when trying to account for regularities and consistent patterns of change over time, such as the 'clear conceptual shift in children's performance' at about the age of 4 (Carpendale and Lewis, 2004, p. 90). For these patterns to be replicated consistently, according to this model, it must also be the case that processes of social interaction and relationship-building follow fairly consistent pathways across the population of children in general. Indeed, some support for the 'interactionist' or 'constructivist' position may be provided by studies involving children with rather different characteristics to the norm, such as D/deaf children, who have been observed to perform less well than others on 'false-belief tasks' (Steeds *et al.*, 1997, p. 192). This might at least partly be attributable to restrictions on their opportunities to interact with parents and others; for autistic children, however, organic explanations of difference are reputedly more plausible (Baron-Cohen, 2001).

What we can conclude from this brief overview is that psychological constructs and explanations of childhood reflect a process of grappling with tensions between functionalist and interactive models of development, which is, as yet, unresolved. A number of different explanations of children's intellectual and social development are advanced here, but none appear conclusive; nor are they mutually exclusive, as previously observed. Indeed, studies which show that children are able to combine sense-making techniques across differing social contexts (for example, Khabbache, 2005) may indicate that an explanatory model which incorporates parallel and interactive processes of growth and learning is more likely to be appropriate.

Sociological accounts: the big picture?

Although it may appear at first glance as if they represent a very
different perspective, sociologies of childhood have arguably followed a very similar 'developmental' path to that of psychology.
'Mechanistic' accounts of social organization and patterns of childhood have increasingly given way to those stressing the 'organic'
nature of human interactions (following Durkheim, 1947). Despite
their ostensible differences of orientation and methodology, there is
also a degree of convergence between sociologists and psychologists
around the provisional and unfinished nature of many attempts at
global explanatory accounts of childhood and child development.

A number of observers have commented (Corsaro, 1997, for example) that the breadth and depth of studies on children in sociology
have expanded substantially in the recent past, but that this is very
much a contemporary phenomenon. It is reported that the historical emphasis of mainstream sociology was very much on 'socialization'
and the processes by which children were transformed from innocent
and uncivilized beginnings to achieve their full status and potential as
adult citizens: 'All accounts of this character begin from an essential
and given model of human conduct and then seek to explain childhood as if teleologically related to that pre-established end' (Jenks,
1996, p. 10). This is largely due to the implicit normative assumptions
in much sociological thought based in conventional functionalist perspectives, which essentially saw the child as akin to other 'deviants'
(Jenks, 1996, p. 20), who can only be understood and responded to as
a standardized 'proto-adult'. As sociology itself became infused with a
wider range of critical perspectives, so did its approach to the study
of childhood (Jenks, 1996, p. 50). At the same time, as wider social
changes have led to the 'destabilization of adulthood' (Lee, 2001,
p. 19), so, too, has the idealized adult citizen lost ground as the benchmark against which children's lives and experiences can be measured
and judged. This change of perspective is linked explicitly in some
quarters to the emergence of post-modern thinking: 'In place of the
abstract, universal self, a postmodern culture asserts selves that are differentiated and individuated by class, gender, race, sexuality, ethnicity, nationality, physical and psychological ableness, and on and on'
(Seidman, 1998, quoted in Moss and Petrie, 2002, p. 23).

There is a parallel process operating here, whereby historical certainties in terms of the ordering of social and personal relationships
have become increasingly destabilized at just the same time, and

probably for very similar reasons (Giddens, 1991), as our understandings of children and their childhoods have also become more diverse and contested. Established 'truth regimes' (Lee, 2001, p. 122) no longer retain the capacity to define the object of study and generate unchallengeable answers to the questions of 'what children are like', and what they *should* be like.

As a consequence of this kind of decentring of knowledge and power, it has become sociologically respectable to recognize and validate a wider range of viewpoints, all of which are capable of generating legitimate ideas and knowledge. These of course include children's perspectives, and sociology has become increasingly active in pursuing the question of how children construct and understand their own life experiences. This has led to a process of alignment with the children's rights movement which is engaged in a similar process of seeking to give them a voice. And, in academic terms, we have seen this extended to an attempt to develop a committed sociology *for* children (Mayall, 2002, for example).

Corsaro (1997) has sought to articulate the process by which children engage in the production of knowledge and relationships, both between themselves and with other (adult) members of society. In the process, they become 'interpretive' and active participants in creating the social world (Smith, 2000a):

> The focus is on *childhood* as a social construction resulting from the collective actions of *children* with adults and each other. Childhood is recognised as a structural form and children are social agents who contribute to the reproduction of childhood and society through their negotiations with adults and through their creative production of a series of peer cultures with other children.
>
> (Corsaro, 1997, p. 43)

This argument, drawing on structural accounts of the production and reproduction of social relations, finds strong echoes in the 'generational' accounts of childhood initially articulated by Mannheim (1952) but developed and elaborated by Alanen (2001; 2004) more recently. The shift of focus involved in these analytical developments means that children and their social relationships become the '*center* of analysis' (Corsaro, 1997, p. xiii), no longer being subsumed under other conceptual and empirical categories 'such as families or schools'. Corsaro's insights are nicely illustrated by his account of his own experiences as a researcher in a pre-school setting in

Italy (where he was a foreign presence in several respects). He was able both to observe the complex worlds the children constructed between themselves ('The bank with money', 1997, p. 2), and to gain an insight into the reversal of established roles with the children coming to see themselves as his teachers (1997, p. 92).

The recognition of children's distinct and independent status as social actors has important implications for the way in which sociology addresses them. It is, of course, by no means new to think in terms of the 'social construction of reality' (Berger and Luckman, 1967), but the place of children within this frame of reference has only gradually been recognized. What has emerged more recently, though, is a proliferation of sociologies of, with and 'for' children. However, as children and the notion of 'childhood' have come to the fore, so some of the differences of emphasis between analytical perspectives have been flattened somewhat. It has been argued instead that studies of childhood should be interpreted in terms of their alignment with a number of distinct 'discourses' (James *et al.*, 1998), reflecting different 'meta' theoretical assumptions, and leading to rather different conclusions. To assimilate all contemporary sociologies of childhood with a unified 'social constructionist' position would be erroneous. This mistake might lead to the conflation of some quite important distinctions between alternative viewpoints *within* childhood sociology, as in the following example:

> The new childhood sociologists base their theory on this ... proposition, that children should be regarded as constructions of their particular society ... There is no definitive or universal account of what childhood is or what children should be. All is relative and depends on the particular constructions of childhood of different societies or of the same society at different times and the expectations associated with children (and adults) resulting from these constructions.
>
> (King, 2007, p. 196)

The 'new' sociologies of childhood are, in fact, rather more subtle and varied than this caricature, being distinguishable along a number of axes, as James *et al* (1998, p. 206) have already enumerated. Sociologists of childhood are thus able to debate important distinctions between the structural and cultural factors which shape children's lives, and which create the conditions for their own interpretive and creative responses (Smith, 2000a). While we might agree that it is no 'mere coincidence' (King, 2007, p. 195) that the emergence of the children's rights movement has been mirrored by burgeoning theoretical interest in their lives and, indeed, their perspectives on their lives, this does not mean that sociology has lost its ability to think sociologically in this context.

Different analytical perspectives have been captured, for example, through the elaboration of four distinct explanatory 'discourses' which are all 'alive and well': the 'social structural child'; the 'socially constructed child'; the 'minority group child'; and the 'tribal child' (James *et al.*, 1998, p. 200). Each of these falls at a different point within a complex set of well-established theoretical dichotomies: 'structure and agency', 'identity and difference', 'continuity and change', and 'global and local' (James *et al.*, 1998, p. 199). Thus, for example, wider structural changes in the ways in which childhood is addressed, educated, regulated and controlled do not simply reflect new and emerging developments in the ways in which childhood is thought about and 'constructed', but are likely to operate in an interactive and generative fashion to engineer changes in *both* the experience of *and* ideas about being a child. Prout argues that this is a dialogic process which requires a degree of insight and flexibility in attempts to unpack and understand it:

> Childhood has been deeply implicated in, affected by and destabilized by contemporary social, technological and economic change. It started with the crisis of representation that has occurred around childhood. This both draws on and feeds back into the constitution of real childhoods, blurring the boundary between childhood and adulthood that modernity put into place. There is ... a simultaneous trend towards a common global conception of childhood but also a growing awareness of its diversity.
>
> (Prout, 2005, p. 33)

This can readily be illustrated by the contested nature of adolescence, where the assignation of identities to those in that category necessitates a resolution of the essentially normative question of whether and in what circumstances they are defined as 'children', 'young people', 'adolescents', 'youths', or even fellow citizens. The 'new sociology of childhood' has opened up an area for critical inquiry which had not previously been considered in depth, and it is misleading to suggest that it is entirely self-contained, and 'ignores any accounts of events that lie outside this narrow perspective', as King (2007, p. 211) does. Rather, this developing field of study has both marked out new approaches and recognized the importance of engaging with more established traditions both within and beyond the discipline of sociology: 'Childhood is necessarily caught up in patterns of change because it is integral to society, history, economics – in fact to life in all its many-sided complexity' (Prout, 2005, p. 34).

Childhood: towards an interdisciplinary future?

This is a good base for reflecting further on the possibilities of bringing together very diverse insights and perspectives on childhood, in order to achieve a stronger and more cohesive theoretical grounding. We may not be able to resolve some perennial issues (such as the 'nature' vs 'nurture' debate), but we may be able to identify healthy possibilities for continuing dialogue and critical discussion on the key questions of what we know (and can know) about children's lives, what we need to find out and what methods of 'knowing' are applicable to the subject matter.

In this spirit, some have tried to quantify the contribution of different influences to children's characteristics or behaviour. Thus, based on one twin study of the incidence of juvenile delinquency, it has been suggested that 'genetic effects' account for around 18 per cent of variation in individual levels of delinquency, while the remainder can be attributed to 'shared' (26 per cent) or 'non-shared' (56 per cent) environmental factors (Taylor *et al.*, 2000, p. 437). This kind of causal differentiation might be seen as highly convenient, if we were to accept that these elements could be separated out accurately in this fashion, investigated independently, and then reintegrated to provide working models across the range of childhood experiences and activities. This is not the case, of course, and as we have seen, most disciplines appear to accept the interactive nature of antecedent factors on outcomes for children. Integrating investigative and analytical frameworks requires a more detailed strategy, though. Arguing from within the 'new sociology' of childhood, Prout, for example, recognizes that efforts to both acknowledge and then 'bracket off' biological aspects of childhood represent an 'unhelpful' form of 'dualistic opposition' (2005, p. 57). The material world cannot be sidestepped or wished away. Some sort of interactive and collaborative dynamic must be predicated between what appear to be radically different modes of understanding and knowledge generation, all of which are themselves contested internally, of course.

Prout suggests that we should start by thinking in terms of 'complex systems', which 'contain different levels: the molecular; the cellular; the organism, and society. Reciprocal relations take place between all these different levels and the system (and its various levels and regions) develops (non-teleologically) over time' (Prout, 2005, p. 94). The levels, in turn, are not 'pre-given', but constituted through the 'networks and flows' that infuse them, which in the case of social networks, includes 'people, texts and things', and in others include components such as 'molecules', 'genes' and 'the physical environment'. The implications of this are that we must allow for an explanatory framework which is complex, interactive, multi-directional and does not necessarily prioritize any one 'level'.

Notions of networks and flow (Urry, 2000, for example) have become influential factors in the search for comprehensive and elaborate explanatory systems across a wide range of social phenomena. It is unsurprising that childhood should have become a site for developments of this kind in the attempt to supersede rather narrow and polarized debates such as those between 'nature' and 'nurture'.

At the same time, this kind of 'realist' approach offers more mileage than those which seek to resolve inherent explanatory tensions by positing a phenomenological synthesis of 'mind and body' (Turner, 1984, p. 53). Alternative conceptualizations of childhood, as either corporeal or social, are not collapsed into one, but are to be seen and understood as existing in interactive tension with one other, with a complex pattern of influences and impacts 'flowing' in either direction.

This kind of dynamic formulation of changes in children can be identified across disciplinary boundaries too; for example, the notion of 'plasticity' has become prominent in biological accounts. Increasing recognition of this attribute of the brain has influenced thinking about the educational process, tangentially also casting new light on prior conceptions of child development. Thus:

> The adult brain is flexible, it can grow new cells and make new connections, at least in some regions such as the hippocampus. Although laying down new information becomes less efficient with age, there is no age limit for learning.
>
> (Blakemore and Frith, 2005, p. 9)

Changes in the brain are not necessarily determined according to chronological age, but by other factors, such as the 'use' of certain functions, and adaptation to the 'environment' (Blakemore and Frith, 2005, p. 123). As specific skills are developed, so does the relevant part of the brain, but equally, the brain can adapt to changing demands, so that: 'With every new experience, your brain slightly rewires its physical structure'(Blakemore and Frith, 2005, p. 133). For Prout, this translates into an appreciation that the body is both 'socially and biologically unfinished' and that 'the body and society work on each other' (2005, p. 105). This introduces another important element into our framework for understanding, and this is children's capacity to 'work' on and transform themselves, both in terms of their social identities and their physical being, arguably from infancy:

> There is increasing evidence . . . that infants are not blank slates . . . but come equipped with remarkable minds programmed to be receptive to and to make sense of what is going on around them in both the social and physical worlds.
>
> (Matthews, 2007, p. 323)

While there is some indication that the capacity to make complex emotional and moral judgements may be age-related (Healy, 2004, p. 84), and the influence of significant physiological transitions such as puberty cannot be overlooked (Coleman and Hendry, 1999), these changes in our understanding do not suggest that children are pre-programmed, but that their childhood experiences, physical changes, identities and social worlds depend on an interlocking series of interactions, in which they are involved as 'interpreters' and 'actors' as well as receptors of pre-existing messages, stimuli, codes or con-structs. Self-consciousness, and therefore a concept of themselves (and others) as children is thus a key attribute which children bring to the constructions of the world and their place within it. Children quickly acquire an understanding of themselves *as* children, recog-nizing the importance of size (Corsaro, 1997), knowledge, skills and age (Moss and Petrie, 2002) as relevant factors in the construction of their relationships with other children. Children are 'scientists', involved in their own explorations, making their own interpretations and developing and revising their own explanatory accounts of the world and their relationships (Gopnik, 1996).

So, 'plasticity' is a feature of their social and intellectual as well as physiological beings: 'If children appear disorderly this is not because their activities simply lack order. Rather it is because their activi-ties contain a profusion of different orders which they can move between very rapidly' (Lee, 2001, p. 141). According to Lee, tran-sitions based on age are not so much a process of development towards a fully mature adulthood, but a 'slowing down of the pace of change' between different states of being. The range of possibilities and opportunities to move between identities seem to be fewer for adults, and in this sense social change mirrors physical change rather than being in opposition to it. As we age and grow, there are more 'fixed points' and a greater degree of certainty, based on decreasing pace of change and increasing resources in terms of knowledge and physical capacity.

Within this broad explanatory framework, though, there remains a capacity to account for specific variations (historical, evolutionary, social or cultural) in the way in which childhood is understood and experienced at different points in time and in different places.

Prout (2005) uses the term 'hybridity' to describe the necessary shift to achieve a fuller and better integrated understanding of childhood, so that, for example, 'the distinction between being and becoming' (2005, p. 143) is eradicated, and it can be recognized as 'a multiple set of constructions emergent from the connection and disconnection, fusion and separation of . . . heterogeneous materials' (2005, p. 144). As a result, too, he notes that this implicitly removes the 'taken-for-granted' distinction between childhood and adulthood, which are no longer separable on any arbitrary, discipline-specific grounds. Instead, this categorical separation 'should be problematized and the attempt made to understand how and why the distinction arises, what the materials and processes are that construct it and how its shifting boundaries are constituted and reconstituted' (2005, p. 144).

Despite these observations, the scale and persistence of the generational divide should not be underestimated (Mannheim, 1952; Alanen, 2001; 2004). However, if childhood cannot easily be distinguished from adulthood analytically, it becomes all the more challenging to address the task of enumerating those specific attributes of this particular 'life stage' which are generalizable across divides, which are 'internal' and which are 'external' to the child and whether these are socially, physiologically or psychologically determined.

Note

1 False belief tests are typically used experimentally to ascertain the extent to which children are able to attribute mental capacities to other people, by recognizing that others are capable of having a different ('false') understanding of the material world to their own.

PART II

Childhood in Context

5

Children, the State and Social Policy

Child welfare: making assumptions about children?

In this part of the book, I will move from the predominantly academic focus on defining and understanding childhood to the rather different issue of the 'construction' and treatment of children in the social policy and welfare domains. This is not to suggest that these two 'worlds' have no connection. It is demonstrably the case that academic insights have on occasion informed child care policies (the Sure Start programme in the UK, for example). At the same time, persistent concerns about protecting, nurturing and controlling children have acted as the focus for large areas of policy-oriented research activity, as in the case of Bowlby's (1953) extensive study into the question of 'maternal deprivation' and its consequences. Nonetheless, by distinguishing between these fields of inquiry and shifting attention to the pragmatic and the practical, we may gain further insights into the basis on which childhood is defined and shaped in a material and contextual sense.

This, in turn, will help us to consider a number of further questions, such as the extent to which policy and welfare practices fundamentally determine children's experiences and shape childhood, as well as the matter of whether or not such interventions are based on sound evidence rather than preconception. As we proceed through subsequent chapters, on children and the economic sphere, and children and the media, further light will be shed on the question of whether and how children's lives are shaped by external (social) influences, rather than their intrinsic characteristics. This will give a rather different slant on the issue of whether or not childhood is primarily an 'adult' construction, mediated by powerful social forces, or is rather a unique life stage, to which policy and practice are tailored, *post hoc*, so to speak.

First, attention will turn to the origins and development of contemporary state practices, especially in the 'developed' world (eg, Hendrick, 1997), and their connections with underlying assumptions and knowledge about the nature of childhood and the needs of children. I will consider the increasingly sharp focus on children as a distinct constituency in recent times and in specific contexts (see Chapter 2), and the ways in which this has been articulated in law and practice. As will become clear, these developments are related to a number of central tensions in our perceptions of children (as 'angels' or 'villains', for example, Fionda, 2005). Indeed, it may appear that many of the theoretical and ideological differences discussed earlier are played out in divergent forms of policy and intervention in child welfare (King and Piper, 1990). This has been particularly sharply in evidence in the sphere of youth justice, for instance (Jenks, 1996; Smith, 2007).

By drawing on a number of illustrative examples, the aim will be to identify trends and themes in the sphere of child welfare policy and practice, which may be seen to apply across substantive areas of intervention, and geographical and political divisions. On this basis, the chapter will address the underlying issue of the 'universality' of childhood, as viewed through the lens of state policy and activity. Does the widespread common currency of childhood (for example, as represented in international instruments such as the UN Convention on the Rights of the Child) offer us any greater degree of confidence in the belief that there is something special and specific about being a child? Or, are there other drivers for this apparent convergence of policy agendas and shared visions? Might important differences between children and their childhoods be obscured in this way of thinking about their well-being and treatment?

Models of childhood in policy

A number of sources have suggested that policy debates and welfare interventions with children are shaped by implicit but conflicting normative models of children and their characteristics (Jenks, 1996;

Daniel and Ivatts, 1998; James and James, 2004). Thus, for example, contemporary developments might be 'indicative' that 'certain structural shifts in the thinking about the place and position of children have occurred in British society' (James and James, 2004, p. 38) as one model (paternalism) cedes ground to another (rights-based). Indeed, there is a broad measure of agreement that policy changes in relation to families and children have reflected wider ideological shifts and social trends (Carney, 1999; Hendrick, 2003), although these do not always flow in the same direction.

Jenks has suggested that what is played out in the policy arena is a polarized conflict between caricatures of children as either naturally good, or evil, with problematic consequences:

> Thus, between, on the one hand, the clamour for punishment, revenge and retribution and, on the other hand, demands for understanding and loving care, it would seem that public perceptions of what children need are indeed in disarray.
>
> (Jenks, 1996, p. 132)

This dynamic tension reveals an inherent instability in the ways in which children are understood and provided for by the state. This uncertainty appears to be compounded by the emergence of a 'postmodern' society, in which all knowledge and expertise is fleeting, contingent and contested. It has been suggested that 'contemporary' policy agendas are best approached as negotiable, localized and specific exercises in fitting appropriate interventions to highly variable and disparate needs (Carney, 1999, p. 64).

Hendrick (2003), too, has taken an approach which sees child welfare as the (provisional) resolution of conflicting views of children's natures and needs. He depicts these conflicts in the form of 'three guiding dualisms – mind/body, victim/threat, normal/abnormal' (2003, p. 1). Thus, for example, the Victorian era saw a prevailing interest in regulating the child's body, and promoting the physical health of disadvantaged and sometimes 'cruelly treated' (2003, p. 3) children. The subsequent emergence of psychology as an influential discipline was associated, Hendrick believes, with a shift towards concern for mental stability and well-being, exemplified by the post-war growth in the influence of the ideas of Bowlby (1953) concerning children's 'attachment' needs. Fears about the consequences of insecure attachments have permeated much of the policy agenda relating to the 'needs' of children in the UK as a result (Department of Health, 2000, for example), and guidance literature on 'good practice' in social work with children and families underlines these concerns:

> Attachment theory offers a compelling set of ideas about how children develop close relationships with their main care-givers, how they attempt to adapt and survive in their particular care-giving environment, and how their behaviours and coping strategies can be understood as functional . . .
>
>   Underpinning all practice using an attachment perspective is the provision of relationships in which the other is experienced as available and responsive, consistent and understanding.
>
> (Howe, 2001, p. 205)

Similarly, historical shifts can be identified in the treatment of children predominantly as either 'victims' or 'threats', with each stereotype tending to dominate at different times, such as the 'moral panic' about child abuse which followed the death of Maria Colwell and subsequent inquiry in the early 1970s (see Parton, 1985). Hendrick (2003, p. 11) makes the important point that these foci of concern are highly specific, contrasting the public concern about the death of one child through mistreatment in the UK with the very many millions of children dying at the same time throughout the world of 'predictable and preventable causes'. So, 'Was the public expression of concern directed at the child as a *victim* or as a *symbol*, a representative of what was felt to be a more disturbing and widespread phenomenon than her own death?' (Hendrick, 2003, p. 11).

Similarly, in the contemporary era (the early twenty-first century), the predominant concern has been the *threat* represented by children and young people, rather than their needs, characterized by Hendrick as the 'enveloping' of 'victim' status by a preoccupation with the possibility of children becoming sources of harm to others (2003, p. 12).

A number of other authors have suggested that in modern Western societies, the changing pattern of policy and practice in relation to children can be described in terms of dominant, although not exclusive, 'value positions' (Fox Harding, 1997). Thus, at certain points, such as the 1970s, UK government policy was dominated with a concern to 'protect' children, while in the following decade (the 1980s) there appeared to be a clear change of emphasis towards a 'laissez-faire' approach to the family. Both of these positions, though in opposition on one level, could be said to take an 'adultist' view of children, in contrast to others which would emphasize the child's needs ('family support') or rights ('children's rights'), and which can be identified in certain aspects of policy in the UK (Sure Start, in the former case; and the Children and Young People's Unit, in the latter, for example), and more centrally in other countries, notably Scandinavia (Khoo *et al.*, 2002).

Changes of emphasis in child welfare policy can be ascribed to a number of factors, of course, and they are open to different characterizations. So, whereas Jenks (1996, p. 132) might refer to the current climate as being one of 'disarray', Hendrick prefers to describe the position as 'complicated', but not out of control: 'New Labour as a political party, as the governor of policies and, to the extent that it has one, as a political philosophy, is nothing if not complex' (2003, p. 234). In this sense, the UK government which spanned the turn of the century is reported as being deliberately 'ambivalent', seeking to bring together a number of competing strands of belief and interests into some sort of alignment, but not into a state of perfect equilibrium or consensus. It might be said to have been trying to ride the post-modern tide rather than being submerged by it. As a result, policies for children can be expected to incorporate contradictions, perhaps even intentionally.

There is no doubt that the New Labour government sought to take 'childhood and children seriously' (Hendrick, 2003, p. 236), investing substantial additional spending in this particular segment of the population, and making explicit commitments to 'tackle' child poverty and enhance educational opportunities. Reshaping childhood therefore became a central plank of the government's wider 'modernization' agenda, and in order to assimilate the different aspects of children's characteristics and circumstances, several linking themes were enumerated. Notably, the concepts of 'welfare' and 'justice', and 'rights' and 'responsibilities' were now presented as being complementary rather than contradictory: 'The new child – all children – is to be obedient, disciplined, hard-working, academically well educated, and tutored in the reciprocity of responsibilities and rights' (Hendrick, 2003, p. 238). In policy terms, this meant that entitlements of all kinds would be dependent on complying with societal standards and expectations; by the same token, failure to meet these standards might well prompt regulatory sanctions, loss of entitlements or penalties of one kind or another:

The attempt to take this kind of integrated and inclusive approach to policies for children has been epitomized in the UK context in the *Every Child Matters* initiative (DfES, 2003), which proposed a holistic approach to meeting children's needs and promoting their 'well-being'. The overarching policy document for this project tried to develop a schema within which competing agendas could be harmonized, and sought to provide the infrastructure for a more unified and effective approach to child welfare which would still provide sufficient flexibility to meet individual need: 'We need to focus both on the universal services which every child uses, and on more targeted services for those with additional needs' (DfES, 2003, p. 6).

According to this vision, children's interests could best be met by providing a framework of universal services, such as health and education, within which 'specialist support' (DfES, 2003, p. 9) could be provided where additional concerns arise for individual children. This rather elegant 'fudge' represents an attempt to assimilate competing models of childhood, but without addressing underlying questions about the tensions between universal and specific needs, whether in terms of children's background and characteristics, or in terms of the relationship between generalized and targeted interventions. Similar attempts to bridge this divide are evident in policy developments elsewhere, including Ireland, for instance (Buckley and O'Sullivan, 2007). Whether we see this as a constructive attempt to 'put [childhood] back together' (Hendrick, 2003, p. 242), or to provide a superficial gloss over a state of chaos (Jenks, 1996), it does represent one attempt to make sense in practical terms of a continuing fracture between polarized conceptualizations.

Wyness (2000), too, has argued that policy in relation to children (and families) is characterized by a sense of moral ambiguity, stemming from the increasingly 'contested' understanding of childhood itself: 'Children who were either ignored or came into view as "necessarily" and "naturally" incompetent are now seen in more contested terms as both socially exploited and . . . agentic' (Wyness, 2000, p. 28). The changing landscape translates in this account into a messy array of policies directed towards children *and* their parents. In the educational sphere, for example, children's 'incompetence' is taken for granted, and it is parents who 'are expected to know what their children's needs are and are to be free to express [their] rights within an education market-place' (Wyness, 2000, p. 43). On the other hand, in child welfare settings, following the Children Act 1989, children have 'become more prominent participants in child-care matters and thus are intimately involved in decision-making processes that directly affect their welfare' (Wyness, 2000, p. 49). So, the degree of autonomy offered to children in key decision-making processes in their lives may vary from setting to setting, suggesting unresolved questions about their status in relation to the family and other (state) institutions.

While in one sense the insertion of parents and the family into the discussion is a further complicating factor, for the present, it is significant in illustrating the continuing tensions within child welfare policy:

> There is no clear-cut policy agenda with regard to the relationship between parents, their children and institutions with an interest in childhood. Policy, if anything serves to confound these relationships and produce moral ambiguity.
>
> (Wyness, 2000, p. 36)

It is clear that this moral ambivalence is reflective of a wider process, whereby 'the images of the child that a parent, school or society have constructed' (King, 1999, p. 15) shape normative assumptions about her/him. The normative, prescriptive dimension of policy thus reflect underlying, if not always articulated, beliefs about children's 'nature' and their level of maturity and competence. It is because these are in dispute that policy comes to be characterized by 'holes' and 'knots', where it conveys 'contradictory messages' (Fox Harding, 1996, p. 223).

We can conclude, then, that the field of children's policy is highly contentious, and that it is a site in which competing beliefs and attitudes about children are played out, sometimes with considerable urgency. However, some (James and James, 2004) would argue that the precise form these debates take is situationally specific, and that in the UK, in particular, they are quite tightly constrained by certain underlying preconceptions, such as the independence of families (see also Fox Harding, 1997) and a developmental ('deficit') model of children themselves. Thus, children's policy has been framed by a conceptual framework which excludes children themselves from the debate, and constitutes them as a disenfranchised interest, in the same way as other marginalized or oppressed social groups: 'We would ... contend ... that the lack of agency of children (in the sense of their ability to effect change) reflects their minority group status' (James and James, 2004, p. 104). It is not therefore an inherent lack of competence or maturity which inhibits children from having a say and influencing law and policy; but rather, this is the consequence of inequalities in power and social relations, with adult interests exerting material control over children's lives in ways that are in fact recognized by children themselves:

> The children relate their vulnerability to having their feelings hurt to the unequal power relationships between children and adults. These inequalities mean that adults are able to respond to children with physical, behavioural and emotional actions, in ways that are denied to children.
>
> (Mason and Falloon, 2001, p. 106)

This is not to suggest that these power relations are rigid or immutable, however. There is evidence of change over time (James and James, 2004, p. 105), and this might lead to a renegotiation of the fundamental determinants of 'childhood' itself.

Competing models of childhood in social policy?

Of course, approaches to policy for children within one country at a particular point are likely to be specific to their context, both geographically and temporally (see earlier chapters). Thus, the models of childhood brought to bear in the policy domain may also be both more diverse and more contingent than it might first seem. Some have suggested that children (or certain groups of children, at least) have recently been the subject of a progressive process of 'responsibilisation' (Goldson and Muncie, 2006) which has superseded the ' "child in need" construct' (2006, p. 214). By holding children and young people to blame for their anti-social behaviour, this movement has effectively blurred dividing lines between childhood and adulthood. Associated with this has been the emergence of the '"adult-child", the "child" whose recalcitrance betrays their very child-status and, as such, is no longer deserving of legal safeguards and compassion' (Goldson, 1999, p. 24). In this domain, by contrast with mainstream or 'normal' childhoods, adult status is attributed to children from a relatively early age. That this is not solely a UK issue is borne out by reports early in 2009 that France, too, is considering lowering the age of criminal responsibility to 12.

Far from representing an amalgam of different perspectives, UK (or at least, English and Welsh) policy and practice in relation specifically to children who offend appears to be based on a highly partial view. In this sense, there is a concrete process by which childhood is being eroded, as others have suggested (see previous chapters), even if it has not quite 'disappeared'. Even in this context, though, there is evidence of differing and sometimes competing strands of policy and ideological perspectives (Muncie, 2002).

Once other jurisdictions are considered, it becomes clear that there is considerable diversity in the way in which justice systems deal with (and think about) children and young people (Muncie and Goldson, 2006). Wide variations are noted, for example, in the age at which different countries treat young people as being capable of demonstrating criminal responsibility, with the United Kingdom at the lower end of the age range, and Scandinavian countries at the upper extreme (Muncie and Goldson, 2006, p. 200). This can be taken as tentative evidence of cross-cultural variations in the ways in which childhood is defined. However, the picture seems rather more complex and uncertain than this, with competing strands of thought evident over time and within jurisdictions:

> Modern juvenile justice appears as ever more hybrid: attempting to deliver neither welfare or justice but a complex and contradictory amalgam of the punitive, the responsibilizing, the inclusionary, the exclusionary and the protective . . . Within this mix, possibilities for transition and change are forever present. In the USA and Canada we may now be witnessing the beginnings of some exhaustion of extreme penal populism. In Finland and Italy decarceration and tolerance continue to remain in some ascendancy.
>
> (Muncie and Goldson, 2006, p. 214)

Some common international trends and some distinct differences in orientation and practice can be identified. A widespread consensus in favour of a 'welfare protectionist' approach to young offenders has progressively broken down towards the end of the twentieth century across many developed Western nations, with the focus of intervention shifting from the 'need' of the young person to her/his misdeeds (Muncie and Goldson, 2006, p. 197). This trend is consistent with the previously identified trend in the UK towards 'adulterization' (Muncie and Goldson, 2006, p. 199), with countries as diverse as Holland and Canada making parallel moves to remove some of the previous protections offered to child offenders in judicial proceedings. Within a broader pattern of right-wing and coercive policy shifts, the treatment of young offenders is characterized as a progressive process of 'justice-based . . . repenalisation' (Muncie and Goldson, 2006, p. 205).

Despite this, some penal regimes have stood clearly at odds with this trend, especially in Belgium and Finland. While these, too, may be subject to challenge (Put and Walgrave, 2006, p. 125), they do represent a quite distinct strand of thought. Belgium 'was indeed one of

the very few [countries] in the world to provide a purely rehabilitative system for its young offenders'; while,

> in Finnish public policy, juvenile crime and 'children in trouble' are still
> viewed as problems arising from social conditions, and these problems
> should be addressed by investing more in health services and in general
> child welfare – not in penal institutions.
>
> (Lappi-Seppala, 2006, p. 194)

From this, two observations follow: first, that there is a degree of
cross-national variation in approaches to the treatment of youth
crime; and, second, that these differences may reflect embedded
assumptions about the nature of childhood and appropriate forms of
intervention.

   In light of this, it might be helpful to consider broader comparative analyses of welfare policy. In the case of developed nations, at
least, the prototypical framework for this kind of analysis has been
attributed to Esping-Andersen (1990), despite some subsequent criticism and revision (Esping-Andersen, 1999; Bonoli *et al.*, 2000). In
its initial phase of development, this framework posited three 'ideal
types' of welfare system within developed Western capitalist econo-
mies: the 'liberal welfare regime'; the 'social democratic welfare
regime'; and, the 'conservative welfare regime' (Esping-Andersen,
1999). These incorporated divergent practices, especially in terms of
social security provision, which in turn represented differing ideological perspectives and 'working assumptions'. This schema incorporated competing models of the family, and, by extension, children's
place in relation to it. Thus, for example, it is held to be the conservative or corporatist regimes (Germany and Italy are offered as
examples) which are most likely to ascribe a central role in welfare provision to the family (Esping-Andersen, 1999, p. 85). Others
attribute the primary role to the 'market' (the USA, the UK, other
'Anglo-Saxon' states) or to the 'state' (Scandinavia). The place of
children, and responsibility for them, would seem to vary depending on these broad distinctions. For instance, the extent and nature
of child care provision might very well depend on different implicit
models of parenting, attachment and development. It is noted that
Scandinavian countries, in particular, have followed a distinct pathway towards 'de-familialization' (Esping-Andersen, 1999, p. 55),
whereby the burden of responsibility for providing care as well as
income support for children has been transferred progressively to
the state. Children in these systems are also more readily attributed

independent rights, as opposed to those which see parents or the family as the focal point for intervention, even though Qvortrup (1997) has questioned the true extent of children's independent recognition in official documentation and policy initiatives.

These varying approaches to family policy might be thought to reflect deeper underlying assumptions about the nature of childhood, and the appropriate place of policy in providing for children's well-being (Phipps, 2001). Cross-country comparisons seem to suggest a degree of consistency between patterns of beliefs about what is best for children, welfare provision *and* children's experience. So, Norwegian children are less restricted in their activities than those from the USA or Canada, they have fewer accidents or injuries, and they are at the same time less fearful: '"Being free of fear" seems a compelling dimension of child well-being. Norwegian children are much less likely to be anxious/frightened than are children in the other countries under study' (Phipps, 2001, p. 93).

A more child-centred policy regime is associated with distinct improvements in the quality of life and, thus, the experience of childhood itself. The conclusion to be drawn is that 'value differences are connected to differences in policies' and 'that outcomes for children differ' (Phipps, 2001, p. 95). Welfare practices in relation to children can be seen to be related to some quite fundamental social beliefs such as the view that 'people live in poverty because they are lazy', which is directly linked to the 'design' of 'programmes for children'.

A different slant on inter-country comparisons is provided by those who view the child as historically 'invisible' in policy debates. Accordingly, it is suggested: 'Social policy is not for children' (Skevik, 2003, p. 423). Differences of treatment can only be inferred from the ways in which 'families, mothers (and sometimes fathers)' are addressed by welfare institutions. Clearly, the underlying assumption that children should be treated as 'objects' rather than 'subjects' of policy itself incorporates a certain pattern of beliefs about childhood agency and competencies, although this is progressively coming into question (Skevik, 2003, p. 424). Despite this common starting point, differences are observable between national welfare regimes in their conception of, and approach to, children: 'Norway has a policy towards parents and children; the UK has a policy towards families' (Skevik, 2003, p. 436). In other words, one welfare system recognizes children in their own right, whereas the other tends to see them only as a constituent of a larger object of policy interventions, the family.

This distinction can be demonstrated by examination of variations in benefit and child maintenance arrangements between
the two states. Children's entitlement is treated as a separate issue
from their family setting in Norway, but in the British context
that is much less evident in benefits policy, with the exception of
Child Benefit.

It is argued, too, that such variations are reflected in other aspects
of policy and practice. Thus, the comparatively early commitment to
children's rights in Norway, and the associated establishment of the
position of Children's Commissioner, are indicative of a distinctive
position on the independent rights of children (Fox Harding, 1997).
Equally, and more strikingly, attention has been drawn to the dis-
parity of response between two similar but not precisely comparable
cases, one in Norway and one in England, in which children were
killed by other children (Hattenstone, 2000). In the former, where
the children concerned were admittedly several years younger, the
response was framed in conciliatory and educational terms, while in
the latter, it was dealt with in a process represented predominantly by
'justice' and punishment models of intervention. While it is difficult
to base too much on comparisons between individual cases whose
superficial similarity conceals significant differences, this example has
been seen as further evidence for the claim that alternative models of
childhood, children's rights, children's needs and assumptions about
their underlying characteristics will each become influential in different policy contexts. These do not appear to be completely arbitrary, but represent cultural and attitudinal variations, giving further
support to the notion that typologies of welfare and their associated ideological underpinnings offer a plausible explanatory frame
(Esping-Andersen, 1999).

Papadopoulos' (1996) analysis of welfare support in Greece also
lends support to the 'typology' thesis, concluding that in that country, by the mid-1990s at least: 'Children and young people are still
conceptualised within the legislative and policy context as totally
dependent on family and a notion of 'child as partner' or participant
in decisions ... is totally absent' (Papadopoulos, 1996, p. 184). This line
of argument is not accepted universally, however, with some claiming
that the typologies advanced are themselves unclear or insufficiently
robust (Bonoli *et al.*, 2000, p. 17), while others have advanced empirical evidence to suggest that child welfare provision cannot easily be
distinguished in the ways predicted by the explanatory models on
offer (Bradshaw, 2005). Expenditure on income benefits for children

cannot simply be 'inferred' from 'regime types' (Bradshaw, 2005, p. 29), with spending more readily associated with patterns of social expenditure, and redistributive policies. Thus:

> Those countries that make most effort to transfer resources horizontally have the most generous child benefit packages. Nations make choices. The policies that they choose have an impact on the financial burdens borne by parents raising children.
>
> (Bradshaw, 2005, p. 29)

Whether these choices can be said to reflect a consistent view of the responsibilities of the state towards families and children is another matter. Some clearly believe that it makes sense to consider different regime types in terms of their ideologies of childhood (Papadopoulos, 1996; Fox Harding, 1997; Skevik, 2003), whereas others tend to view outcomes as rather less coherent and instead dependent on the conjuncture of competing perspectives and policy agendas (Hendrick, 2003; Bradshaw, 2005).

As interest in the subject grows, more recent contributions also caution us to avoid tendencies towards ethnocentric models. In Latin America, for instance, it is reported that health and welfare practices in relation to children have drawn 'successively and sometimes simultaneously from indigenous traditions, colonial patterns, state-building concerns, technical developments, racial and medical ideologies, and domestic and international innovations' (Birn, 2007, p. 699).

Children, social policy and models of childhood: a case study of the UK

As we know, there has been considerable interest in the question of whether models of welfare can be identified which reflect prevailing assumptions and ideologies under different regimes (Esping-Andersen, 1990). Existing attempts to explore child welfare systems have offered some evidence to support the argument that there is a degree of consistency between ideologies and policy interventions. However, this relationship is by no means clear-cut or straightforward (Hendrick, 2003; Birn, 2007). One way of investigating this complex issue has been to consider empirically the influence of competing models of childhood *within* rather than *between* legal and welfare systems (Daniel and Ivatts, 1998; James and James, 2004).

Thus, explanations for policy change are sought in the shifting balance of influence between competing assumptions about children.

Attempts to explore this territory are particularly pertinent in the case of Britain, it is argued, because its policy agenda for children has historically been 'implicit' rather than clearly elaborated (Daniel and Ivatts, 1998, p. 4). In purely organizational and strategic terms, the policy responsibility for children in the UK has historically been 'scattered and fragmented', with no 'mechanism for co-ordination' (Daniel and Ivatts, 1998, p. 5). As we shall see, very recent developments may have changed this position somewhat, but the underlying argument is that:

> In the absence of any explicit framework of aims and principles, policy towards children is developed according to a set of implicit assumptions and values, often embedded in wider concerns such as the relationship between the state and the family, or the future of the nation.
>
> (Daniel and Ivatts, 1998, p. 5)

Children's presence in policy debates and initiatives is essentially restricted to one of three previously assigned roles, drawing on wider discourses and constructions: child as 'threat; victim; and investment' (Daniel and Ivatts, 1998, p. 11). These characterizations are not necessarily in direct conflict, but certainly 'overlap' providing a range of potential justifications for intervention in the family. This classification draws on Hendrick's (1994) earlier study of nineteenth- and twentieth-century child welfare. In his account, policy for children is constructed largely in the light of the dynamic interplay between their perceived status as 'victim' or 'threat' (Hendrick, 1994, p. 8), such that:

> Despite numerous advantages accruing from the ostensibly protective Acts the victims were rarely allowed to reap the benefits of sympathy for their condition without the suspicion of what they might become if, in the nineteenth century, they were left unprotected by charitable organisations such as Dr Barnardo's or, in the twentieth century, by the State. The child victim was nearly always seen as harbouring the possibility of another condition, one that was sensed to be threatening.
>
> (Hendrick, 1994, p. 8)

This duality seems to be a perennial feature of the ways in which policy addresses the child, notably in areas of intervention such as youth justice, and special education.

However, this recurring tension also served an additional purpose, in his view, which was to act as a focal point for the third conceptualization of the child as a site for 'investment' (Hendrick, 1994, p. 14). Children's problems and the need to take action to address them were thus mediated by a future-oriented concern to create the next generation of healthy and productive members of society. Critical periods of policy change and increased levels of public spending may be associated with this; for instance, substantial state investment in child health and education followed the exposure in the Boer War of endemic unfitness and unpreparedness among the armed forces. Further periods of positive 'investment' in children can be identified following the Beveridge Report of 1942, and the findings on child poverty revealed by the Commission on Social Justice in the 1990s (Daniel and Ivatts, 1998, p. 15). At other times, though, as issues of threat or victimhood have receded into the background, the principle of children as a legitimate focus for 'investment' by the state has seemed less compelling. For Daniel and Ivatts (1998, p. 14) the default position has been to see 'children more as a private indulgence than a public responsibility', to be provided for and controlled within the family. Likewise, for Hendrick (1994, p. 14), the inter-war period was a time of cutbacks which saw a comparatively reduced level of concern over 'malnutrition and ill-health' among children.

Periodic intensification of the commitment to 'invest in children' has resulted once again in an upsurge of activity in the early years of the twenty-first century, with the highly interventionist approach of the New Labour government. Alongside its ambitions to end child poverty, this administration also made major commitments through schemes such as Sure Start, and more recently, its *Every Child Matters* initiative. This is noteworthy because it ties together Hendrick's three conceptualizations of childhood under the umbrella of the 'five outcomes' to which policy should aspire:

> Every Child Matters: Change for Children is a new approach to the well-being of children and young people from birth to age 19.
>
> The Government's aim is for every child, whatever their background or their circumstances, to have the support they need to:
>
> - Be healthy
> - Stay safe
> - Enjoy and achieve
> - Make a positive contribution
> - Achieve economic well-being.
>
> (http://everychildmatters.gov.uk/aims,
> accessed 15 Feb. 2008)

Subsumed under these aims are notions of protecting children from harm ('victim' perspective) and ensuring that they behave responsibly ('threat'), and the mechanism for achieving this is to be a well-funded corporate and collaborative commitment from all those agencies with a responsibility for children's well-being ('investment'). In this sense, at least, there has been a discernible shift in emphasis towards the idea of a comprehensive approach to children in their role as the collective future of the nation.

On the face of it, this represents a break with earlier approaches, as children become recognized as the focal point for policy-making in their own right. In the same way as has been the case in other states, such as Norway, for many years, so a 'child focus' has emerged in recent UK initiatives: 'Undoubtedly the most significant political development for children's rights has been the election of more "children friendly" Labour governments in 1997 and again in 2001' (Franklin, 2002a, p. 3). This child-centred approach has been reflected in the explicit expectation that children themselves will have an active role in the policy-making process, and there have been a number of concrete developments in support of this, including the establishment of the Children and Young People's Unit, the posts of Children's Commissioner (at different times and with rather different remits in the four countries of the UK), and a range of mechanisms intended to obtain and act on children's views. Thus:

> [Statutory agencies] will need to involve children and young people in this process, and when inspectors assess how local areas are doing, they will listen especially to the views of children and young people themselves.
>
> (http://everychildmatters.gov.uk/aims, accessed 15 Feb. 2008)

Similar trends are clearly observable internationally, following the adoption of the UN Convention on the Rights of the Child in 1989. Responses to this kind of development have been mixed, however. Parton (2006), for example, agrees that there has been a significant recent shift with childhood becoming both a 'catalyst' for public concern and a 'key site for government intervention' (Parton, 2006, p. 98), to the extent that the triangular relationship between children, the family and with the state has been significantly altered. The prioritizing of children's needs and interests may have advantages to the extent that they come to be seen as actors in their own right, but there are negative consequences, too. As the machinery of intervention becomes increasingly sensitized to child-related concerns, the possibility of collateral damage also becomes greater. Now, 'the systems are so extensive, the definitions of concern so broad' (Parton, 2006, p. 185) and professionals are so clearly accountable, that these organizational and professional interests may come to dominate at the point where decisions are made about where and how to intervene: 'While children are being placed at the centre of the new services, there is a great danger that the services will not be child-centred' (Parton, 2006, p. 185). In similar terms, as we have seen, recent trends in youth justice have been described as involving a process of 'responsibilizing' children and young people, so that they are held to be accountable for their actions in increasingly similar ways to adults (Goldson and Muncie, 2006, p. 224). Restorative justice initiatives, for example, can be seen as both positive, to the extent that they include young people in addressing the problems arising from their behaviour, and damaging to the extent that they are associated with punitive and exclusionary sanctions (Haines and O'Mahony, 2006, p. 120). As is often the case in child welfare policy, we are faced with a paradox. Measures to enhance children's centrality and influence in the process of policy-making are at the same time associated with a greater emphasis on their accountability; this, in turn, exposes them to interventions which impose new restrictions and controls.

Despite substantial reservations about the limitations and sometimes counterproductive outcomes of the 'children's rights' agenda (Muncie, 2002; Freeman, 2002), there is some support for the idea that a fourth 'model' of policy formation for children is now becoming established, in the UK and internationally (John, 2003). Thus, alongside the notions of children as 'threat', 'victims' and 'investments', children are now appearing 'in policies' and in policy-making 'as persons in their own right' (Fox Harding, 1997; Skevik, 2003, p. 426).

As already noted, the UK itself has been slower than some countries (Scandinavia, Austria, and parts of the developing world) to recognize and respond to the 'children's rights movement', but there is reported evidence of a consistent and widespread trend:

> Children across the world are now seeing themselves as partners in the challenge to improve conditions in the world for everyone. They are repositioning themselves, not as powerless and dependent but as partners in a new relationship with adults involving reciprocal responsibilities.
>
> (John, 2003, p. 222)

While a moment's thought will probably bring to mind many contemporary examples of children's rights being denied in the most
brutal and extreme ways possible (at the time of writing genocide in
Darfur is a prominent illustration of this), formal recognition of their
place in the policy-making process is indeed becoming clearer and
more explicit, for example, through their direct representation at the
UN Summit on Children in 2001 (John, 2003, p. 69). As John notes,
too (2003, p. 217), new technologies also offer them scope to use
informal means to 'subvert' and transform existing power structures
and hierarchies. At the other extreme, might it also be the case that
'street children' who experience the most oppressive forms of social
exclusion are gaining some capacity, albeit limited and compromised,
to organize themselves and articulate their own programmes for
change (Ennew, 2002)? The identification of this group of children
as either 'threat' or 'victim' has, in the past, resulted in brutal repres-
sion or ineffective service provision; so the assertion of a different
participative model of change in Brazil has become 'an icon for
popular understanding of what children's participation can mean'
(Ennew, 2002, p. 395).

Models of child welfare – models of childhood?

Returning to our central theme, it may be helpful briefly to reflect
on the relationship between conceptualizations of childhood in general and the ways in which children are addressed through the various policy frameworks applied to them. It may be significant, for
example, that the emerging interest in children as social 'actors' in
their own right coincides with the contemporary development of
psychological and biophysical models which emphasize their capacity for independent thought (Gopnik, 1996, for instance).

It is interesting to note that internationally, there has emerged
a high level consensus about the interests and needs of children as
represented by the UN Convention on the Rights of the Child
(UNCRC). This incorporates a range of rights, entitlements and protections which are believed to be applicable, irrespective of age, characteristics or context. The organizing principle for the convention
is the notion of 'evolving capacities' (Lansdown, 2005). This offers
the notion of a sliding scale, whereby children's need for protection
diminishes as their individual and social competencies are enhanced.
The convention is also designed to be flexible enough to allow
these assumptions to be applied selectively, given that children's

opportunities and competencies will vary according to their social, environmental and cultural settings.

Interestingly, this approach coincides with some of the observations that we have already made. Children acquire and develop understanding and skills differentially, and it is because of this that they have certain underlying rights to be protected from birth. These protections and their level will vary as children age, but there is nothing programmatic about this, and variations across a range of dimensions need to be taken into account.

The UNCRC also accommodates a quite nuanced view of the interaction of parallel processes in childhood, whereby the need for special treatment is modified by children's own experiences, access to resources and physical development. As far as possible, then, the convention represents a coherent and credible attempt to represent in practice the complexities as well as the uniformities of children's lives in situ.

Whether or not childhood is a social construction, greater attention does seem to be focusing on the 'evolving capacities' of children themselves to understand and shape the world around them. This is depicted, for instance, in the form of a 'picture of the human infant gradually forming and coordinating distinctions between his or her perspective and the perspectives of others' (Carpendale and Lewis, 2006, p. 253). Children are thus assumed to able to generate shared meanings and social understandings from a relatively early age; by extension, therefore, it might seem logical to make use of these understandings and their direct experiences of 'childhood' to inform the policy-making process.

This, in turn, has significant consequences for the way we think about both children and policy. In the same way that other movements, in the fields of disability, gender, ethnicity, sexuality and religion, for instance, have asserted their own demands to take an authoritative role in policy-decisions affecting their interests, perhaps children should be viewed as having similar collective interests. How would this impact on the construction of education systems or models of income maintenance, if the logic of children's rights and the recognition of their social competence are followed to their logical conclusions? Or are children already beginning to exercise this sort of choice and control through the informal networks and systems they initiate in their own interests (Mayall, 2002; John, 2003)? Does the emergence of a common voice and collective organization indicate that children are coming to recognize that there is a material basis for their shared interests and identity?

The underlying suggestion here is that we may actually be witnessing a progressive convergence between the ways in which children are represented in public policy, especially at the global level, the ways in which they see themselves, and the increasing recognition across a range of disciplines of their specific characteristics and distinctive capacities. This is not to suggest that such aspirational goals are reflected in the realities of many children's lives, however, and the disparities between policy and the real world obviously pose major and continuing challenges for those committed to applying knowledge and understanding effectively in children's interests.

6

Children and the Market

Children's relationship to the global market: producers and consumers

Having raised the question in the previous chapter of children's capacity to articulate their own policy objectives as a collective interest, this chapter addresses similar issues from a rather different perspective, that is, the relationship between children and the market economy. Much recent attention has focused on this in two key aspects: children as *consumers*, and children as *producers*. Thus, the way in which children are seen as a potential market for goods and services has generated considerable academic interest, mirroring that of commercial concerns which have identified what appears to be a lucrative opportunity for profit. At the same time, and in ironic counterpoint, the experience of other children as sources of (often very cheap) labour to feed growing demand for consumer goods has also been a matter of growing debate and policy activity.

In order to pursue these questions, it may be helpful to draw on a three-fold model which seeks to conceptualize children in distinct 'phases' as: 'consumers', 'interpreters' and 'actors' (Smith, 2000a), and which thereby represents distinct aspects of their relationship with the wider economy. Thus, they are addressed directly (and indirectly) as potential purchasers (or influencers of purchasers, namely, their parents) by advertisers; and, in a different context, their place as producers and sellers of goods and services may be equated to their position as 'actors'. At the same time, mediating between these roles,

105

children must also make sense of the external messages conveyed to them, and, as far as they are able, draw on these representations in order to exercise choices about how to act.

Using this analytical framework will help us to clarify and explore some important distinctions and commonalities in the way in which children fulfil their roles as economic agents.

Children learning to be consumers

From an early age, children begin to participate in market transactions:

> There's an Easy-Shop just down the street, and I go there sometimes and get things in the afternoon after school before Momma gets home. I sometimes have supper fixed and set the table before Momma gets here.
>
> (Shandra, aged 8, quoted in McNeal, 2007, p. 122)

The sheer scale of consumption by those under the age of 18 has generated massive commercial interest in developing and engaging with this sector of the population as a distinct sector of the market (Shah, 2008). It is estimated that in the United States, children themselves spend massive amounts each year (those aged up to 11 – $18 billion; 'teens'– $160 billion), and that they 'influence' a similar level of expenditure by parents: 'Advertising to children is big business.' There is thus a very direct and instrumental interest in the processes by which children can be recruited as purchasers of a wide range of products (and sources of 'influence' on yet more extensive buying choices by their parents, carers and others), including, of course, specific child-oriented goods such as sweets and toys, but also, and sometimes controversially, other products, such as fashion items, electronic media, and music. Children are also, it should be noted, consumers of a range of products which are prohibited to them, either generally, such as illegal drugs, or on specific age grounds, such as tobacco and alcohol.

There is a predictable connection between the emergence and recognition of this distinct 'market' and a growing interest in understanding how messages can be conveyed to children in order to turn them from potential to actual consumers of specific products or activities:

> Retailers have accordingly become more 'child-oriented' in their sales techniques; spending on advertising directed at children has grown exponentially; and there has been a marked increase in more general promotional activities aimed at children, not least in schools.
>
> (Buckingham and Tingstad, 2007, p. 51)

Insights from disciplines such as sociology and psychology are utilized to inform commercial decisions about the most effective way to engage and persuade children. This in itself has become the focus for intense debate, both practical and ethical. One enthusiastic promoter of 'marketing' to children (McNeal, 2007) has mapped out a developmental model of the different ages of the child *as* a consumer. Marketing strategies and messages must, according to this model, be adapted to the different levels of knowledge and comprehension demonstrated by children according to their age. As a consequence, approaches to children as consumers are sometimes compartmentalized according to whether they are 'preschoolers', 'tweens' (8–12 year olds), or in the older age range as a slightly scaled down version of the adult market, whose adult aspirations might themselves be targeted (fashion, identity and 'fitting in', for example).

Children are viewed as progressing from a state of relative incompetence, to one in which they can apply near adult insights into the meanings and intent of advertising messages directed towards them. This requires the acquisition of 'two key information-processing skills' (Kunkel *et al.*, 2004, p. 5), that of being able to distinguish 'at a perceptual level' between commercial and other forms of subject matter, and that of being able to 'attribute persuasive intent' to what is communicated to them, and to treat it sceptically. These skills are viewed as developing 'over time as a function of cognitive growth and intellectual development'. Whether children gain these capabilities as a result of processes of maturation or as a result of learning from experience is not explored here, but it is plausible to suggest that the necessity of treating sales messages with scepticism comes from dashed hopes and lived disappointments rather than innate processes of cognitive maturation.

Nonetheless, what is demonstrable is that children's understanding of the ways they are addressed by 'commercials' changes over time, reflecting their acquisition of the role of fully-fledged 'consumer'. Children below the age of 4–5 show little awareness of the 'concept' of the commercial, treating them as similar to other programmes they may watch on television. As they do become aware of the distinction between advertisements and programme content, this is usually reflected first in an appreciation of substantive differences – commercials are 'funnier' or shorter than other programmes (Kunkel *et al.*, 2004, p. 6).It is only as they get older that children are said to recognize that advertising has a 'persuasive' intent, and it is also argued at this stage that this is 'linked to the development of the child's relevant cognitive capabilities' (Kunkel *et al.*, 2004, p. 9), rather than the sheer quantity of television advertising viewed, since this does not seem to have any influence on children's understanding of the purposes behind advertising.

Not only are developmental stages thought to be observable in children's emerging capacity to assimilate advertising material, but this study also draws attention to some of the ways in which they then respond to commercial messages. Children demonstrate good recall of advertising messages, and cite these sources as primary influences on their product preferences. In this context, experience does matter, with greater exposure to particular products likely to lead to positive attitudes; endorsements from celebrity figures also appear to have a persuasive effect (Kunkel *et al.*, 2004, p. 10). Children are influenced not just as direct purchasers, but also in the way that they may be able to persuade parents of what to buy:

> Research shows that children's purchase-influence attempts have a relatively high degree of success. Frequent parental yielding to children's purchase requests has been reported . . . In sum, although the process may be indirect, television commercials targeted at children are highly effective at accomplishing their intended goal of promoting product sales.
>
> (Kunkel *et al.*, 2004, p. 11)

Implicit here, too, in advertising practices and their outcomes, is a belief in children as essentially passive and malleable, open to manipulation and persuasion, and with limited capacity to adopt or exercise a critical perspective towards the messages of commercials. Moreover, experience in the form of 'heavy' television viewing is associated with the emergence of materialistic attitudes.

This comprehensive investigation of advertising practices in the USA suggests that children, especially younger children, do not have the capacity to view advertising material critically, they 'tend to accept commercial claims' (Kunkel *et al.*, 2004, p. 16) and this is more likely to be translated into 'purchase requests for heavily advertised products' than is evident with older children or adults.

This analysis and its conclusion – that more should be done to protect children from exploitative advertising – suggest a view of children as essentially vulnerable and immature. They are held to be cognitively underdeveloped, and thus both inherently persuadable and at the same time unable to exercise an independent or critical view of what is being presented to them. Others (for example, Schor, 2004) broadly agree with this analysis, while portraying a somewhat more complex picture. Children are, for instance, found to be capable of viewing advertising critically from about the age of 8 (Schor, 2004, p. 67), but advertisers have reflexively incorporated this knowledge into their strategies, so that: 'a back-and-forth dynamic has evolved as advertisers respond to kids' mistrust in order to circumvent it' (Schor, 2004, p. 67). The production of a 'consumer culture' among children is seen as an insidious and multi-faceted process. Thus, for example, ideas of 'kid empowerment and antiadultism are used to sell ostensibly mundane items such as snacks and cereal' (Schor, 2004, p. 123).

So, with some irony, it seems that some children are specifically targeted in a way that emphasizes their independent capacity for autonomous thought precisely in order to persuade them to take a particular consumer role. As marketers have come to recognize the substantial purchasing power of 'tweenagers', for instance (Pilcher *et al.*, 2004), they have also sought to tailor their messages to this specific group. Postmodern thinking may have played a part here, with the assumption of a 'weakening of previously established' generational boundaries and traditions (Pilcher *et al.*, 2004, p. 8).

Others have emphasized the importance of dialogue with children, in their own right: 'Tweens hate to be sold to, but love to be respected. They want to be listened to, heard and understood. Marketers should spend time with them: listen to them; talk to them; discover how they dream' (McDougall and Chantrey, 2004, p. 14). This portrayal suggests an almost magical (but somewhat implausible) transformation at around the age of 8, as children move from a naïve and uncritical response to advertising material to one which is characterized by an active and critical sense of awareness. 'Tweens' (roughly 8–13) are portrayed as active and inquiring, and must be engaged by marketers on these terms. They 'still want to explore and experience, and this is just as true of brands as it is of other things' (McDougall and Chantrey, 2004, p. 10). At the same time, this account notes, they are subject to significant levels of 'peer pressure'.

Approaches to marketing which recognize children as participants in dialogue and as partners in the construction of distinctive trends in fashion and consumption seem to display a rather different view of childhood to those which might see children more straightforwardly as targets for 'bombardment' with advertising (McDougall and Chantrey, 2004, p. 10). Different perspectives on children as

consumers may thus be expressed in polarized and somewhat emo-
tive terms. For some, it is suggested that

> [The marketing enterprise] is little more than exploitation of childhood
> innocence: children, it is argued should be kept free of the corrupting
> influence of consumer culture, since the market is inherently inimical
> to their natural interests and needs ... However, others see consumer
> culture as potentially empowering for children: no longer restricted by
> the paternalistic imperatives of adults, children are now free to register
> their needs in the marketplace, and are increasingly seen as sophisticated,
> discriminating consumers.
>
> (Buckingham and Tingstad, 2007, p. 52)

This polarization can also be recast in the form of a conflict between
different perspectives in the study of childhood (Cook, 2005). A fundamental tension is identified between the 'exploited or exploitable child'
and the 'empowered child' (Cook, 2005, p. 156). In the contemporary
era, it is argued, it is the site of children's consumption that is the focal
point for this conflict to be played and out. This is partly because consumer culture is all-pervasive, at least in the developed world (Langer,
2005, p. 261), and this sets the parameters for the development and
assertion of personal and collective identities. Thus: 'symbolic resources
for children's self-formation are increasingly 'commercial' in origin and
children's capacity for spontaneity and creativity is exercised within a
commercially constituted life world' (Langer, 2005, p. 262). Children's
identity is formed through a process of reflection and negotiation, with
self and others, which locates the individual within a particular context
and establishes a specific sense of 'self' (Langer, 2005, p. 263). Modern
childhood identities are developed within a certain framework, which
both makes assumptions about children and constitutes their terms
of reference. '[The] market is ... one of several structuring forces that
categorise, define and calibrate children', reputedly (Buckingham and
Tingstad, 2007, p. 54). More strongly put, [A] generation has grown,
formed within, by and for the market rather than by and for society' (Seabrook, 2007). According to this view, children have become
detached from other anchoring points, such as 'place, function or
purpose' and are left to engage and construct themselves, their peer
relationships and their culture solely within the framework generated
by the market and its modes of communication and ideology.

Rather than being passive objects, on one hand, or active autonomous beings, on the other, the suggestion here is that the market
works to construct a form of childhood which incorporates both

aspects. Children's active self-expression is to be encouraged, but only to the extent that it reflects a renegotiation and realignment of their pre-assigned roles as consumers.

Children as producers – a different world?

Of course, the other side of the coin (literally) is the process of producing goods for the market. While the focus on children as consumers has tended to revolve around those who are relatively affluent and living in wealthy societies, the issue of child labour is very often framed in terms of the exploitation of children in poorer countries (UNICEF, 2005), or historical examples drawn from pre-industrial and industrializing societies (Bennett, 1991; Zelizer, 1994). Here, the stereotypical illustration has often been that of the exploited child making trainers in an Asian factory which are subsequently marketed and sold as designer goods to other, affluent children in the West (see Bartlett *et al.*, 2005, p. 936). In other words, two very different childhoods are connected and mediated by the common process leading from production to purchase of this one line of fashion products. While factory work is by no means the most prevalent form of child labour (UNICEF, 2005, p. 22), it is a useful starting point for our consideration of the experience and impact of children's 'work'. Given the extent of their involvement in economic activities across the world, we may be forced to reconsider many of our contemporary assumptions about what constitutes childhood, and what distinguishes it from mature adulthood. On the other hand, recurrent childhood themes such as the issues of vulnerability and exploitation are reinforced by the evidence uncovered here.

As UNICEF (2005, p. 7) points out, the very term 'child labour' incorporates an assumption that this is not an appropriate form of activity for the young. However, many millions of children start work as soon as they can because of poverty, and as a way of supplementing meagre family incomes. It is estimated that more than 350 million children between the ages of 5 and 17 are involved in work across the world, and of these, only around 80 million (23 per cent) have 'reasonable jobs' (UNICEF, 2005, p. 21). Some 180 million (51 per cent) 'are involved in the abuse of the "worst forms" of child labour', including slavery, sexual exploitation, forced labour and other very hazardous occupations, and this number is more heavily concentrated among the younger members of the age range. There are significant geographical variations, with 41 per cent of

5 to 14-year-olds in Africa doing paid work, compared to 21 per cent in Asia, and 17 per cent in Latin America and the Caribbean (UNICEF, 2005, p. 22). Most (70 per cent) are said to be involved in agricultural work, but others are involved in the 'informal economy' (street selling, for example) or in the production of goods for export.

It should be noted that, as well as age and geographical variations, other patterns are also identifiable, significantly on the basis of gender and minority group status. Thus, it seems that girls are more likely to leave or be withdrawn from education earlier, while they are also more likely to be engaged in certain forms of exploitative work, such as domestic service, or sex work (UNICEF, 2005, p. 13). Other discriminatory forces ensure that certain groups are forced out of education and into the labour market, such as low caste children in South Asia, and Roma children in Europe.

These international findings suggest a number of important points. First, it is clear that child labour is a very widespread, endemic and routinized phenomenon. Second, it involves certain groups disproportionately. Third, it has a dramatic material impact in shaping childhood, for instance, by taking the place of formal educational activities. And, finally, it is associated with very substantial levels of exploitation and mistreatment. Children as producers, then, appear to exist in a highly problematic and skewed relationship with their wider societies and the (global) economy. As children appear to be constrained in their choices of activity and future aspirations by economic circumstances and external pressure, so we may need to adopt a similarly restricted view of what constitutes childhood for them.

In the same way as attention has been focused on the problematic nature of child labour in the contemporary global economy, so also the history of children's work in developed countries has been a subject of significant interest. Children's involvement as contributors in the workplace was well established by the time of the Industrial Revolution, but this nonetheless had a dramatic effect on their lives. The more unpredictable but in some ways less harsh and demanding rhythms of agricultural labour were supplanted by the intensity of the manufacturing process: 'The working day for children during the 'brisk' or busy time could keep them at the machines for up to sixteen to eighteen hours in conditions made intolerable for many by strict discipline enforced by physical punishment' (Bennett, 1991, p. 7). This was not something that went without criticism, being described in some quarters as a form of slavery. Children were frequently the victims of workplace injuries as well as being subjected to serious beatings (Bennett, 1991, p. 11).

This experience was replicated in other developing countries of the time, including the United States (Zelizer, 1994). It is reported that the US census of 1900 found that as many as one in ten children aged 10–15 was 'gainfully employed' (Zelizer, 1994, p. 56), but even this was an underestimate. Industrialization had made a major contribution to this figure, being responsible for an increase of 'over a million' child workers between 1870 and 1900. This trend was borne of the demands of manufacturing enterprises, on the one hand, and persistent poverty, on the other: 'The useful child, therefore, provided a unique economic buffer for the working-class family of the late nineteenth century' (Zelizer, 1994, p. 60).

As in the contemporary global context, however, child labour in the past became a matter of considerable concern, focusing on a number of important questions; children were believed to be forfeiting educational opportunities while at the same time experiencing exploitation, poor health and harm. The response to this has been a gradual enactment of enhanced protections for children paralleled by increased investment in their education. A series of legislative reforms and structural changes was introduced from the late nineteenth century onwards. Children's working hours and legitimate places of employment were regulated, and formal education took the place of paid work for increasing numbers to progressively higher ages (Newman, 2000). Of course, in keeping with the discourses of development and modernization, children are believed to be considerably better off under the welfare regimes of contemporary industrial societies (McKechnie and Hobbs, 1999).

Idealization of these trends has had a number of consequences, though. First, it cements in place assumptions about the preferred state of childhood:

> The 'true' nature of childhood was to be defined by home, school and dependence. Work, while essential for the self-esteem and identity of adults, was perceived as having an entirely opposite effect on children, being a source of potential danger not just to their health, but to their very souls.
> (Newman, 2000, p. 330)

Childhood is seen through this lens as undergoing a process of continual improvement, or 'liberation', with the living conditions, entitlements and protections available becoming progressively better as industrialized capitalist societies have continued to develop. The point is made, however, that children are not the only beneficiaries of modernization and reform. Changing economic needs have also played a significant part, so that education became an important means of preparing them to take on different productive roles (Zelizer, 1994, p. 112). Newman (2000, p. 332) also claims that 'the protection of children' and changing expectations of them owe as much to 'expediency' as anything else. For Newman, the status of children in modern societies reflects a process of 'sacralizing' them, as much in the interests of adults and their sentimentalities as in the interests of children's well-being. He concludes that this is unlikely to be sustained in the longer term, however, because of the evidence of 'substantial changes' in the domestic economy (Newman, 2000, p. 335). In this way, too, the contingent nature of one particular cultural form which idealizes children as dependent and in need of nurturing and protection is thrown into relief and leads us to re-evaluate the 'assumed superiority of cultures' that do not offer children the opportunity to participate in the economy as workers and producers, but merely as consumers.

Partial and ahistorical idealizations of children's place (or absence) in the economic arena are also called into question in a rather different way by investigations into the actual extent of their involvement as workers in developed welfare states, which is found to be both more extensive and, indeed, more exploitative than conventionally believed:

> The developed countries look to their own past development and highlight the way in which children were used in an array of economic activities including factory work and mining. The implication of this view of children at work is that the developed economies have solved the problem in their own countries in times long past.
>
> (McKechnie and Hobbs, 1999, p. 89)

Any involvement of children as employees is assumed to be found only among a small minority, to encompass 'light' and non-exploitative work, and to be subject to effective legislative controls and policy frameworks to enforce the necessary safeguards (McKechnie and Hobbs, 1999, p. 90).

By contrast, these authors point to the substantial evidence available concerning children's working practices in those very same modern developed countries. When looking, for example, at employment levels of children around the UK, they have found rates of 'between 32 and 50 per cent' in some form or other of current work (McKechnie and Hobbs, 1999, p. 91). While much of this may be represented by 'children's jobs' such as newspaper delivery, 'it is not uncommon to find children starting work at 4.00am and working several hours before going to school' (McKechnie and Hobbs, 1999, p. 93). Children were also found to be working in a range of 'adult employment' settings, such as garage work, a sawmill, and building sites. So, not only is there evidence of very extensive employment of children, but in many cases, too, this is found to be exploitative, whether in terms of long hours, unsatisfactory or dangerous work settings, or low pay.

While they are not directly involved in the 'market', another group of children who can be said to be engaged in productive economic activity are young carers, whose extensive range of activities effectively subsidizes the welfare state to a very considerable extent. Aldridge and Becker (2002, p. 208) have estimated that there are 'as many as 50,000' young carers in Britain who are providing what they term 'substantial' levels of assistance to parents or other relatives in their own homes. This level and intensity of support offered by children to others have only relatively recently been acknowledged in research and policy, but we now: 'know that young carers perform a range of caring and other duties, from basic domestic work to nursing tasks that include intimate caring (toileting, bathing), administering medication, lifting, as well as acting as interpreters between parents and welfare professionals' (Aldridge and Becker, 2002, p. 209). In this role, as in other more conventionally understood economic activities, children's position is seen as essentially ambiguous, with some sources claiming that their caring experience leads to them becoming 'parentified' (Aldridge and Becker, 2002, p. 217), as responsibility for nurturing and physical care shifts between generations. While this suggestion has been questioned, there does seem to be a degree of '*duality*' about children's experiences, whereby they are asked to take on additional responsibilities normally ascribed to adults, while also undertaking conventional childhood activities such as schooling. While the context is very different, children's place as 'producers' in this respect may also bear similarities to that of children engaged in manual labour in developing countries, who are making a distinct and necessary economic contribution to family well-being. This duality of roles has been reflected in popular responses, too, with 'young caring' being the subject of two contrasting media portrayals. The 'little angel' story ... and 'the little victim' narrative once again contrast views of the child as an active

and conscious 'producer' of social welfare with those which see her/
him as essentially vulnerable and exploited.

Modes of childhood: towards a theoretical model?

As we have seen, contrasting assumptions about and experiences of childhood are identifiable in the different ways in which children are engaged
in economic activity. They may be seen, for instance, as a 'market' which
can be targeted, drawing on psychological insights, and thereby they
develop into consumers. On the other hand, the focus might be turned
to their productive activities and the ways in which they become contributors (paid or unpaid) to the broader social economy. Implicit in
these perspectives are theoretical assumptions about children and child
development which appear partial. It is therefore important to seek to
develop a conceptual framework which enables us to view children and
their lives from an integrated perspective, and which does not fragment
or fracture different aspects of their experiences.

Of course, the dichotomy between children as consumers or producers is mirrored by a series of other dualisms, whereby they are
portrayed one-sidedly as perpetrators or victims (Jenks, 1996; Fionda,
2005, for example). Importantly, though, their lives, as a whole and in
their distinct phases, do not reflect such simplistic characterizations,
and this is demonstrable in empirical as well as theoretical terms. Two
contrasting examples can be drawn upon to illustrate this point.

The first of these revisits a source already touched upon. This
is Corsaro's (1997, p. 2) description of a quasi-commercial activity being carried out by a number of pre-school children in Italy.
The author was carrying out a piece of research through participant
observation, when he noticed 'three children marching around the
yard carrying a large, red milk carton', which contained a bucket
filled with rocks. He thought that they were using it as a kind of
boat, but they corrected him, informing him that it was, in fact, a
kind of mobile bank. They then went through a process of determining that he wanted to make a withdrawal and counting out what he
needed in the form of rocks (worth 10,000 lire each), before heading
off with the bank, presumably to make the next 'house call'.

As he observes, this episode indicates that:

> Children are active, creative social agents who produce their own unique
> children's cultures while simultaneously contributing to the production
> of adult societies. [The children] weren't supposed to play with the milk
> carton but they didn't like the adult rule, so they played with it anyway.

> They created a highly unique 'travelling bank' – an idea taken from the adult world but extended and given new meaning.
>
> (Corsaro, 1997, p. 4)

Importantly, then, children had made their own observations of the economic world, made own sense of it, and then reconstructed their own version of it at a relatively young age. They had assimilated some of the rules of money and banking, while also incorporating a number of refinements of their own, suggesting quite a complex and multi-faceted relationship with the world of banks and commerce, consistent with the conceptual framework set out at the beginning of this chapter.

In a different, albeit non-commercial, context the relationship between children's roles as consumers and producers of culture has also been explored helpfully (Barrett, 2003). The starting point was the emergent concern with globalizing forces associated with 'computer-mediated technologies' (Barrett, 2003, p. 196), which are linked with 'the commodification of children's culture' even in 'the kindergarten'. Children's worlds are populated with consumerist messages, from their backpacks with pictures of popular television characters to their learning and creative materials carrying all sorts of commercial messages. However, this particular study, focusing on children's consumption and use of musical influences, went on to address 'the ways in which children select from the musical worlds they encounter in order to construct and 'engineer' their own musical narratives' (Barrett, 2003, p. 197). Children's understanding and creation of music are shaped by their exposure to key television programmes, it is suggested, in this case (Australia), *Play School* and *Hi-5*. Both programmes are associated with a wide range of products which they are seeking to 'market' to children, although it is interesting that they appear to address young children in different ways. *Play School* is more traditional, drawing on nursery rhymes, and with a fairly undramatic format. However, in this programme, 'the child is encouraged to participate through the inclusion of songs that are familiar', which are 'presented in ways that encourage joining in' (Barrett, 2003, p. 203). *Hi-5* is much more contemporary in feel, being based on a pop concert format, although space for participation is much more limited and highly structured. In the study described here, the attempt was made to explore the ways in which these 'major musical reference points' (Barrett, 2003, p. 204) were utilized in children's own music-making. It was found, for example, that children were prepared to make their own songs, in some but not all cases. These songs appeared to integrate musical sources with their own experience. For example, a girl who lived on a farm recited songs about animals, as well as her own daily routines. The author of the study concludes that the songs created by this particular child (Chelsea) 'reflect an understanding of traditional nursery rhyme and song material as it is presented to children' (Barrett, 2003, p. 205), albeit drawing on her personal life experience:

> It is clear that Chelsea, as with other children of her age . . ., is an active producer rather than simply a re-producer of her musical culture and her musical narratives.
>
> The textual content of Chelsea's songs revolves around the themes of her daily life, those of 'going to mummy', 'going for a walk and going back home', 'having lunch', 'going to bed', 'mummy singing a lullaby' and 'then it's morning time'. The characters that populate these songs are those of her domestic situation: the sheep, the rabbits and the dangers they are prone to (cats will eat you), Mummy and Barbie.
>
> (Barrett, 2003, p. 205)

While children in this context are addressed as potential or actual consumers of music and other products, they are in fact 'constructing meaning' for themselves and utilizing these cultural influences to express themselves. Indeed, the very variety of competing styles in children's television actually offers the child a 'rich palette' (Barrett, 2003, p. 206) of sources from which 'she constructs her own musical narratives'.

Accounting for this interactive and creative process requires us to think of the child as more than a one-dimensional construct. In effect, s/he is at one and the same time, consumer, synthesizer and producer of culture, ideas and material things.

My own earlier attempt to make sense of this tension was prompted initially by concerns about globalization and the apparent homogenization of many aspects of childhood experience (Smith, 2000a), drawing on the ideas of Giddens (1991), in particular. It seemed here that the interpenetration of many aspects of production, consumption and culture meant that children, like other members of the global society, were becoming increasingly exposed to an array of interchangeable messages or stimuli, almost irrespective of the setting, in the same way as Barrett (2003) observes. Children, like adults, appear to have become the objects of a process of 'commodification'

(Giddens, 1991, p. 197), whereby the impetus towards economic growth under capitalism generates 'standardized consumption patterns, promoted through advertising and other methods'. Against this backdrop, and especially in the context of developmental assumptions about children's levels of competence, it might be expected that these consumerist messages are simply received, processed and acted upon in a more or less unilinear and predictable fashion. However, as we have observed, children do appear to be capable from an early age of deviating from the script and amending their responses. This is reflected not least in those aspects of their use of new technology which supersede those of their adult counterparts: 'children are quite frequently ahead of adults both in media awareness and technical competence ... – they understand the 24-button remote control, and they know where it is!' (Smith, 2000a, p. 4).

Indeed, the counterpoint to the globalization thesis, expressed through theories of post-modern fragmentation, rather suggests that children may need to be a step ahead, as their individual lives and circumstances become more complex, precisely because of the sheer array of 'inputs' they are likely to receive from different sources. The competitive and, indeed, disparate nature of the market itself points towards inconsistency and unevenness in children's experience of it – whether as consumers, or producers, subject to the demands of a casualized economy.

Fragmentation is reported to affect children in a number of ways, not just as economic beings, but because other aspects of their lives are also increasingly likely to be in flux, due to family change, migration, or social and economic upheaval. It is reassuring, then, as Giddens (1991, p. 199) again observes, that individuals can be observed to 'actively discriminate' between different types of information and 'interpret' it 'on their own terms'. We must therefore adopt an integrated framework for understanding the different aspects of children's lives, which sees them as, at one and the same time, 'consumers', 'interpreters' and 'actors' (Smith, 2000a, p. 5). From this stem some important considerations for the ways in which children are addressed, engaged and encouraged to participate in the social world. The implication here is that they have a capacity to exercise and act on a 'critical' view of the world and what is presented to them. Thus, for example, 'set against the passive and malleable consumer is another persona, the questioning and creative interpreter' (Smith, 2000a, p. 7), who will, of course, go on to act in ways which are not entirely predictable or programmable. As Giddens observes, it is in these complex processes of sense-making and action that individuals begin to chart distinctive personal biographies and a sense of self.

Ironically, the problem for children might not be located in their undeveloped capacities or their malleability, but in the limited and often partial material provided to help them in the sense-making process. In McNeal's (2007, p. 289) view: 'Children are assuming more responsibility for consumer behaviour decisions in their households and are doing it with no increase in information on which to make those decisions.' Children are therefore seen as having the capacity to make choices and to act in their own right, but not to be afforded sufficient information or advice to enable them to do so appropriately. This in turn might lead us to the view that it is the external environment which should be called into question for its partial treatment of children, rather than their own inherent limitations. If our construction of the child as a competent being, able to acquire, process and act on information rationally, is accurate, then responsibility for the distortion, disruption and misrepresentation of childhood must lie elsewhere. Equally, we cannot think only in terms of partial solutions to the problems of childhood, whether in the form of protection or control measures, because these, similarly, reflect only a restricted view of children, and their internal processes.

Constructing the economic child

We might be drawn to the conclusion that children's place in the market is largely shaped by external forces which hold a one-sided and sometimes exploitative view of them. Indeed, it may be the case that childhood itself is defined to a considerable extent by children's relationship to the economy. At the same time, children demonstrate the capacity to make sense of and respond to these influences, to the extent that they are able to do so, depending on their level of prior knowledge and experience and the resources available to them to assert themselves independently.

Thus, John (2003, p. 177) recounts the example of Mexican child workers who have been able to express their views and negotiate some form of compromise between their economic activities and their educational needs. It might appear from some perspectives that they should be protected from the exploitative demands of their employment setting. However, '[The] adults who had grown up as street children were emphatic about how essential it had been for

them to find ways of earning money.' Children's capacity to negotiate and reframe external pressures and to resist being defined one-
dimensionally should not be underestimated: 'listening to the child
labourer's realities has represented a start on a process of empowerment' (John, 2003, p. 175).

Representing children in this way and recognizing their capacities
may reflect a change in their economic relationships with the wider
society which is mirrored in the changing way they are conceptualized. Does the interactive nature of their engagement with the
market also help to account for the ways in which children become
'knowing' consumers? They form independent opinions and 'demonstrate a growing autonomy from their parents in terms of the
products they choose and their methods of choosing. We have also
seen examples of children assuming an authority to modernise parents' tastes' (Boden, 2006, p. 8). While this may be the case, Boden
also acknowledges that children 'are faced with a series of objective
and subjective constraints' that are highly influential on their behaviour as consumers. Children's decisions and actions therefore appear
to be mediated by a variety of structural and interpersonal factors,
giving further support to the notion that this must be understood as
an interactive process.

In analytical terms, this might suggest that it is more helpful to
think in terms of patterns and tendencies in the landscapes and experiences of childhood, rather than seeking out uniformities which can
be generalized across the population as a whole. We cannot dispense
with the idea that childhood has common features, but it seems
increasingly likely that the way it is negotiated depends on a wide
range of contextual influences and localized choices, including those
structured by the demands and constraints of the economy. As already
demonstrated (Chapters 3 and 4), there are good grounds for thinking that these influences have a direct impact on the internal lives of
children as well as the external worlds that they inhabit and create.

7

Children and the Media

The role of the media in children's lives

Just as children's relationship with the economy is important, so, too, it is essential to consider their interactions with the media, especially in our 'digital age'. The recurrent questions of how childhood is defined and lived are highly relevant in this context, given the pervasive reach of a wide range of means of communication throughout children's lives. They are clearly a target for specific economic reasons, such as the marketing of goods, activities and services, as we saw in the previous chapter. But beyond this, the media has a central role to play in learning and socialization processes, on the one hand; and, on the other, acting as a focal point for children's own creativity and independent forms of communication and relationship-building. The various platforms available provide both a means of constructing and shaping childhood, and a vehicle for children's own growing ability to express themselves autonomously and in their terms.

The centrality of the media to children's lives in modern times gives rise to a number of questions. Is this a highly specific historical phase, indicating that contemporary childhoods are, almost by definition, fundamentally different from those in former times, when the media were not so pervasive? In other words, has childhood been revolutionized by the emergence of new forms of communication and information technology? Or are these undoubted innovations and the ways in which they are used more appropriately understood as ephemeral, representing new dynamics and challenges, but none-theless leaving the childhood experience essentially unaltered?

The aim of this chapter is to explore these questions in light of what we know at present about the relationship between children and the media, of all kinds. In order to pursue this goal, I will con-sider a number of subjects of interest, including:

- media constructions of childhood;
- media influences on children;
- children's 'constructive' use of the media;
- specific issues of topical interest, such as the question of media violence and children.

Constructing childhood? The role of the media

In one sense, the role of the media in creating perceptions of child-hood brings us full circle, back to the work of Ariès (1962), whose ideas were strongly influenced by the depictions of children in picto-rial form. He notes, for example, the virtual absence of children and family scenes from calendars prior to the sixteenth century (Ariès, (1962, p. 342), suggesting a parallel development of portrayals of fam-ily life with that of the concept 'of childhood' itself (Ariès, 1962, p. 364). Of course, the dynamics of the relationship between repre-sentation and reality remain unclear, although strong moral and reli-gious themes were evident in many depictions of children and family life (Ariès, 1962, p. 360).

In the modern era, with the burgeoning of the media, a much wider range of imagery is evident, across the full spectrum of chil-dren's lives (Holland, 2004). Nonetheless, the important distinction between idealized portrayals of 'childhood', since the Middle Ages, and the changing experiences of children themselves remains clear, suggesting a degree of disjuncture between the image and the real-ity: 'Alongside the joyous images from advertising and consumer magazines, many contemporary narratives of childhood are bleak and deeply disturbing' (Holland, 2004, p. xi). According to this source, then, we should not expect there to be a direct correlation between the 'image' and underlying reality; portrayals of children are con-ceived as aspects of an interactive process, through which meanings come to be created '*between* an image and its makers and its users' (Holland, 2004, p. 4). Underlying this argument is an assumption that the production and dissemination of images of childhood are purposeful, intended to convey certain impressions and promote specific messages, rather than simply an attempt to represent 'real life':

> This imagery obsessively sorts and classifies, as if afraid of interpretations which might run out of control. With absolute conviction it stresses those vital indications which separate children from adults, work from play, happiness from unhappiness, appropriate from inappropriate appearance and behaviour.
>
> (Holland, 2004, p. 5)

The images of children to which we are exposed are described as '*desired* images' (Holland, 2004, p. 7), that is, they are intended to convey a certain characterization of what it is to be a child, or what childhood *should* be like. Thus, we are likely to find that representations which are awkward, embarrassing, inconsistent, or which undermine preconceived notions may not readily be expressed. This does not mean necessarily that the only portrayals of children we will encounter will represent innocence and goodness, but rather that they will tend to emphasize consistent stereotypical characteristics, polarizing ideas of childhood rather than reflecting its ambiguities and uncertainties. It is unsurprising, in light of this, that we can identify a series of strong and resonant themes in the childhood images Holland catalogues.

Innocence, for example, has been a pervasive theme over a lengthy period of time, feeding, indeed, into the consumerist agenda: 'The image of innocence was an eminently exploitable commodity. It could be associated with cleanliness and purity, and could contribute to the new marketing technique of branding' (Holland, 2004, p. 12).

On the other hand, other, darker images of wayward and threatening children ('bad boys', Holland, 2004, p. 116) can also be found permeating newspaper and TV reports. Children are here presented in a series of threatening poses, with graphic and shocking characterizations mirrored in a series of equally disturbing nicknames, such as 'Balaclava Boy', an 11-year-old who reportedly 'terrorised a Hartlepool estate' in the year 2000 (Holland, 2004, p. 122). These children need to be rescued from depravity, and restored to their natural state of innocence, according to one reading of these disturbing images. They are sometimes pictured with their parents, who are shown demonstrating understanding and forgiveness (Holland, 2004, p. 129), despite their outrageous appearance.

It seems that media constructions of childhood must above all demonstrate coherence and internal consistency. They are without nuance. Kitzinger (2004) argues, for example, that definitions of child sexual abuse are essentially contingent, depending on contemporary understandings of childhood. So, the modern 'western concept of childhood innocence' is a key factor in determining how 'assaults against children' are viewed, and what the appropriate response should be (Kitzinger, 2004, p. 33). Depictions of, and responses to, paedophilia can be shown to have changed significantly over a relatively short period of time, she suggests, based partly on shifting views about children's rights and capacity to make decisions on their own behalf (Kitzinger, 2004, p. 34). It was media attention which played a significant part in redefining sexual acts between adults and children as abusive: 'The USA had front-page revelations about "the reality" of abuse, including incest, from the early 1980s onwards' (Kitzinger, 2004, p. 35). While this clearly paralleled similar developments in professional understandings of child sexual abuse among social workers and police, it also appears to have been part of a wider process of reframing the relationship between children and adults, and reasserting the primacy of childhood 'innocence'.

At the same time, the media search for childhood innocence has been confounded by an alternative and opposing stereotype, the 'knowing' and 'threatening' child (Holland, 2004, p. 116). Age and gender may be invoked partly to explain the discrepancies in these depictions of childhood, but it remains difficult to account for 'children as young as 11 amongst those running wild on a Sheffield estate', reported in a feature in the *Mail on Sunday*, accompanied by 'photographs' showing 'young boys pushing a stolen car or leaping in front of the flames, in a spectacular image of mayhem and destruction' (Holland, 2004, p. 122). As Jenks (1996, p. 127) also observes, citing *The Sunday Times*, the media have problems of 'classification' when relatively young children (sometimes girls, too, like Mary Bell some years previously) become involved in 'violent acts', such as the killing of James Bulger. According to Jenks, the media response in this kind of case is one of 'conceptual eviction' (Jenks, 1996, p. 128), whereby children involved in acts of extreme violence are removed from the category of 'child'. An alternative lexicon, incorporating terms such as 'evil', 'devils', and 'adult' is evident in media reports, giving rise to two alternative forms of caricature: children as 'inherently evil'; or the knowing 'adult–child'. According to Jenks, this process of 'splitting off' exceptional and extreme actions is a feature of the project of 'firming up' the boundaries of specific 'conceptual categories' such as 'the child'. Thus, 'In this sense, by refusing children who commit acts of violence acceptance within the category of child, the public was reaffirming to itself the essence of what children are' (1996, p. 129).

Children cannot simultaneously be 'innocent' and capable of anti-social or violent acts, it seems, so mechanisms have to found for attributing them to one category or the other. This strategy also provides for the possibility of a narrative approach, as Jenks shows, whereby media accounts seek to capture a sense of changing times, and very often the 'loss of childhood itself' (Jenks, 1996, p. 131).

Media representations and categorizations of childhood appear to be dominated by two central preoccupations: the search for a consistent and coherent model of what childhood is; and, equally significantly, a focus on what childhood means from a societal perspective. There is a consistent preoccupation with what childhood means 'for us', rather than for children themselves. At the same time, the available categories drawn on by the media are rendered one-dimensional and static, in a way which clearly does not reflect the multiplicity and complexity of real lives, such as we have encountered in previous chapters. As a result, conflicts and contradictions tend to be airbrushed out of the picture, although they cannot be erased quite so easily from the underlying domain of lived experience. Indeed, both print and broadcast media are able to subsume contradictory images without engaging with the challenge of making sense of the implicit oppositions incorporated therein. For both Jenks (1996) and Holland (2004), this paradoxical sense of unresolved ambiguities creates problems for children:

> Given the dominance of particular models of child development in public perceptions of children, models which are both unilinear and on the whole uniform, children are rarely seen as competent advocates of their own experiences.
>
> (Jenks, 1996, p. 135)

Not only do children have little material control over the ways in which they are represented by the media, but the messages embedded within these often serve to underline a sense that their views cannot be trusted or are in some way inadequate, depending on whether they are seen as inherently wicked or dependent and vulnerable. For Holland, this is attributable to their lack of 'power' which means that: 'they suffer the indignity of being unable to present themselves as they would want to be seen' (2004, p. 21), or to provide accounts which illustrate the social and moral variations and inconsistencies which characterize their lives and experience. The very complexity of their own understandings and the expectations placed upon them make their own sense-making a much harder task to undertake.

Addressing children: do the media believe their own rhetoric?

As well as seeking to capture the nature of childhood in representational form, the media also have a more active relationship with children, clearly. Buckingham (2000, p. 8) distinguishes between two kinds of media discourses, those *about childhood*, and those produced *for children*, and it is to this area of activity that I now turn. As we have seen, this is partly inspired by an awareness of children as a potential market for consumer products, or as a potential source of influence on parents'/carers' purchasing decisions. In addition, of course, children are a target audience for media outputs of other kinds, and thus the ways in which they are addressed and influenced should be informative. Here indeed, we must face up to the important question of the media role in creating or shaping (as distinct from 'reporting on') the very 'childhoods' which generate shock and outrage from the very same outlets. As concern grows about the influence of violent images, for example, arguments also rage about who is responsible for this, and who should take responsibility for addressing it:

> Interpretations of ... changes in childhood – and of the role of the media in reflecting or producing them – have been sharply polarized. On the one hand, there are those who argue that childhood as we know it is disappearing or dying, and that the media – particularly television – are primarily to blame ... On the other hand, there are those who argue that there is a growing generation gap in media use.
>
> (Buckingham, 2000, p. 5)

Simultaneously, it seems, children's unfettered exposure to adult material through TV and film diminishes the boundaries of knowledge, experience and behaviour between the generations. Yet children's access to, and command of, a whole variety of new technologies (the internet, electronic games, mobile phones) have also maintained a distinct realm of interaction and creativity which is closed to many adults.

Marsh (2007) reworks this distinction in terms of two alternative categories applicable to children in the context of their media involvement. They can be seen as 'media saps' or 'media sages', who are either passive victims of 'manipulation by ruthless media corporations' (Marsh, 2007, p. 15) or have 'more expertise with the new technologies than the adults themselves' (Marsh, 2007, p. 19).

Inevitably, the reality of the matter is more complex (Marsh, 2007, p. 20). Children's use of different media sources is recognized as extensive, but they do access a range of these rather than being dependent on exclusive forms of input. Even very young children are likely to have access to a variety of sources and technologies – with 98 per cent of homes with young children having a television and video/DVD player, and 81 per cent owning a laptop or desktop computer. The mean age of the children in Marsh's study was 3 years 4 months, but they were already 'engaged in screen use' (television, console games, hand-held games or computers) for a mean timespan of 126 minutes a day (2007, p. 8). Although watching television forms the largest part of these activities, it is significantly outstripped by playing with toys, so does not seem to be irretrievably displacing these other types of activity (2007, p. 9). Aside from watching television, these young children were also found to be spending time on computers (53 per cent on a typical day, 2007, p. 11), and they 'were being inducted into mobile phone use' (2007, p. 12) even though they were not using mobiles independently. While their use of media was clearly not exclusive, these children 'were saturated' in the material disseminated. This might lead one to the conclusion that children, especially young children, may well be at risk of becoming 'media saps', who are simply absorbing and reproducing the images, ideas and messages relayed to them. The implications may be all the more significant given what we have already observed about 'sensitive periods' in brain development (see Chapter 4).

Children may be thought to be particularly vulnerable to the influence of television advertising, for example. Their involvement with the media might also be thought of as restrictive in other ways, such as the creation of an 'asocial' childhood, where their principal relationships would be with the screen and its characters. However, the evidence from this study (Marsh *et al.*, 2005) did not really justify these fears: 'few children conform to the stereotype of the media-addicted individual, adrift from the landscapes of social life' (Marsh *et al.*, 2005, p. 16).

Where children were viewed as actual or potential 'media sages' by their parents, their developing capacities were seen as an important safeguard. However, there was a degree of ambiguity about this finding, and Marsh (2007, p. 20) concludes that parents, as well as early years practitioners, tended to hold multiple or contradictory views about the impact of the media on children. The complexities of this relationship may be 'overlooked'.

Others share the view that the adoption of extreme positions on the subject of children's media use will only produce 'a partial picture that may be increasingly untenable for interpreting childhood in complex societies' (Drotner, 2005, p. 56). Similarly:

> A developmental perspective does not come up with a simple value-judgement on whether television is good or bad for children … It is a staple object of thought for children, on which they display and exercise their growing capacities of mind to a degree that their parents and teachers appear to barely suspect.
>
> (Hodge and Tripp, 1986, p. 98)

Again, this should not really be surprising given what we know about children's cognitive abilities and the processes by which they learn, especially through the acquisition of knowledge which they may initially take as 'given', but only until they find evidence to the contrary.

Hodge and Tripp's (1986) early study of children's television use noted some interesting variations, especially on the basis of class, leading to the conclusion that the interaction between children and media sources is mediated in quite specific ways. The authors' observations led them to the conclusion that working-class 'children are socialized into different ways of thinking about TV as about other things' (1986, p. 98), and that, in particular, their 'transformational' facilities were less well developed than those of children from other social classes, suggesting a (relatively) greater likelihood of passive acceptance.

The view that children's interactions with media are mediated by their circumstances and those around them is certainly shared by others, including Marsh *et al.* (2005), who suggests that even 'globalized discourses' like those of the Disney films are 'adapted for local contexts' (2005, p. 13) and are often interwoven with specific family events or associated with certain family members (2005, p. 14).

With some reservations though (see above), children can be seen as an 'active' audience (Buckingham, 2000, p. 115). Levels of sophistication and interpretive capacities should be seen as relative and unpredictable, rather than absolutely determined according to class differentials or other variables such as gender and culture:

> For instance, there is often an implicit assumption that if children are 'active', then they are somehow not going to be influenced by what they watch or read. Yet this does not necessarily follow. Indeed, one could argue that in some instances to be 'active' is to be more open to influence.
> (Buckingham, 2000, p. 115)

Buckingham cites here the example of contemporary advertising which specifically seeks to appeal to children's aspirations to be mature, sophisticated and 'critical.' His concerns here are linked to wider observations about the apparent naïveté of sociological celebrations of the 'competent' child (2000, p. 119), which rather underplays the impact of external influences on children, as well as the limits to competence, which children share in common with other members of society.

Further research by Buckingham and a colleague suggests that children do, however, know what they don't know, and do not inevitably make sweeping claims to media competence: 'children appear to locate themselves within developmental narratives, in which particular kinds of knowledge are "needed" at particular ages' (Buckingham and Bragg, 2005, p. 67). The way children positioned themselves in relation to the representation of sex in the media was found in this case to be part of a careful process of constructing 'counter-discourses' to meet 'adult concerns' (Buckingham and Bragg, 2005, p. 63). They drew on the media as a useful source of information for a number of reasons, including the avoidance of 'embarrassment' or elaborating moral agendas, but also because it offered them the power to choose when to 'research' particular topics (Buckingham and Bragg, 2005, p. 66). There was no sign here of the kind of irresponsibility sometimes attributed to children in this respect, and some would say they did not watch something 'because I don't feel that I need to know about that yet' (Buckingham and Bragg, 2005, p. 67). The authors conclude that the evidence of children's autonomy and competence may be positive, but that it also represents 'a process of engendering a sense of "hyper-responsibility"': children today have been bound to become self-regulating media consumers ... responsible for their own ethical self-development' (Buckingham and Bragg, 2005, p. 74). Buckingham concludes that, in order for children to be equipped to participate in this way, then the wider society does have a responsibility to 'prepare them' for this role rather than simply leave them to negotiate it unaided (2000, p. 207). The power and potential of the media to set agendas, to determine content and to control outputs should not be underestimated, even as the project of promoting children's media 'participation rights' is pursued. Media education has a particularly important part to play in this respect, according to him. This clearly resonates with the wider proposition detailed in the present account that *vulnerability* and active *learning from experience* are equally central and determining features of the lives of all children.

Children as media producers

Having considered children in different ways as objects of the media, either as artefacts or audience, it is important also to move on to consider their place as active producers of media outputs. I have acknowledged, in the previous section and earlier chapters, that children's capacity for taking an 'active' role in relation to external messages should be recognized. However, this point can be extended, such that children are seen as creative initiators of ideas and messages. It is not simply a matter of children responding to a dialogue initiated by the adult media, but it is also about their place in generating their own forms of expression. Clearly, these forms of expression are contextualized by external influences and other media sources, but I am concerned here with children's capacity to take this material and 'transform' (Hodge and Tripp, 1986) it. Accordingly: 'Children are generally sharp and cynical readers of the mass media – as they are able to demonstrate when given the opportunity to be *writers* of such media' (Gauntlett, 1998).

Contemporary interest focuses particularly on the emerging opportunities associated with the internet, mobile phones and other forms of new technology, where children and young people are believed to be more competent and confident than adults. Predictably, this ensures that this is a potent source of adult suspicion and prompts both public concern and official action, including government-sponsored inquiries (Byron, 2008). Underlying these fears, however, are specific issues to do with our deeper understanding of childhood and its essential nature:

Concerns [exist] about the role of harmful or inappropriate material in technology, in how children use online or virtual information or experiences to develop a sense of self – the inner working model of ourselves which drives how we think and feel about ourselves and in turn affects how we behave (e.g. emotional regulation, impulse control, self monitoring). For example, within some virtual worlds there is the potential to develop a new identity (called an 'avatar') and this raises the question of how this might affect a young person's sense of 'self'.

(Byron, 2008, p. 34)

Like other, earlier expressions of concern about television (see Livingstone and Bovill, 1999), this kind of characterization seems unable to shake off the underlying belief that children are ultimately subject to the influence of these media, rather than exercising choice and control over them. This gives us an insight into adult concerns *about* children's use of 'new technologies', but it tells us rather less about the nature of that experience from the child's point of view.

It is recognized that this is an area of human activity, where both numerically and in terms of their competence, children probably dominate. Although the picture is constantly changing, it has been acknowledged that children's internet use substantially outweighs that of adults (Livingstone, 2003, p. 148), and that is mirrored in parents' comments about relative levels of aptitude: 'I don't think she is quite as competent as some, but she is certainly better than we are' (parent, quoted in Marsh, 2007, p. 19).

We are cautioned against making complacent assumptions about the 'nature and extent' of children's expertise (Livingstone, 2003, p. 149), and it is pointed out that there are bound to be differential rates among children of both access to, and use of, the internet (Livingstone and Bober, 2004). Children's use of these technologies is also mixed, spanning: 'studying/homework', 'email', 'playing games', 'chat sites' and 'hobbies and interests' (Livingstone, 2003, p. 149). Some of these uses are more proactive and creative than others, and this partly contributes to tensions between parents and children, and between parentally approved and non-approved uses of the internet: 'The ... struggle between parental strategies and children's tactics suggests a "digital generation gap"' (Livingstone, 2003, p. 149).

Indeed, given the rapid growth in availability of the internet and other new forms of technology, questions of control and ownership have quickly become prominent, alongside other, significant considerations, such as whether the nature of childhood itself might be changing as a result. Do 'the opportunities facilitated by the Internet represent a significant change in young people's lives or, less dramatically, simply a new means of achieving familiar ends?' (Livingston and Bober, 2004, p. 396). In seeking to answer this very question, these investigators conducted a survey of children and young people's internet use. Like their parents, children and young people appear to believe that they are more competent in using the internet than adults ('My dad hasn't even got a clue. can't even work the mouse', Nina, 17, quoted in Livingstone and Bober, 2004, p. 403). It may be partly for this reason that they are enthusiastic about making use of this new opportunity to express themselves, on their own terms. While 'education and learning' may be the reasons parents/carers facilitate internet access:

> Children and young people themselves are . . . far more excited by the Internet as a communication medium than as a learning resource . . . as with the mobile phone . . ., it is email, chat and, especially, instant messaging that has taken off so rapidly in recent years, leading many to identify the Internet as a young person's technology precisely because of the transformation it appears to be having on their language, on the conduct of social relationships and on the peer network in general.
>
> (Livingstone and Bober, 2004, p. 405)

In some ways, this is redolent of other debates about children's needs and wishes to have private spaces and places (bedrooms, play areas, bus stops and street corners) which are theirs alone, and where they can determine the nature of their lived environment and what goes on there. Their use of the internet may be one way of trying to address these aspirations in 'virtual' form. In this sense, then, we are witnessing the re-emergence or reshaping of a perennial site of tension between the generations, and children's attempts to use the internet independently is nothing new. In some ways, indeed, this development is a source of reassurance for parents/carers, as children typically remain physically present within the home whilst using the internet, and this is of less concern than fears for their 'physical safety' (Livingstone and Bovill, 1999, p. 15). In other respects, of course, children's worlds become less restricted, with the capacity to extend their range of contacts and friendships and the (virtual) networks to which they have access (yet another source of parental concern, of course) far beyond the immediate neighbourhood. As elsewhere, irony abounds here; as children's physical 'range' becomes more circumscribed, their global networks and identities become much more widely diffused, open and 'out of control'.

These brief reflections on the use of new media by children, and their active articulation of new forms of expression and identity, lead us back again to some of the broader theoretical issues we have considered previously. Thus, for example, the depiction of children offered to us here emphasizes their creative and distinctive character as 'social actors', while also helping to shed light on some of the tensions within this portrayal (James and James, 2004). The commonalities evident in the establishment of more or less exclusive and more or less global social networks among children suggest that there is something about the use of, and experience of new technology which is potentially common to all children ('minority group' child; James and James, 2004, p. 59). However, the evidence of differential access and use, allied with earlier findings about differential 'transformational' capacities equally suggests that there may be significant variations in children's performance of the role of social actor: 'Within the "tribal" model the commonalities of childhood are down played and instead the diversities in children's experiences – those wrought by age, gender, class, health and ethnicity for example – are highlighted' (James and James, 2004, p. 59).

Importantly, James and James suggest that it is not the task of analysis to opt for one or other of these positions, but to see them as operating in tandem and in tension with each other. It is possible, to identify both globalizing and individualizing tendencies in children's exposure to, and creative use of, emerging technologies. Our challenge, is to identify the shifting nature of the dynamics between positions or 'models' of childhood, and to understand how they combine 'at any given time and in any particular social situation' to 'shape their daily lived experiences' (James and James, 2004, p. 61).

Practical examples of this kind of project can increasingly be identified as children's role as 'media producers' is captured by the contemporary research (Gauntlett, 1998; de Block, 2004). For instance, new media can provide migrant children with a distinctive 'language' in which to express themselves to others internationally (de Block, 2004, p. 3), while also enabling them to explore and account for cultural differences and stereotypes. This is indicative of an emerging contemporary resource by which children can retain (or recover) a sense of their distinctive identities and origins, while still exploring difference and diversity in ways which generate new shared understandings and a stronger sense of generational solidarity.

Violence, the media and children: a case study

Before concluding this discussion of the relationship between children and the media, it will be instructive to consider one concrete

illustration, and that is the vexed subject of violence and its purported effects on children. This example, while of intrinsic interest,
also allows us to reconsider the questions of influence, interaction
and self-expression which addressed earlier. Indeed, it brings to the
fore once again the array of (often competing) implicit and explicit
assumptions about the malleability of children's minds, their innate
characteristics, and their ability to make sense of and act independently in the face of external stimuli.

There is no doubt that the effect of media violence on the young
has been a long standing and heavily researched area of controversy (Browne and Hamilton-Giachristis, 2005). Although most of
the research in this area is psychological in orientation, rather than
sociological (Boyle and Hibberd, 2005), its outputs have revealed a
significant diversity of opinion. Some argue that there are demonstrable and substantial effects of exposure to violence on children
and young people (Anderson *et al.*, 2003; Anderson, 2004; Bartholow
et al., 2006). Video games, in particular, are a matter of contemporary concern: 'as more studies of violent video games have been conducted, the significance of violent video game effects has become
clearer . . . The magnitude of these effects is also somewhat alarming'
(Anderson, 2004, p. 120).

The effects of exposure to violence can be measured both in terms
of behavioural outcomes, and in changes in the electrical activity
levels in the brain (Bartholow *et al.*, 2006), leading to the conclusion
that there is a causal connection and that continued exposure desen-
sitizes young people to the effects of violence, and thereby renders
them more prone to aggressive behaviour.

On the other side of the coin, it has been contested that the evidence of one or more causal links produced over a period of time
has not been convincing (Cumberbatch, 1995; Freedman, 2001). In
expressing extreme doubt about the quality and meaning of previous
studies, one commentator has observed: 'This body of research is not
only extremely limited . . ., but also suffers from many methodological problems . . . the measures of aggression are either remote from
aggression or of questionable value' (Freedman, 2001, p. 7). Doubts
have also been expressed as to the real-world applications of findings from a particular branch of experimental psychology (Boyle and
Hibberd, 2005, p. 31).

A more nuanced account suggests, that the impacts of 'violent
imagery' on children can be identified in terms of 'short-term effects
on arousal, thoughts, and emotions, increasing the likelihood of

aggressive or fearful behaviour' (Browne and Hamilton-Giachristis, 2005, p. 708). Other differences are also discernible, for instance, with a more substantial effect of media violence on boys than girls, and the effects are persistent, suggesting that there may be 'a stronger influence of media violence for those with a predisposition for aggressive behaviour attributable to personality ... or situational factors ... or both' (Browne and Hamilton-Giachristis, 2005, p. 708). So, violent images of one kind or another are believed to have an amplificatory effect, compounding influences and inclinations already present in the child's background.

This study and other commentaries, though, have also sought to take a wider view, arguing that research needs to place existing evidence 'within a wider cultural and social context' which sees involvement with specific activities such as 'video games as one element of a young person's engagement with a range of media and social factors which may influence behaviour' (Boyle and Hibberd, 2005, p. 35). Buckingham (2000) concurs, arguing that much previous research has been misconceived, thinking only in terms of 'violence' as a measurable phenomenon whose effect on its object can be tracked straightforwardly. The causal models involved are simplistic and assume that influence flows in a particular direction, but

> this research in fact fails to prove its central hypothesis: that media violence makes people more aggressive *than they would otherwise have been*, or that it causes them to commit violent acts *they would not otherwise have committed*.
> (Buckingham, 2000, p. 130)

This is not to suggest that there is no connection between exposure to images of violence and violent behaviour, but rather to question the necessity of any simplistic causal dynamic. Large-scale surveys, for example, have been able to demonstrate an association of some kind. Thus: 'those who view more than four hours of TV daily are 7 per cent more likely to get in a fight during the year than those who watch less than one hour' (Kline, 2005, p. 90); interestingly, this correlation is stronger for girls than boys. However, it is also noted here that 'aggression is a complex form of social interaction' (Kline, 2005, p. 91), which is probably learned from a variety of sources. In most cases, too, use of the media is itself 'mediated' by other influences, such as peers and family members. It is thus plausible that media effects may be variable, depending on the social 'assets' available to children, and the extent to which risks are interactive or cumulative (Kline, 2005, p. 91). The potential value of an 'eco-logical' understanding of differential childhoods is opened up at this point (Bronfenbrenner, 1979), revealing the possibility that psychologies (and even neurologies) of childhood may differ according to the complex interplay between the individual and social and environmental factors. Causal explanations themselves may be more situationally specific than previously thought, only holding true for *some* children, displaying *certain* characteristics, in *particular* circumstances.

Buckingham's approach broadens the focus of debate, arguing that the effects of media violence cannot be viewed in one-dimensional, behavioural terms, but must be evaluated to the extent that it has '*emotional*' or '*ideological*' effects, too (2000, p. 134). Once again, these effects are seen as variable, and it is held to be possible for the same content to prompt a range of contradictory reactions:

> Television can provoke 'negative' responses such as worry, fear and sadness, just as it can generate 'positive' responses such as amusement, excitement and pleasure – and, indeed, it often generates 'positive' and 'negative' responses at one and the same time.
>
> (Buckingham, 2000, p. 134)

Buckingham also makes the point that children's engagement with violent material demonstrates 'knowing' and discriminatory qualities. They can, and do, distinguish readily between fictional and non-fictional violence, and, indeed, between genres, too. Children approach this material consciously and with a degree of 'media literacy' which involves applying 'responses to stressful situations' carried over from 'real life' (Buckingham, 2000, p. 135). These techniques are not always performed entirely successfully, and thus some fictional material, that is, certain 'horror movies' can be quite unsettling, while others can be treated readily as comedies, and therefore dealt with comfortably (Buckingham, 2000, p. 137).

This brings us back to a recurrent theme. Children's responses to external influences, whether from the media, peers, school teachers or their parents and communities, are not simply reactive; and this is evident from a relatively early age. Their ways of dealing with these 'inputs' are: 'simultaneously "cognitive" and "social": they involve forms of internal self-awareness and self-control, but they are also manifested in social performances of various kinds, both in the immediate context of viewing and subsequently in talk' (Buckingham, 2000, p. 135).

As Buckingham comments, this kind of self-conscious and proactive use of media paints a rather different picture than do the claims about the relationship between stimulus and response evident in much of the experimental literature. So, children recounted to him the ambivalence of their responses to horror films, which were experienced as simultaneously 'scary' and pleasurable (Buckingham, 2000, p. 140). He describes children manipulating videos to both relive the 'scariest or most "violent" moments' for enjoyment, while this also helps them to analyse the material and 'conquer ... fear' (Buckingham, 2000, p. 140). At the same time, clearly, this kind of process reinforces the appreciation that this is representational material which is quite distinct from real life, which cannot be paused or replayed. Thus:

> The ambivalence and complexity of children's experiences of horror should lead us to question many of the assumptions that are frequently made about it ... To be sure, children do often get frightened or disgusted by horror films, but then so do adults. The notion that the experience is therefore necessarily negative or traumatic, or indeed that it inevitably 'depraves and corrupts', is no more valid than the idea that it is somehow automatically therapeutic.
>
> (Buckingham, 2000, p. 141)

Nor, of course, does it suggest that children's modes or range of responses differ fundamentally from those of adults. They may simply be less experienced in interpreting and responding to the range of representations and messages they encounter.

A more appropriate conclusion, according to Hodge and Tripp (1986) would be to see media violence as a catalyst, that is, as something which may trigger a range of actions or reactions, which are not predictable, consistent or unilinear. They conclude that attempts to 'control' the levels of violence to which children are exposed through television, in particular, are both impractical and unlikely to lead to any clear-cut behavioural changes (Hodge and Tripp, 1986, p. 212). This does not conflict with other evidence of variable and unpredictable effects thrown up by a series of studies on the subject (Cumberbatch, 1995), and should deter us from drawing simplistic conclusions.

Conclusion: children's ambiguous relationship with the media

This brief overview has enabled us to consider the relationship between children and the media from a number of viewpoints, and to generate a number of significant observations. First, it is a relationship which is complex and contested, almost inevitably given the pre-eminence of the media as a feature of contemporary society. In light of this, it is unwise to be dogmatic in the conclusions to be drawn, despite, or perhaps because of, the polarized and essentially unresolved nature of these debates. Rather, we must recognize both the materiality, and therefore, significant impact of the media, on the one hand, while also accepting that children have been shown to have the capacity to analyse and respond to its messages, however bold and overbearing. In some respects, too, children appear to have deliberately sought out contexts and styles of media communication where they are 'in control' and determined to set the agenda.

Once again, this opens up wider questions about the way in which childhoods are constructed, and the internal processes by which children change and develop. To see these as mechanical and predictable is unsustainable, given what we now know about the (varying) capacities of even quite young children to draw on what they experience, and to 'transform' it (Hodge and Tripp, 1986). Is it better to think in terms of differentiated 'distributions' of resources and capabilities among children, mediated contemporaneously by common processes of experience, knowledge acquisition and growth?

PART III

Childhood: Universal or Contextual?

8

Childhood:

An Adult Conception?

Is there an 'adult' view of childhood?

In this final part of the book, the aim is to develop a broader analytical understanding of the terrain of childhood, reflecting on some of the key debates and challenges in this area, and seeking to draw out common themes and key points of difference and diversity. This discussion is at least partly framed by considerations touched upon previously, based on a 'generational' analysis (Mannheim, 1952; Alanen, 2001). As acknowledged in the previous chapters, one of the central features of childhood is the way in which it is addressed by adult interests, in policy, in marketing and in the media. This might be indicative of a structural division between the generations, whose origins and dynamics need to be understood.

Adult conceptualizations and depictions of children's lives will be the focus of the present chapter, and children's own perceptions and experiences *of* childhood will be the central theme of Chapter 9. This will assist in the further task of identifying and overcoming the inherent limitations of starting (almost always) from an adult viewpoint and then attempting to derive authoritative and accurate conclusions about what it means to be a child. If we consider other areas of social life, the idea that one group can both properly appreciate and speak for another is highly questionable. This clearly applies to disciplines such as disability studies, feminism or investigations of ethnicity and cultural diversity. At the very least, adult approaches to understanding childhood as an entity must be evaluated critically; and, at the same time, we must also accord legitimacy to the perspectives and analyses offered by the objects of study, children themselves.

To start with, then, I will consider in more depth some of the ways in which conventional approaches have sought to categorize children and represent them as fixed and predictable objects of inquiry. In this context, we should be reminded of the clarion call of the Butler-Sloss Inquiry into allegations of child sexual abuse in Cleveland, NE England: 'the child is a person, not an object of concern' (Butler-Sloss, 1988, p. 245). In different ways, commentators have had a tendency to adopt restricted and determinate views of children, their needs and their abilities; these must be unpacked in order to obtain a fuller and more suitably nuanced view of childhood and change processes.

The invisible child: neither seen nor heard

To begin with, I will reflect on the argument that children are some-times excluded from view, aggregated numerically and conceptually with other social groupings, such as the family:

> Familialization ... implies keeping children hidden in the family, inac-cessible to the public gaze. For children, this can be detrimental. From a cultural point of view it must be regarded as a major shortcoming, which however seems consistent with the position of children in modern soci-ety, economically and symbolically.
>
> (Qvortrup, 2005, p. 10)

Children appear to share this experience with other collectivities which are sometimes missing or misidentified (for example, where the genderless term 'parent' often stands for 'mother'). The neglect of specific consideration of children as a constituency has important policy consequences: 'the marginalization of children in the econ-omy (and economics) leads to (or is at least instrumental in preserv-ing) the marginalization of children in the welfare state (analysis), too' (Wintersberger, 2005, p. 217).

As Qvortrup (1997) has demonstrated, there is a well-established tendency for welfare systems to include the child by proxy, as part of a larger household unit, usually the family, of course. Thus, as Wintersberger observes, children tend to be overlooked 'both con-ceptually and practically' (2005, p. 215). Others, including parents and professionals represent them, in effect, and decide what is in their interests, and, at the same time, act as the mediating agencies through which these interests are met. I noted in Chapter 6 that there was significant evidence to support this viewpoint, for instance, in the spheres of child health and education, where parents are treated as the 'consumers' of services.

In the same way in which Pahl (1989) has identified women's distinctive financial interests and contribution as obscured historically, so children's place in the economic and welfare systems has been diminished, possibly also for ideological and/or structural reasons (Alanen, 2001). As indicated in earlier chapters, children are significant contributors to the global economy, in both developed and developing nations, albeit in rather different ways. However, this has often been ignored or just taken for granted. Thus, children who are carers make a major unpaid contribution to the national economy (Aldridge and Becker, 2002; Baldwin and Hirst, 2002), but the invisibility of their economic role is mirrored by the equally overlooked nature of the consequences, such as material poverty and restricted lives. A number of adverse outcomes have been identified, including: 'impaired educational development ... isolation ... lack of time for usual childhood and leisure activities ... lack of recognition, praise or respect ... limited horizons or aspirations for the future' (Baldwin and Hirst, 2002, p. 158). While there is some indication that this picture may be changing (Baldwin and Hirst, 2002, pp. 162–3), problems persist, of lack of awareness and recognition, and consequently absence of effective services and support.

The issue of children's lack of visibility can be identified as problematic in a number of other respects, too. Indeed, the cloak of invisibility permeates the world of child welfare, usually in relation to groups who are socially excluded, or are denied services. Poignantly, this is reflected in children's accounts, too, as reflected in the title of one report on self-harm (*'I feel like I'm invisible'*, Dow, 2004). There are many examples of children's needs being overlooked or subsumed into concerns about the well-being or the behaviour of adults, often their parents. Where parental substance use is concerned, the focus is on adult criminality and health needs rather than child protection concerns (Kroll and Taylor, 2000). Despite well-documented links between substance misuse and child mistreatment, parenting problems and family violence, these connections often go unrecognized, it seems. Many welfare professionals evaluating their own practice are reported as saying that they: 'felt conscious that due to pressure of work and organizational imperatives, they were retaining neither a clear child protective stance, nor a holistic approach to the problem' (Kroll and Taylor, 2000, p. 97).

While there seem to be many possible professional and organizational reasons for this, the authors of this study have concluded that prevailing approaches enabled: 'child protection concerns to lurk just out of sight' and that children are in danger of becoming effectively 'invisible within the professional network' (2000, p. 98).

It has also been observed that sometimes children's interests do not come to the fore in cases of domestic violence, where abuse perpetrated by one adult (usually male) on another (usually female) takes centre stage, while the meaning and consequences for children are treated as secondary issues. An overview of research in this area found, among other things, that children: 'are more aware of problems than parents realise', even when they don't really understand what is going on (Gorin, 2004, p. 1). At the same time (Gorin, 2004, p. 3), it seems from children's accounts that some professionals do not engage with them, and do not 'speak directly' to them. These concerns about being overlooked are mirrored elsewhere. In another study of domestic violence undertaken from children's perspective, it was reported that:

> No child had purely positive things to say about the police, and many noted that the actions taken had been ineffective or that they had felt invisible to the officers who responded to the call (despite guidance in most areas recommending checking on the children's safety and needs, and even where it was the children themselves who had made the call).
>
> (Mullender *et al.*, 2002, p. 105)

The metaphor of invisibility can be applied, too, to other aspects of children's lives. Many, it seems, are falling out of the (universal) education system in the UK. By their final year of schooling, many have 'dropped off the school roll' (Skidmore *et al.*, 2007, p. 6). In fact: 'There is a hidden figure. It is a statistic that the official records don't reveal, because they themselves aren't really aware of it. This is the number of pupils who simply don't make it into the exam room.' Thus, there were reported to be some 36,300 school students in England and Wales in 2006 who were either missing from the system entirely or were simply not entered for GCSE exams (Skidmore *et al.*, 2007, p. 7). This group of young people is found also to be well-represented in a number of other 'categories', such as young carers, young parents, looked after young people, those involved in crime and those with disabilities (Skidmore *et al.*, 2007, p. 14). In sum, as with the population as a whole, children in difficult educational circumstances tend to be concentrated among those who are defined collectively as 'socially excluded'. Ironically, they may have become 'visible' in these groups, while still remaining out of sight within the formal education system. The question of how children can be simultaneously 'visible' and 'invisible' finds echoes in Lee's (1999) account of the 'ambiguities' of childhood which has been shown to be another recurrent motif.

In other parts of the world, ambiguities of status are associated with being 'on the street'. Children who live on the streets are 'out of place' (West, 2003, p. 3). There is a distinctly normative tone to the idea of 'street children', who are not where they *should* be, according to conventional adult assumptions:

> [The] ideal or stated aim in many countries may be for children to live with parents and attend school, while the reality may be very different ... Street children generally do not attend school but they do work. They may not be registered or have official identity, they may not receive any public education or health care, they may be harassed by police, have no opportunity for recreation or play, and certainly are not consulted in matters that affect their daily lives.
>
> (West, 2003, p. 3)

Thus, the idea of invisibility is problematic, in that children are, in fact, highly visible in some respects, whilst they are unrecognized in others. They may become the object of police attention by virtue of their presence on the streets, but they may be absent from official records, because their very existence has not been recorded anywhere. In fact, as observed elsewhere (Goldson and Muncie, 2006), when children do become visible in these ways, it often results in them losing 'child' status, as when they are assigned adult criminal responsibility for their actions (Jenks, 1996).

So, an important question arises: to whom, and under what circumstances do children become 'visible' or 'invisible'? This is both a normative and a conditional status. Children may not be seen because they are involved in activities which are deemed unsuitable; and they may not be acknowledged because to do so would be to recognize the inadequacies of the conventional institutions of society. They may, for instance, be involved in activities which are commonly agreed to be unacceptable, such as 'work in factories or sweat shops, serving as drug couriers, or in brothels or other forms of sex work'

(West, 2003, p. 10). In this sense, they are clearly not invisible to everyone, but they are out of sight to respectable society. Indeed, adults may have a vested interest in their invisibility, albeit for contrasting reasons. Those who are exploiting them illegally do not wish this to be known, but equally, respectable society itself may not wish to be reminded that it is failing some of its youngest citizens by leaving them vulnerable to exploitation and abuse.

This is not an issue exclusive to poorer countries or communities, of course, and in other circumstances there may even be an active 'invisibilization' process under way, whereby children who are felt to be problematic, or in some way unacceptable, are removed from the picture. This may be evidenced in a number of ways, such as the very limited representation of disabled children (and adults) in the media; or, by the process by which problematic pupils are excluded from school and therefore do not appear on the school's record of achievements (or failures!).

For organizations such as Save the Children, the unwillingness to take account of their interests, or sometimes just to acknowledge their existence, represents a much wider and more systemic failure to recognize, their distinctive rights as a social grouping. A major policy investigation in 2003, for instance, concluded that there had been a collective European failure to respect children's rights, and to deliver on existing commitments to them. This was attributed to a 'lack of awareness' of the centrality of the issue (Save the Children, 2003, p. 3), and it was suggested that policy processes tended to obscure rather than highlight the specific interests of children. Some stark realities were noted: 'Astonishingly, animals' rights are defined in the EU treaty, but children's are not. There is no comprehensive legal base to promote the interests and priorities of children within EU law' (Kinnock, quoted in Save the Children, 2003, p. 6). This was found to be reflected at the level of the European Union in the absence of action programmes exclusively targeted at promoting children's well-being.

These indications of omission and exclusion in relation to children suggest a broader process by which the organization of social perceptions and knowledge about them may be skewed in some ways, sometimes accidentally, sometimes more deliberately. So, recognizing that their well-being is sometimes compromised and they may be exposed to exploitation and abuse also requires society and its power-holders to acknowledge their own shortcomings; it may be more comfortable not to have to confront this reality. At the same time, clearly, where children are being exploited and abused, there is a direct interest on the part of those who are harming them in their remaining 'out of sight'.

Put another way, whereas it is tempting to idealize childhood, and to hold on to normative visions of what it should be like, it may be uncomfortable and challenging but necessary to confront the evidence that some (in fact, many) childhoods do not in any way meet these stereotypical aspirations. For present purposes, this leads us to consider some important questions about the ways in which perspectives on childhood can be distorted if we rely solely on those which adopt a one-sided adult standpoint, not least because the power to define what is and what should be is not distributed evenly, and there will certainly be vested interests at play.

Thinking in terms of generational power relations may offer some important insights: 'in order to detect the range and nature of the agency of concrete, living children, the exploration needs to be oriented towards identifying the generational structures from which children's powers (or lack of them) derive' (Alanen, 2001, p. 21).

Accordingly, the process of defining and delimiting childhood depends as much on the nature and quality of intergenerational structures and relations as it does on any innate characteristics. Power and inequality become key components of the analysis of adult–child relations, not just in terms of specific examples of exploitation and oppression, but also in the general sense that they are embedded in the production and reproduction of social relations. The interaction between these structural dynamics of exclusion and those 'universal' features of childhood I have identified, such as physical immaturity, and limited knowledge and experience, may be seen to compound the sense of 'vulnerability' adumbrated here as a common feature of 'being a child'.

Glimpses of the child: seen but not heard?

Building on 'generational' arguments, Alanen (2004) has suggested that the problems that follow from the failure to consider children's welfare needs can be summarized in two ways: in the form of an absence of 'knowledge', paralleled by an inadequate development of theoretical understanding. Where information and ideas are sought in relation to children, these are determined by adult priorities, and are therefore biased and not child-centred:

Some attention has, certainly, been focused on children ... within welfare research and the welfare policy domain, but *this has tended to be on a single issue*, such as *poverty, child labour*, or comparisons of a single *child welfare system*, such as child benefits or day care arrangements.

(Alanen, 2004, p. 8)

That is to say, it is specific aspects of children's lives which have been the subject of investigation, from above, and usually from a distinctive disciplinary perspective. Alongside this has been a tendency, according to Alanen, to view children in research and policy in an instrumental manner, in the sense that childhood is viewed purely as a 'preparatory stage' for their future development and for adult life. Children in this respect are viewed not in their own right as 'beings', but merely as 'becomings' (2004, p. 8).

Lee (2001) has picked up on this distinction to reflect on its implications for our approach to childhood. The distinction between 'adult "human beings"' on the one hand, and 'child "human becomings"' (2001, p. 7), on the other, suggests a fundamental form of differentiation between 'different types of humans', in his view, which is a key feature of our conceptualization of childhood as essentially incomplete, and as a dependent, developmental stage of life, which serves essentially as preparation for taking up the status of full and finished adulthood.

Adulthood thus acts as the kind of 'standard' against which childhood is to be measured and judged. Thus, so 'long as adulthood could be treated as a fixed point that everybody understood, childhood could be defined in relation to this certainty', and 'children were often defined as whatever adults were *not*' (Lee, 2001, p. 8). As he recognizes, this position incorporates a number of major assumptions, not least that adulthood itself conforms to some kind of standardized, finished state, which is really no more than a 'convenient fiction', and which is increasingly becoming exposed as such as adult lives themselves have become more 'flexible', diverse and unstable (Lee, 2001, p. 21). Despite these trends, a series of conceptual building blocks persist which give shape to our thinking about childhood. Adult 'independence' is contrasted to childhood 'dependence', for example; and, even where these fixed positions are modified, underlying distinctions are maintained, such that adult 'dependency' is seen as 'accidental, or circumstantial' whereas children's dependency is 'natural' and inevitable (Lee, 2001, p. 23). Alongside dependence, we also find the notion of growth or development *towards* maturity and independence. The finished adult state offers the benchmarks against which this process can be measured and managed. Children's journey towards completeness can thus be captured in the form of identifiable physical and psychological changes, educational achievements and acquisition of adult competencies and status. It is therefore a short step to the establishment of an array of machinery and processes for assessing and evaluating this kind of progress. There is, unsurprisingly, a very substantial body of seemingly authoritative literature which takes this approach to child welfare and development as a given (see, for example, Fahlberg, 1994; Beckett, 2002; Aldgate *et al.*, 2006). We are thus informed that this is the 'natural' order of things, underpinned by historical experience:

> The concept of childhood progressing through a series of stages is not a contemporary device or construction. The division or categorization of human life into different periods, which incorporate childhood as well as adulthood, are to be found in writings as far back as the seventh century CE.
>
> (Rose *et al.*, 2006, p. 163)

The basis is established for a prescriptive model based on quantifying and distinguishing 'distinctive periods of change' according to a range of identifiable characteristics, which is valuable for 'parents' and 'professionals' alike (Rose *et al.*, 2006, p. 164). While acknowledging recent criticisms of the 'constructed' nature of the developmental process, this depiction remains rooted in notions of measurable progression, across a number of areas, such as 'physical change', 'social behaviour' and 'understanding and intellectual capacity'. This one-sided approach to defining children's needs and structuring their lives, manifests itself in observable differences in the ways in which adults and children engage in and make sense of the same activity, such as schooling, where testing and gradation take on a much more significant meaning for teaching staff than for their charges (Christensen and James, 2001, p. 73).

Foucault's (1979) work provides a distinctive theoretical frame for this way of understanding and organizing children's 'development' in the educational sphere certainly, as Lee (2001) recognizes. Historical investigation demonstrates the emergence of a systematization of education and schooling, according to which objectives and procedures are precisely specified and structured. Space and time came to be carefully and explicitly organized over the school day to ensure standardized and common progress towards socially desirable educational (and behavioural) goals:

> A mass of people with their own interests, desires and personal likes and dislikes was thereby disciplined into an orderly collection of pupils who, for the most part, would then abandon their own activities to be led, passively, by the teacher.
>
> (Lee, 2001, p. 79)

Within this setting, learning goals could be subdivided into specific, quantifiable stages, whereby 'standard expectations' could be established, prescribed input provided and 'progress charted'. Thus, the 'speed and success' of children's journey towards competence could be assessed, and any variations from the norm identified and addressed speedily. As Alanen (2004, p. 10) has recognized, the importation of these kinds of quasi-objective measures of children's 'progress' has significant implications in terms of their 'normative' content.

The focus on educational development also captures quite nicely a further consequence of the use of the 'standard adult' as the benchmark against which to judge childhood change, and this is the choice of partial and particularized indicators, among which would be those of physical growth, psychological maturity and moral development as well as educational achievement. Children, in this sense, are objectified, and certain features of their lives brought to the fore at the expense of others. Children are not, for example, expected to be responsible for their material circumstances or housing status, but these may have a more substantial impact on their growth and development than more obviously child-oriented services such as health, child care or education. Children's 'proxy' status within the family has been recognized as a further mediating and distorting factor in our attempts to gain a clear and comprehensive picture of their lives (Daniel and Ivatts, 1998). It is argued that the very 'language of social policy' tends to be organized around the needs of the family rather than children as a distinctive constituency.

While this problem can partly be attributed to prevailing ideologies of the family, the consequences can be unhelpful: 'the fact that children are subsumed within the term 'family' prevents them from becoming the primary focus of policy' (Daniel and Ivatts, 1998, p. 11).

More accurately, it might be concluded that it is only certain aspects of children's lives which become the focus of social policy in their own right. In all other respects, such as care, maintenance, moral guidance and protection, the family is expected to take primary responsibility. While there may be justifiable reasons for ensuring that children are provided with protection and care, and 'their status as dependants is not exclusively a negative one' (Qvortrup, 2005, p. 9), there are certain unhelpful consequences of this elision of children's interests with those of the family. Thus, the 'good reasons for protecting children against exploitation and subjugation do not justify depriving them of a right to conceptual autonomy' (Qvortrup, 2005, p. 10). Indeed, aggregating children with families 'can be detrimental'. This is illustrated forcefully in the case of housing policy which treats children as bare household statistics and makes no direct connection between housing and other needs, such as those of 'friendships' and continuity of schooling (Daniel and Ivatts, 1998, p. 142). Indeed, falling into one (undesirable) category in housing terms may have positively harmful consequences in other respects: 'There is some suggestion ... that with schools' reputation being increasingly dependent on their pupils' test results, many schools are reluctant to accept homeless children, who are likely to perform badly in tests' (Daniel and Ivatts, 1998, p. 142). This evidence has been replicated over a considerable period of time in many geographical settings (for example, Gregg, 2003; Kelly, 2007). Daniel and Ivatts conclude that poor housing and homelessness are fundamentally damaging to many children, and that 'there is a strong case' for making the claim that better housing conditions for poorer families 'would achieve more for children's welfare than other social policy reforms' (1998, p. 144).

Children's distinctive status and welfare may be subsumed under policy goals in other respects, too. For example, early years' care and education services tend to conceptualize children and childhood in ways which are limited and partial. At different times, they may be seen as a site of investment, as potential members of the workforce, as representatives (of their parents and families), or as an economic obstacle, in terms of the restrictions imposed on parental employment opportunities. The suggestion has been made that 'despite the fact that children head the list of potential beneficiaries ... the wider debate about early childhood services' has prioritized 'the needs of the economy and society', or 'parents' (Daniel and Ivatts, 1998, p. 148). Lee (2001, p. 77) agrees that education of children has been viewed as an aspect of social life best characterized as a 'site of investment', directed towards their future potential, rather than current status. Moss and Petrie (2002) argue that this kind of approach to service provision 'for' children is more or less endemic. Children's

services are 'atomized', as evidenced by the wide range of govern-
mental and other bodies and policy silos through which their needs
are addressed, precisely because they are constructed from particular
adult perspectives, whether these be economically driven, or focused
more on social ends, such as crime control or producing the next
generation of 'good parents'. Thus:

> An important component of the construction of children's services is
> instrumentality. Provision is made for a specified purpose, in the name of
> which the child is acted upon to produce outcomes, which are both pre-
> determined and normative. Moreover the 'customers' for these services
> are first and foremost adults.
>
> (Moss and Petrie, 2002, p. 63)

This preoccupation with pre-determined externally imposed objectives is associated with an equivalent emphasis on determining 'what
works', to be judged against behavioural, developmental and educational outcomes criteria, rather than process measures, such as whether
or not children are happy and fulfilled in what they are doing in the
present. Resources often provided explicitly *for* children are not, in
fact, 'provided as places for children to live their childhoods and to
develop their culture', although they do find ways of adapting situations to these purposes 'subversively' (Moss and Petrie, 2002, p. 63).

It is time to return to the problematic issue of the lens through
which we choose to view children and their experiences, and the
ensuing implications for the way in which we make judgements about
their lives, development and achievements. There may be differences
of opinion as to the consequences of the various 'partial' approaches
discussed here: some might think in terms of 'generational' inequalities
and unbalanced power relations (Alanen, 2004), while others seem to
suggest a more fluid and 'ambiguous' set of relationships and expectations, reflecting wider developments and relationships in a post-
modern age (Valentine, 2004, p. 35). The common ground, however,
would appear to be that a one-sided characterization of childhood is
just that, and may have significant and damaging implications for the
ways it is thought of, and the ways in which children themselves are
treated and live their lives (Lee, 2001, p. 63).

Dealing with 'difference'

From an adult viewpoint, then, some children are invisible while
some are only partially and sporadically visible. There is a third group,

however, and these are children who are only *too* visible, because their behaviour or characteristics actually appear to locate them *outside* childhood. In other words, by their behaviour, or in some cases their appearance and characteristics, they present a challenge to established normative assumptions about what constitutes childhood and the pathways it should follow. Children in this category include those who are identified as young offenders, for example, but there are others, too, whose presence may be troubling or challenging, such as those who are 'too clever', those with disabilities, or those whose sexuality is problematized.

For some (see Jenks, 1996), the strategic adult response is one of identity substitution, whereby children who represent a challenge to conventional assumptions are redefined as something else, according to a particular 'label' which obscures their child status. The subject of crime and disorder is a fruitful setting for this kind of analysis. While there are clearly important differences between jurisdictions, recent developments in the UK illustrate this quite clearly. The growing concern over children's 'anti-social' behaviour has been associated with a process of detaching those concerned from their childhood status, and redefining them as 'tomorrow's criminals' (Squires and Stephen, 2005, p. 29), and this is only part of a wider trend towards the 'adulteration' (Muncie and Goldson, 2006, p. 199) of young people who offend, and the putative 'end of adolescence' (Jones, 2008).

As we have already seen, this is not a fixed position and views about children's status vary both historically and geographically, but nonetheless, there is a degree of consistency across contemporary developments internationally (Muncie and Goldson, 2006, p. 199). This 'responsibilization' process has been concretely illustrated by the relatively recent abolition in England and Wales of the principle of *doli incapax*, which until 1998 gave explicit recognition to the distinctive status of 10–14-year-olds as not yet being attributable with full adult responsibility for any criminal act they might commit (unless it could be proved otherwise). This change in the law effectively meant that the level of culpability attached to a 10-year-old offender would be equivalent to that of any adult responsible for a similar offence. That this should be recognized as special treatment of a particular problematic group (young offenders) is further supported by the evidence that across a range of other legislative provision, 'childhood' extends to a considerably higher age.

The abolition of *doli incapax* could certainly be seen as a modern-day reworking of a recurrent struggle between principles of 'welfare' and 'justice' in the treatment of young offenders, but we are also invited to consider the wider question of whether it is simply 'an erosion of childhood in youth justice policy' or reflective of 'wider sociological perceptions of what it means to be a child' (Fionda, 2005, p. 20). In some formal senses, the former appears to be the case, as childhood status in general remains applicable to anyone under 18 (who is covered by age-specific child law, for example, and cannot take part in the democratic process by voting). In other words, what is described as the 'erosion' of conventional understandings of childhood is selective, and applies only to certain 'outgroups', such as those who break the law (Fionda, 2005, p. 27).

An alternative view is offered by Brown (2005), who believes that there are two intersecting processes at play here. One of these problematizes youth and childhood in general, and the other is selective, focusing on the distinctive (and often undesirable) attributes of specific sub-groups. This distinction has, she argues, facilitated well-established processes of differentiation and discrimination based on characteristics such as gender, class, ethnicity and culture, as well as age. By the late nineteenth century in Britain: 'The preconditions for a universalizing discourse of youth were in place: a youth which was either to be the standard bearer and upholder of a Great Nation, or the scourge of the future and the harbinger of doom' (Brown, 2005, p. 16). Childhood in general is seen as a time of 'risk' (threat and vulnerability), but at the same time this is exacerbated by the establishment of specific categories within that broader population. The reasons for this are not necessarily well meant:

> The making special of certain groups by defining them as representing childhood or adolescence may no longer be seen as simply a benevolent process based upon the special needs of a biologically driven life cycle. The coincidences of history and discourse are too many.
>
> (Brown, 2005, p. 24)

Brown suggests here that there are identifiable aims and objectives underlying the processes of attaching problematic labels to certain social groups, which are politically and morally driven. The practical consequences of this tendency can be seen in the persistent tension between treating young people as 'victims' or 'villains' (Packman *et al.*, 1986). This faultline has permeated systems and practices developed to respond to the problems of children and young people for at least a century (dating back in legislative terms to the Children Act

1908, certainly). In England and Wales, it still remains embedded in the structural and policy tensions between government departments and agencies responsible for promoting children's welfare and dealing with their crimes respectively (see DfES, 2003; Home Office, 2003). While it is relatively straightforward to frame children's welfare needs in terms of dependence, vulnerability and (adult) threats, and thus to attribute them collectively with victim status, once they become categorized as 'villains', different rules and discourses apply. Brown (2005, p. 123) suggests that there may be a form of 'acceptable victimhood' which is associated with certain expectations about what it is to be a child, for example, being physically weaker than adults, less knowledgeable about risk and danger, and probably more trusting of others. This classification coincides with our recurrent observations about aspects of childhood which appear to be held in common by children, transcending specific historical, spatial and temporal settings. Gender, though, also comes into play here, in light of conventional assumption that girls are more passive and vulnerable than their male counterparts.

Victims who do not meet these expectations and are not stereotypical, however, are less readily acknowledged, both in individual cases, and in terms of the statistical evidence of who is at most risk of suffering certain types of crime (Smith, D., 2004). Both national crime surveys and local investigations 'show conclusively that, despite young people's undoubted widespread involvement in petty offending' of certain types, their involvement in serious crime is 'minor' and this 'is far outweighed by their vulnerability as victims' (Brown, 2005, p. 122). There is a very substantial overlap, however, between being a 'victim' and being responsible for the commission of an offence; young people who break the law are also found to be more likely to be the victims of crime (Smith, D., 2004). Indeed, there may be a causal link between these two ostensibly disparate aspects of young people's lives (Brown, 2005, p. 127). The problem for Brown is that the evidence about: 'victimization ... sit[s] very uneasily with the tenacious adherence to a punishment culture which appears to be central to contemporary British attitudes' (2005, p. 124). The artificial distinctions made can only be sustained, it seems, by maintaining an ideological and substantive barrier between the characteristics of childhood (and their putative victim status) and those associated with adult attitudes and attributes, such as criminality. Girls, then, are by and large assumed not to be capable of, or responsible for, crime, with the result that they are largely absent from both official figures and criminological discourse in the role of offender (Brown, 2005,

p. 130). Current estimates suggest that female young offenders comprise around just 15 per cent of the total number officially processed (Feilzer and Hood, 2004, p. 125), and where they do come to police attention, they are more likely to be diverted from prosecution (Feilzer and Hood, 2004, p. 159). However, a much larger proportion of girls or young women say that they have committed an offence 'ever' (East and Campbell, 2000) which suggests that there may be a tendency for official processes to reinforce prior assumptions about their status and qualities. The 'typical' young offender is thus constituted as male, and in many cases 'black', in the popular imagination, in official reports, and in criminological discourse (Brown, 2005, p. 137). This classificatory process may also be associated with a tendency to associate archetypal childhood attributes with aspects of the idealized female persona, such as passivity, suggestibility, and physical weakness.

This, too, reflects a wider project of detaching the attributes associated with the commission of crime from the notion of childhood. Self-confident and aggressive masculinity becomes the lens through which the actions of young offenders are viewed:

> Aggressive normative heterosexuality, individualism, competitiveness and other attributes of delinquency in (male) group settings may be understood as ways of aspiring to hegemonic masculinity; if legitimate avenues are unavailable or unattainable then illegitimate ones are usually attainable.
>
> (Brown, 2005, p. 140)

It appears that the 'denial of childhood' is very much a subjective as well as an external feature of young males' lives (see Merton, 1957), especially for those who are unable to retain aspirations to follow a 'normal' developmental pathway, by way of successive educational achievements, for example. That is to say, their sense of identity may be closely entwined with the specific repertoire of 'adult' behaviours available to them in their concrete circumstances.

As Fionda puts it, the eradication of 'child-specific procedures for dealing with youth crime' (2005, p. 32) reflects the 'contemporary construction of childhood' itself. What has been in evidence in recent times in the UK is a reassertion of what she terms 'pre-sociological' notions of the child, leading to the predominance of 'adult-centred' ideas: 'children are debased and rendered inferior and attributed with expectations of innocence and childishness which may or may not be realistic'. Criminal acts mean that they are literally acting 'out of character', and thereby invoke 'authoritarian' measures of social control. In order to ensure that children stay within the morally and ideologically constructed boundaries of childhood, implicit and sometimes explicit restrictions are legitimately placed on their activities, and indeed, their whereabouts. As Lee (2001, p. 66) observes, with the legislative changes of the Crime and Disorder Act 1998 'the potentially "antisocial" activities of children' might now amount to no more than 'being on the streets' after 9 pm 'without adult supervision'. Thus the array of new court disposals introduced in the UK since 1998 (such as ASBOs, curfews, and dispersal orders) could reasonably be viewed as a means of reconstructing or at least reinforcing dominant conceptions of what being a child should entail.

In this sense, the ideological purposes of these measures (some of which, such as the Child Safety Order, have barely ever been used) may be at least as important as their direct impact:

> It is striking ... that current responses to urban deprivation focus so closely on children's conduct and movements. [These] policies ... are intended to ensure that children stay in their proper place: school during the day and the family home at night.
>
> (Lee, 2001, p. 68)

In Lee's terms, this represents a reassertion that children should properly 'live up to the role of becomings', that is, as being in an incomplete state of preparation for their full adult identities, when they will acquire the status of 'beings'. There is a certain irony here, of course, because children who assert their right to be seen as independent actors by breaching these legal constraints actually become liable to be treated *as* adults before their time. Irresponsibility is not, in this sense, a sign of immaturity or inexperience, but indicates instead an unwelcome sign of precociousness; whereas in other spheres, early achievement of adult status, for example in educational attainment, might be welcomed, in this context, as with early parenting, it is viewed as unacceptable.

Lee argues that the associated control strategy is directed in particular at 'poor children', precisely because the idealized developmental notion of childhood is so central to the maintenance of social order and economic dominance. Other sources indicate that 'race' and cultural difference are also significant factors in this regard (Garland, 2001). This is certainly the case in terms of the discriminatory treatment of young black males in the criminal justice system (Smith, 2007).

However, conflicts between expectations and behaviour are not merely a problem for those committed to maintaining dominant assumptions; asserting their independent status and rights as 'beings' may actually expose children to harsher forms of punishment and discipline. Lee's response is to suggest that 'ambiguity' is an inevitable feature of childhood, and that the task both conceptually and practically is to work with tension and complexity rather than simply to deny it. Childhood should be seen and understood in this sense as a multiplicity of 'becomings' with a variety of trajectories and end-points (Lee, 2001, p. 141), which may be found to exist in adulthood, too, which is equally 'unfinished'.

Conclusion: adult-oriented childhood: a one-sided view?

In this chapter, we have considered a number of adult strategies to make sense of, categorize, and deal with children and the problems sometimes associated with them. These have variously been described in terms of ignoring them, denying their childhood status, or taking a partial view of specific aspects of their lives at the expense of the whole. The common strand between these strategies is a process of problematizing children, seeking partial and one-sided explanations, and then focusing practical interventions only on these aspects of childhood, at the expense of other relevant factors. This suggests that there may be an underlying tendency towards ideologically driven 'generational' (Alanen, 2004) polarization grounded in apparently natural demarcations based on chronological age and physical growth, as well as less tangible and more contestable attributions such as developmental level, and maturity. However, the consequences of this are a series of inconsistencies and anomalies, whereby children are viewed as 'incomplete' and immature in some respects, while in other circumstances are treated by the law and social institutions as fully responsible adults. The reasons for this may be structural (Brown, 2005; Fionda, 2005), or they may be rooted in complexity and increasing 'uncertainty' (Lee, 2001, p. 136). Nonetheless, this is inevitably problematic for those children who find themselves the 'objects' of adult concern (Butler-Sloss, 1988). The picture will certainly be incomplete if no account is taken of how children themselves construct and make sense of 'childhood', which is the subject of what follows.

9

What Do Children Think about Childhood?

The child's perspective is vital

Inevitably, this book is written from an adult perspective, but this should not prevent us from trying to explore the meaning and experience of childhood from the viewpoint of children themselves. Indeed, if we are to consider properly some of the more contentious aspects of the subject, then it is important to give some space to their perceptions and accounts. To what extent, for example, should we value and give recognition to the meaning and value for children of living in the present ('being' in Lee's terms, 2001), as opposed to the tendency to take the future-oriented view which is apparent in much developmental and educational literature?

In recent times the child's viewpoint has been recognized increasingly as both valid and valuable in its own right, and as a source of insight into the meanings and dynamics of childhood itself. Children are not seen merely as objects of inquiry in relation to their unrealized potential, or developmental progress, but as a source of knowledge and understanding about the forms and meaning of a variety of social interactions. Childhood, it seems, can now be recognized as an important source of social understanding in general, rather than simply as an adjunct to reputedly more significant investigations into the mores and dynamics of adult society. Perhaps what happens in childhood can offer us insights into adult relationships and needs across a range of disciplines and life settings.

A substantial body of research has been developed with a specific focus on childhood, in its own right, which has taken the methodological view that there is intrinsic value and meaning in what children do, how they behave, and how their bodies function from their own perspective (for example, Christensen and James, 2000; 2008; Lewis and Lindsay, 2000). From this type of work has emerged a mass of evidence about children's lives in general, specific aspects of these, and the ways in which they are affected by differing social structures and dynamics. We are thus increasingly well placed to begin the task of making sense of childhood in the light of children's own accounts.

A view from below: child–adult relationships

As is apparent from earlier chapters, children have the capacity to make sense of and interpret social interactions from a relatively early age. This suggests that they are able to attribute deliberate intentions to the actions of others, specifically adults (Carpendale and Lewis, 2006). In light of this observation, their understandings of what adults are trying to do to them, *as* children, are clearly of considerable interest and significance. Thus, for example, Mayall (2002) has devoted attention to the child's view of her/his relations with parents. Children's accounts offer a consistent view of how their lives are organized and how they see parents' roles in this, she claims. Parents are key determinants of childhood, because they are believed to have the power to define the shape and nature of their relationships: 'Parental definitions constitute them as children. While, according to young people, these definitions vary somewhat between families, it is through their parents' behaviour that people learn to do childhoods' (Mayall, 2002, p. 45).

The dynamics of these relationships have specific consequences in that children provide 'gendered' accounts of the ways in which parents behave towards them. Household management and interaction are understood to be the domain of mothers rather than fathers. The place of fathers and their relationships with children are more ambiguous in children's minds, especially in a context of significant levels of family change, where fathers could be seen as abdicating their responsibilities if they leave the family home (Mayall, 2002, p. 46).

Children are reported as seeing themselves as having certain 'childhood' rights to free time and control over their own activities, but at the same time, they are aware of their responsibilities and their apprentice status, learning and preparing for future adult roles:

Peter: We're the ones that have to take care of ourselves. Like when we live by ourselves we will.
Adam: So we're like keeping ourselves healthy, by doing things ourselves.
Ann: It's my body, so it's my job.

(Conversation between 9-year-olds,
quoted in Mayall, 2008, p. 113)

For some, active contributions to the family project are features of their lives from an early age; as noted previously, they are and see themselves as active contributors to the 'family enterprise' (Mayall, 2008, p. 47) from as young as 5 years old. This could be interpreted as a relatively straightforward sign that young people are being inducted into prescribed roles from a relatively early age, and that they are being effectively trained for conformity. However, Mayall suggests that there is a degree of ambiguity about this process; children are learning to fit in and to become 'good enough' members of the family, but they are also working on a parallel exercise, 'the project of their own life'. They therefore appear to subscribe to 'the socialization thesis – childhood is in part preparation for adult life, and childhood is a journey during which one learns', but this is also a process in which they believe that they share 'agency in their own socialization' (Mayall, 2008, p. 47). In other words, children appear to be self-consciously aware of the ways in which they are being inducted into family and social norms, expectations and roles; so, the part they play in adopting (or, in some cases, rejecting) these is active and deliberate. This is not a purely dependent or responsive relationship, but one in which they see themselves as having a real part to play. This is paralleled by children's perceptions of parental authority, it seems, with children both acknowledging and validating parents' decision-making capacity, while also seeking scope for negotiation over issues such as 'free time', household tasks and control of one's 'own use of time and space' (Mayall, 2008, p. 47).

Children's understanding of the 'relational' nature of their childhoods thus appears to be clear and at the same time quite sophisticated. Issues of current and future gender roles seemed to be quite well understood by children as young as 9 years old. Thus, Mayall reports the experiences and perceptions of Muslim children who appear to have gained a sense of the tensions between present realities and future expectations, based on the complex interactions between gender, generation and religious conventions:

> The intersections of gender and generation in their lives allowed these girls to experience their current lives, including their domestic responsibilities, as both acceptable and pleasurable. They were already aware that later on issues of career versus traditional women's roles might have to be dealt with, but at present they did not identify conflicts. For the 12-year-olds, these issues were becoming more important.
>
> (Mayall, 2002, p. 52)

By this account, children are able to make sense of and negotiate their place in the family and community across a range of dimensions from a relatively early age, and with a degree of insight and sophistication.

Other sources also suggest that the experience of childhood is one which is 'negotiated', albeit within structures and cultural expectations which are largely already 'given' (Solberg, 1997). Writing somewhat earlier than Mayall, as the emergence of a distinctive sociology of childhood took hold, Solberg aspired 'to break out of the traditional concept of what children are, what children can do and what "age" itself means' (Solberg, 1997, p. 129). Children's accounts of their 'negotiations' seemed to suggest that the pre-existing frames of understanding offered by the concepts of 'play' and 'socialization' were too limited, unilinear and one-dimensional. Solberg found that changing patterns of family life, specifically organized around work and the division of labour, contributed to a reapportionment of responsibilities between family members: 'the children have invaded the home as the mothers have invaded the labour market' (Solberg, 1997, p. 131). As a result, children's 'work' within the home has expanded in scope, with corresponding implications for their assigned roles and status within the family set-up. The changing economic position of women in Norwegian society is reported to have had specific consequences for the ways in which children's (and girls', in particular) responsibilities are determined. In practical terms, where mothers had moved into full-time employment, their children were found to be doing more housework than others. It could perhaps be argued that this represented a process of intensified socialization into conventionally desired roles, especially for girls, but Solberg's findings suggest that this would be too simplistic. Some (but not all) children who play a relatively larger part in the domestic work of the household also seem to take on a more adult status than their peers whose material contribution in the home is more limited. Solberg identifies three different models of family functioning within which the place that children negotiate for themselves is variable. In one case, the child is 'big': 'because of all the work she does and because she manages her own money'. Another child is 'little', because she does very 'little towards the general running of the household' (Solberg, 1997, p. 137). The nature and content of childhoods, then, depend on the processes of negotiation around practical household arrangements, which are initiated by parents and by economic demands upon them, but within which children's perceptions remain significant. The division of labour seems to influence other aspects of the relationship between children and their parents, with those who contribute more also being more likely to establish their own autonomy and independent rights, such as the receipt of an allowance (Solberg, 1997, p. 136). However, the 'connection' between 'social age and work participation is not a necessary one' (Solberg, 1997, p. 137). In some cases, children who work remain closely tied to the parent's supervision, and are not accorded any significant degree of independent responsibility. In another case, children who had gained a considerable degree of independence and freedom within the home found this curtailed when their mother began 'working from home' (Solberg, 1997, p. 140).

Thus, it seems that parents' behaviour and working patterns set the terms for the negotiation of children's standing within the home, and that these are strongly influenced by practical and material factors, such as the amount of time each spends 'at home'. Children take account of established relationships based on parental authority, but, depending on their own roles, they have a degree of freedom to assert their independent interests:

> The children ... are well informed about the rules of the family but their own ways of arranging matters may, nevertheless, be different from the ways their parents do it or would prefer their children to do it. At the age of 12 they are wise enough not to ask for permission too much.
>
> (Solberg, 1997, p. 141)

Children are thus portrayed as organizing and 'negotiating' their childhoods in the light of parental expectations and well-established rules, but the changing practical arrangements of family life also have implications here. Parents need to encourage their children to act a bit more independently because they are not around so much, but the trade-off here is that their 'working agreements' (Solberg, 1997, p. 141) need to be flexible, and sometimes not too explicit. For children, for example, knowing when parents are coming home enables them to 'cover up' activities their parents may not approve of, and maintain the façade of conformity with the rules of the household (Solberg, 1997, p. 140). These processes of negotiation and 'give and take' do not appear substantially different from equivalent adult–adult transactions; it is the uneven distribution of power and resources which seems to shape them rather than any inherent generational differences.

The relationship between children and parental authority has been explored elsewhere (Butler *et al.*, 2005), and here too, the central theme is one of ambiguity, and negotiated relationships. Children at first sight appear to believe that for parents to have ultimate decision-making power is very much the natural order of things:

> I: So what sort of decisions are made about you?
> g11: Whether friends can sleep over here or not ... Having a tidy bedroom ... What time you have got to come in at night ... What friends you bother with ... you know, whether they are trouble or not ... I can't think of any more.
>
> (interview extract, O'Kane, 2008, p. 134)

In addition, those in a parental role can be relied upon most of the time to make 'better' decisions on their behalf (O'Kane, 2008, p. 13). Parents are felt to be able to perform this role better by virtue of their age, understanding and experience. This does not amount to a completely free hand, however, and some children clearly believe that parents' decision-making rights are qualified. For instance, children sometimes know themselves better than their parents: 'I'm very different to my mother, and my mother thinks she knows what I like and if I don't like it, she still thinks I like it anyway' (Jane, 10, quoted in Butler *et al.*, 2005, p. 15). Children seem to believe that it is 'competence' as much as 'status' which justifies parents' exercise of authority, and that this is not just a given, but needs to be demonstrated by their behaviour and understanding, such as their readiness to consider others' opinions (Butler *et al.*, 2005, p. 16).

Thinking about themselves and their capacities, children do seem to develop a greater belief in their own competence with age (Butler *et al.*, 2005, p. 17), and they recognize that this is because they 'have a lot to learn' (Butler *et al.*, 2005, p. 18). Children, then, largely accept parents' rights to make decisions about their lives, but this is not an unqualified position, and there are a number of children and certain contexts where there may be a degree of dissent: 'Children tend to be quicker to defend their right to disagree explicitly and to argue their position more openly in relation to decisions that [are] to do with self-actualisation' (Butler *et al.*, 2005, p. 33).

Where matters of 'identity' are concerned, and children are looking for opportunities to express themselves, they appear more likely to assert claims to make decisions in their own right. So, the choice of clothes, or management of their own bedrooms would be seen by many as important to them, and thus areas where their independent views should be given priority.

There are grounds then for taking the view that children do see their status as distinctive and based on certain structured relationships with adults (parents, primarily), which incorporate assumptions that they have less 'responsibility' and greater freedom, but at the same time less authority or control over their lives (Mayall, 2002). It is viewed and experienced as a natural state of being, although there are certainly ambiguities, complexities and indeed frustrations embedded within it:

> Young people understood childhood comparatively – with adulthood. they drew on their experience in their own and other families to make general points. Through [their] conversations runs a pervasive view that childhood is relatively easy compared to adulthood, although adult control can be irksome.
>
> (Mayall, 2002, p. 114)

Differences do emerge in these accounts, though, with Solberg (1997) emphasizing the structural and material determinants of negotiated childhoods; while Mayall (2002) and Butler *et al.* (2005) place more emphasis on children's acceptance that there is a natural order of things, within which there is nonetheless scope for 'trade-offs' between responsibility and freedom.

Children seem to accept that there may be a justifiable rationale for adults' power over them, based on their lesser experience and restricted knowledge, but they do not accept that this is boundless, unfettered, or always exercized appropriately in their interests.

Do children act independently and 'make' their own childhoods?

Of course, childhood is not simply lived or understood in terms of the interactions between children and their parents or other adults. There are also substantial parts of their lives where they are able to act autonomously to create their own 'worlds', and where 'childhood' may take on a different meaning. In one sense, this aspect of their lives has often been addressed through the conceptual lens of 'play', with its own connotations. In many respects, play is considered to be not really as important as 'work' or 'education', and its inherent value may be underestimated. This derives from two key ideological assumptions: one is the 'work ethic', and the other is the primacy of the 'adult' perspective. What children do when they are playing may thus suffer in comparison to activity which is considered more meaningful because it is economically productive, and is not seen as frivolous. The idea that children's lives, experiences and productions should be valued in and of themselves may be difficult to sustain in the face of such preconceptions. Nonetheless, there has been a considerable amount of work in recent years which has sought to redress this balance and to reflect on the intrinsic meaning and worth of the things children do with each other (Corsaro, 1997; Mayall, 2002; Moss and Petrie, 2002; Marsh, 2005).

It is argued that there are at least two ways in which children's worlds can be distinguished from those shared with or exclusive to adults: in terms of physical distance, on the one hand, and independent 'symbolic' meaning, on the other. As they grow older, children increasingly spend time in the sole company of their peers, and, in doing so, create and sustain their own distinctive cultures and identities. Corsaro argues that these productions should not be devalued because of their childhood origins, but that: 'children and their peer cultures are worthy of documentation and study in their own right' (1997, p. 95). Although their relations with others, including peers, are largely influenced by prior experiences within families, children can clearly be observed to build on and develop these pre-existing concepts and assumptions when interacting in groups. Corsaro suggests that they are involved in an active process of negotiating ideas such as 'ownership' and 'friendship' as they share activities with others. Adult-generated ideas about 'friends' are redefined and negotiated as children begin to relate to others and to make judgements about them. As we know from children's behaviour towards each other in early years' settings, friendships can be highly volatile and unpredict-able over a very short space of time. Indeed, the very intensity and changeability of these relationships may be partly attributable to the limited timescale or lifespan in the context of which they are inter-preted and made sense of – there is a sense of temporal proportional-ity about the scale and dramatic impact of children's experiences.

The rapidity of such change should not, however, be taken as indicative that this kind of 'friendship' is any less real or meaningful to children than its (generally) more stable adult manifestations. It is important to recognize the intrinsic value of children's activities and relationships:

> The simple participant structure of play routines corresponds to a central value of peer cultures: *doing things together* ... It is for this reason that we adults seldom truly appreciate the strong emotional satisfaction children get from promoting and participating in what seems to us to be simple repetitive play.
>
> (Corsaro, 1997, p. 123; original emphasis)

Strandell (1997) has also drawn connections between this lack of awareness and a broader tendency to marginalize the importance of 'play'. Activities that are so defined tend to be seen as inessential and frivolous. Their only real value from a conventional adult perspective lies in their capacity to provide social and cognitive learning oppor-tunities and a means to prepare for later life. Apart from this: 'Play has become the expression of a kind of activity that has no place in real society, something easy that children engage in while wait-ing for entrance into society' (Strandell, 1997, p. 446). This, according to Strandell, has infused not only common-sense understandings, but also the orientation and practices of childhood researchers who have tended to focus on 'language and communication skills' (Strandell, 1997, p. 447), in order to assess the level of children's development towards future outcomes. This kind of instrumental view of chil-dren's activities seems, in her view, to miss the point, which is that 'play' is operating as a much more powerful vehicle by which chil-dren do not simply achieve shared practical tasks, but 'organize their activities and social relations' and 'create social order in everyday life' (Strandell, 1997, p. 457).

In this sense, then, the term 'play' itself is problematic to the extent that it significantly underestimates what is going on when chil-dren interact in this way. That it is not a form of activity which is

structured and organized by adults does not make it any less important to children, or less significant as a facet of the phenomenon that
is 'childhood'. Immediate experience has as much value and meaning
as its consequences which might be identifiable in the form of learning and social skills development. This may help us, too, to understand the meaning for children of attempts to negotiate and sustain
friendships, which can be highly challenging and where apparently
fundamental relationships can change (and change again) extremely
rapidly. With their limited prior experience of such matters: 'maintaining interaction, and making friends are ... demanding tasks for
pre-school children' (Corsaro, 1997, p. 123). This may account for the
fluidity and centrality of these processes in children's lives, and especially in their unsupervised activities. As Corsaro notes, in pre-school
settings there is evidence of teachers and other adult figures spending considerable amounts of time dealing with the issues arising out
of disrupted relationships between children (1997, p. 147). Likewise,
his own observations underlined the importance of negotiations over
friendships:

> The younger children used the word *friend* to attempt to gain access to play,
> to protect shared activities from intruders, to build solidarity and mutual
> trust in the play group, and to attempt to control the activity of playmates.
> Conflict frequently developed regarding the nature of play. In such instances,
> the children often used friendship in attempts to get their way.
>
> (Corsaro, 1997, p. 147)

In some cases, he suggests that this might amount to a '"denial of
friendship" strategy', whereby a child might use the powerful threat
that s/he will not be 'buddies' with someone else any more, in order
to assert control of a situation (Corsaro, 1997, p. 148). Such episodes
could lead to prolonged conflicts and unhappiness, lasting throughout the day; but, equally, they might be capable of quick and straightforward resolution, whereas disruptions in adult friendships may be
less frequent, but much harder to resolve when they do occur. These
experiences for children are not just part of a learning process, but
'rather friendship processes are seen as deeply embedded in children's collective, interpretive reproduction of their cultures' (Corsaro,
1997, p. 149). Their activities and relationships can be seen to have
an intrinsic value, and a kind of internal logic, which may be related
to and influenced by the adult world, but have their own distinctive rhythms, meanings and structures. It can be argued then that

they should be evaluated and understood for themselves, rather than merely as a variation on adult, practices which are implicitly imbued with greater value and validity.

In similar vein, Moss and Petrie (2002, p. 131) complain that 'play is not generally valued or understood by adults, except as a means to an end'; namely, as an activity which contributes to learning and physical and social development. What is known as 'play', in their terms, is actually a 'central activity' for children, carried out 'on the margins' of other aspects of their lives, which are structured and timetabled for them according to other people's agendas. One of the authors reports having watched children involved in some impenetrable activity in a 'dark school playground', going on over a considerable period of time, whilst the adult observers at this particular out-of-school scheme wanted them to be doing something productive and 'worthwhile'. They also note the importance for children of being able to 'play' outdoors and in spaces which they are able to colonize and arrange according to their own priorities. Moss and Petrie take the view that the idea of 'children's spaces' is important precisely because it provides an operational focus for the promotion of distinctive and enriching experiences which are intrinsically valuable:

> The potential of children's spaces can enrich children's lives here and now, recognising the value of childhood as an important life stage in its own right. 'Children's spaces' as sites or forums for children's culture and relationships exemplifies the idea of social spaces *for* childhood, as part of life, not just as preparation for life.
>
> (Moss and Petrie, 2002, p. 123)

Expanding on this point, they argue that there is a political dimension to this issue, with children being at risk of 'oppressive' behaviour from adults, especially in the public service arena (Moss and Petrie, 2002, p. 125); this risk is compounded by the existing structures and requirements which shape large elements of children's lives, such as the common National Curriculum, or the power to curtail their movements through criminal justice legislation. This is a particular problem in the UK, in their view, whereas recognition of children's need for autonomy and free time and space is much more readily recognized elsewhere, such as in Scandinavia (Moss and Petrie, 2002, p. 128).

They are careful, though, to avoid sentimentalizing this issue, recognizing that children's independent activities may incorporate aspects of 'bullying and racism' (Moss and Petrie, 2002, p. 125).

At the same time, they accept that children's cultures are not produced in a vacuum, entirely independently of adults. As Marsh *et al.* (2005) point out, children rely extensively on adult-produced media for their source material in constructing their own roles and identities, while also trying to shape these in their own way. Gender relations, for example, seem to be very readily reproduced through children's own cultural productions, with boys taking on the role of 'Bob the Builder, in action with hammer and chisels', and girls representing themselves as 'Disney' characters, 'dressed in Cinderella or Sleeping Beauty costumes' (Marsh *et al.*, 2005, p. 43). At the same time, it is noted that this is not just a matter of reproducing established norms and identities, because some children could be observed to resist 'the normalization process', presenting 'contested and transgressive models of gendered practices'. Corsaro (1997, p. 151) similarly recounts an example of children running into 'problems in positioning themselves regarding gender' in their own self-constructed role plays. In one example he cites, a conventional 'husband and wife' household partnership was transformed with the result that there became 'two husbands' in the scenario, a state of affairs which was acceptable to them, but not their putative 'wife'. As he states, children draw on what they know to construct their own performances, producing 'typical family routines' (Corsaro, 1997, p. 152). However, these also demonstrate important points of variation from conventional patterns. In particular, self-directed activities allow much greater flexibility of role and behaviour. Both gender roles, and the boundaries of acceptable behaviour become much more fluid and negotiable (Corsaro, 1997, p. 153).

The worlds that children create are therefore strangely familiar, but significantly different from those created for them by adults, which they necessarily utilize as source material but also adapt and reimagine in their own distinctive ways. They are not simply mimicking or reproducing existing patterns of behaviour or relationships, nor are they merely rehearsing for real lives to come; their 'play' has real and immanent meaning, and needs to be recognized as intrinsically worthwhile. Once again, children's *active* presence comes to the fore:

> What weaves its way throughout ... is a clear sense that the children were active agents in these processes of meaning-making, a useful counter to those who emphasis children's consumption practices at the expense of their cultural production.
>
> (Marsh *et al.*, 2005, p. 46)

And, of course adults, too, can learn from children's original inventions, creative ideas and forms of social organization.

When two worlds collide

So far, I have considered childhood from children's perspective, first, as a negotiated response to adult constructions, expectations and norms, and, second, as a project of their own. This is reflected in their attempts to establish their own places, and create distinctive roles and relationships, which make sense in their own terms, but also draw on the raw materials provided, in the form of the existing adult world. At this point, I will move on to consider some of the possibilities for conflict between these perspectives, and what happens, for children, when their childhoods are 'contested' (Wyness, 2000). We might expect from the foregoing that there will be certain 'hotspots' where competing agendas and priorities will necessarily result in intergenerational conflict.

It may be surprising that this is not more common than seems to be the case. Perhaps the divisions between children and adults are less dramatic than some analyses would lead us to anticipate. Education, for example, might be thought of as a potential battleground (Smith, 2000b), but conflicts in this arena tend to be individualized and isolated rather than reflecting continuing and embedded generational tensions.

So, how do children assert their 'right' to a childhood, then? For Wyness, the school is an important site of potential conflict precisely because it is an area of life where 'generational' (Alanen, 2001) power is most directly exercised by adult interests. As he puts it, 'control in school is indicative of the broader social field for children. The school reflects, if not amplifies, the child's lack of social status' (Wyness, 2000, p. 89). The mechanisms by which children's school lives are structured in temporal and spatial terms provide concrete evidence of this, with their days organized and compartmentalized in ways over which they have very little control, and which effectively determine major elements of their childhood experience, underpinned by normative elements of convention, law and policy (James *et al.*, 1998, p. 75). This depiction of the practical organization of time echoes the work of Foucault (1979), who has illustrated its pervasiveness across a wide range of 'modern' social settings, including health care and prisons, as well as the school.

Wyness suggests that it is not just the structure of the school experience that is significant, but also its content. A rigid and prescriptive curriculum based on ideas of standardized content, progression and detailed testing provides little space for children to think, or act, independently. The prescriptive ordering of children's lives in school is further supported by a set of behavioural rules:

> The timetable and the curriculum are overlaid with codes of conduct and modes of self-display, with rules and regulations which are sometimes formalized, sometimes ... obvious to pupils. Behaviour, dress and speech codes limit what pupils can do in class. Arguably, these codes now extend into the relatively autonomous space of the playground.
>
> (Wyness, 2000, p. 90)

In some cases, too, they extend beyond the physical confines of the educational setting, with expectations about dress and behaviour applying to children anywhere they might be seen as 'representing' their school.

Not only are schools organized and run largely to the exclusion of children's active participation, but, if anything, the trend has been towards intensifying this tendency. Indeed, Wyness suggests that there is a progressive process of collusion between schools and parents, based on the idea that it is *parents* rather than children who are the 'consumers' of education in schools: 'pupils have lost the few bargaining powers they once had' (Wyness, 2000, p. 93). One might, therefore, expect to see the school as a natural site for children to articulate forms of opposition, given the levels of constraint and expected deference in evidence. However, there are few signs that children routinely organize themselves in this way, certainly in the UK (although see below). By contrast, though, there are regular reports of mass protests by school students in France about both the organization and content of their education (*The Guardian*, 27 January 2009).

Wyness makes an important distinction between 'subversive' and 'transformative' action. Thus, one strategy commonly utilized by children is to carve out their own spaces and times in order to be able to create their own worlds and to behave covertly in ways which are conventionally unacceptable – reflected, perhaps, in their distinctive patterns of use of ICT in the contemporary era. However, this is to be distinguished from those forms of action which are about wresting control in domains where adults claim authority and the right to exercise power. Here, children's 'deviance' has had much less direct impact, and their opportunities for legitimized forms of participation remain highly constrained, despite the growing rhetoric in support of giving them a 'voice'. Indeed: 'Teachers do not appear to be ... directly accountable to the pupils in class. There are no means by which pupils are able to voice an opinion on the quality of teaching or the content of the curriculum' (Wyness, 2000, p. 96). While pupils do find that they are invited to express opinions about some aspects of school life, such as 'recycling' and 'bullying', they are very rarely involved in other, more central, decisions, such as those concerned with staff appointments or the content of the taught curriculum (Whitty and Wisby, 2007, p. 6). While there are some reported attempts by adult school staff to 'democratize' their schools, these are relatively limited, and it is more common to find children rather despondent about their ability to participate effectively in schools, which are repeatedly found to be 'profoundly undemocratic' (Mayall, 2002, p. 101).

So, there is little evidence in the UK of active engagement of children in shaping and influencing the educational process, either through officially-sanctioned routes such as schools councils, or through adopting the kind of confrontational tactics which are much more evident elsewhere, and have been for many years (Zirakzadeh, 1989).

This is not to suggest that school students are totally passive, or indifferent to changes which affect them. In 2005, for example, 120 students are reported to have walked out of a Norfolk school complaining that they had not been consulted about the curtailment of their lunch break (Couchman, 2006). Peculiarly, Norfolk has something of a tradition in this respect, stemming back to the Burston School strike of 1914, and continuing to the present ('High school suspends protesting pupils', *Thetford & Brandon Times*, 15 May 2008). It may be that such forms of collective protest are more prevalent than we realize and are simply not reported routinely. However, it does seem to be the more widely held view that children's acts of resistance in the educational sphere tend to be isolated, individualized and subversive, taking the form of truancy and disruptive behaviour, which may, in turn, lead to official sanctions such as exclusion (Wyness, 2000, p. 101). These forms of behaviour are transformed fairly routinely into normatively unacceptable forms of deviance. In the end, children's schooling seems to be based on a rather one-dimensional view of childhood, from which children themselves are 'ontologically absent' (Wyness, 2000, p. 104); that is, there is no space for children to act self-consciously and critically in relation to the prescribed format and content of formal learning. Education policy appears to be geared towards producing 'standardized' experiences which bring children 'into line', but does not readily take account of, or encourage their self-expression as active social agents and independent learners.

While schools seem to be unambiguously dominated by adult concerns, with children finding little opportunity to express resistance and to achieve change, there are other contexts where their opportunities to assert themselves may appear more promising, if still problematic. Out-of-school clubs, for example, while often taking place on school premises, offer a much more fluid context within which spaces (and activities) are 'contested' (Smith and Barker, 2000). Research into power relations in this kind of setting suggests that children play an 'active role' in determining what goes on in this sort of setting, and how it is defined. Adults in out-of-school activities were found to be preoccupied with ideas of 'protection' and 'care' (Smith and Barker, 2000, p. 320), but children had very different views, which extended to the ways in which they organized the space available. Thus, while: 'Adult playworkers were keen to stress that they define and control what goes on in clubs' (Smith and Barker, 2000, p. 322), children could be observed to 'transgress' in a number of ways. They also sought to lay exclusive claim to some areas specifically to create privacy and creative space for themselves:

> In a number of clubs one of the favourite activities was to make dens out of furniture, boxes, cardboard or material. Children strictly controlled the micro-environment within the club by prohibiting adults from entering and by sometimes making them too small for adults to inhabit.
>
> (Smith and Barker, 2000, p. 323)

Children also 'contested' the ways in which adults tried to determine what they did in these clubs, as well as how the space was used. They turned drawing paper into aeroplanes, for instance (Smith and Barker, 2000, p. 323). While children's activities and relationships were mediated by established distinctions of age, gender and ethnicity, the common conclusions drawn from this particular study were that children took a decisive part in defining what went on in out-of-school clubs, asserting their right to utilize the space according to their own priorities and preferences: 'although such spaces are created, defined, bounded and controlled by adults, the research ... has highlighted that children attach their own meanings to these institutional settings' (Smith and Barker, 2000, p. 330).

Other spaces, too, are contested by children (and young people), notably 'shopping malls' (Matthews *et al.*, 2000). For a variety of reasons, it is suggested that there may be an increasing number of settings which are not clearly defined as belonging to, or under the control of, one group or another, including physical locations as well as cyberspace. As established work patterns change, or as children as consumers are seen as an increasingly significant group, their presence in commercial areas may also become more ambiguous. Children and young people's use of streets and other public places as sites of interaction and simply 'being' are not new, of course (see Corrigan, 1979), but this remains problematic, and may be increasingly so (but see also Pearson, 1983). In asserting their right to be in public places, children are also seen to pose a challenge. They are 'a polluting presence, because by congregating together they seem to be challenging the hegemony of adult ownership' and control (Matthews *et al.*, 2000, p. 281) of these areas.

Young people's use of the shopping mall is distinctive and suggests a specific kind of lifestyle, which may, of course, be one of the reasons for conflict with the adult world. They do not necessarily spend very much, they may stay in one place ('sit and watch the world go by'; 14-year-old girl, Matthews *et al.*, 2000, p. 286), they may stay there for a long time, and they may congregate in numbers. This is not necessarily a conscious or deliberate attempt to confront other (adult) members of the community, but it does involve the assertion of the right to use 'common' territory for their own ends. Being in the mall is therefore an opportunity to express a particular form of being, a sort of 'in-between' status, in what Matthews *et al.* describe as 'thirdspace' (2000, p. 292). While this may be understood in relatively conventional language of 'transitions' (Smith, 2008), the argument is that young people acting in this way are seeking to establish a distinctive form of identity for themselves:

> We suggest that through their various attempts to assert a right of presence, both 'backstage' and 'on stage', young people assume the mantle of the hybrid. Here, young people are no longer child, living within the safe haven of the home, nor quite adult, with powers to move freely and unassailably within the public domain ... From this perspective, the mall assumes a cultural importance over and above its functional form.
>
> (Matthews *et al.*, 2000, p. 292)

Unlike the school setting, then, these latter spaces reflect a degree of uncertainty and imprecision. It is precisely their contested nature which affords children and young people the opportunity to assert their right to be present, and to utilize the space available in ways which reflect their own emerging and distinctive identities. They are not here subsumed under adult agendas for learning and development; nor do they feel obliged to define themselves according to a deficit model as being not-yet-adult. We should be careful not to idealize these settings or the forms of expression they facilitate, since children are capable of doing bad things to each other quite independently; but at the same time, we are able to gain a glimpse here of 'childhoods' which are more or less owned and organized by their inhabitants, at least temporarily.

Conclusion: children's childhoods

In this chapter I have explored some of the ways and some of the settings in which children make sense of and seek to exert some measure of control over their own lives. In particular, I have focused on the ways in which they come to think about their own status and identity. There are a number of dynamics at play here, reflecting generational power dynamics which are played out differentially depending on the context. In some places, such as schools, adult agendas self-evidently predominate, and childhood is therefore constructed and organized according to established developmental assumptions and power dynamics (Foucault, 1979).

In other places, and at other times, within the family or on the street, different preoccupations and influences are brought to bear. This indicates that core terms such as identity and autonomy must be seen as variable, negotiable and argued over according to the setting. It would be unwise, however, to begin to think in terms of entirely fragmented childhoods with no commonalities or connections between different phases of existence, as is evident, for instance, in the recurrent theme of conflict between generations. We can be sure of one thing, at least: childhood is a 'contested' area of human life (Wyness, 2000).

10

Childhoods:

The Same, Only Different?

The need for analytical coherence

In attempting to provide a summative discussion of the issues raised in so many different contexts, there are a number of significant challenges. It is clearly difficult to establish a common analytical framework for this exercise given the sheer range of disciplines involved in the study of childhood, and the extent of disagreement within and between them. However, without staking out some common ground, the problem of establishing a baseline for our concluding analysis becomes almost insuperable. Some compromises will have to be made in order to enable us to make progress. If so, what are these to be, and how will they impact upon our subsequent deliberations?

Perhaps, for example, we can accept the international definition of childhood as that period of human life between birth and 18, given that the consensus on this is very widely established. However, this in itself entails certain assumptions which are not so easily sustainable. It creates the appearance both of conceptual unity and of a rupture between childhood and adulthood which is more dramatic than the changing phases of childhood itself. Is the transition to adulthood really more significant or dramatic than the onset of puberty (which does not occur at a fixed age point)? If, on the other hand, we decide to subdivide childhood according to certain internal points of transition, what criteria should we apply to determine these? The language of developmental milestones begins to assert itself here, and we are tempted to subscribe to another, fairly standardized, 'story' of childhood. Can we perhaps assume that: 'For all children, development will be sequential – all children will gain competence in certain developmental tasks, in the same order but not necessarily at the same rate' (Aldgate, 2006, p. 21)? In light of the preceding chapters, though, this appears at best to be a major over-simplification, in view of the widely differing cultural norms and practices we have uncovered, as well as also significant physiological and genetic differences.

Despite these strong reservations, in this chapter I will seek first to establish, even if only provisionally, a conceptual framework to underpin our analysis; on this basis, I will then go on to address the fundamental question of which aspects of children's lives are common to them all, and which aspects are distinct and diverse. Following this, I will seek to resolve the associated question of which of these are of the greatest significance, both analytically and materially.

Establishing common starting points

Given that childhood is a contested phenomenon, it is unlikely that very many shared analytical assumptions will emerge. Despite this, there are some common orientations to the subject which are essentially non-contentious. First, almost by definition, studies of children's lives typically incorporate the idea that 'childhood' itself represents a valid analytical category. In other words, it is capable of being conceptualized and discussed as a 'real' subject in its own right. In a sense, this is simply a reflection of the taken-for-granted convention, at least in modern times, that children do have a distinctive place in the life course. For some, this may be grounded in physiological or psychological assumptions about growth and development – the end of childhood is marked by the apparent completion of these processes. For others, however, the *idea* of childhood is more significant, and its status as a social construction is what justifies its analysis as a specific object of inquiry. There is perhaps a degree of irony in the recent assertion of a children's rights perspective in this context, which has called for specific attention to studies of children from *their* perspective. In other words, claims for equal treatment in these terms have in practice necessitated a strong assertion of a distinctive identity, as against other generations, perhaps in the same way as 'black' and disabled groups have done, laying claim to contested identities, precisely in order to assert their own autonomy and claims to power. Some authors have suggested that this is a necessary starting point for considering the position and relationships of children as a specific social group (Alanen, 2001, p. 12).

This, indeed, suggests another common analytical base, in that children and childhood are implicitly viewed 'generationally', that is, they are defined fundamentally in terms of their relationship to adults and adulthood. These demarcations may be seen in the form of developmental stages, or structural differences, but there is nonetheless a consensus about the idea of a clear delineation between these social categories. Not only is there a prescriptive distinction between the child and the adult, but this dichotomy also underpins an analytical approach which considers one in terms of the other. This may involve applying a 'deficit' model, whereby the child is seen as inferior according to certain criteria, such as physical growth or emotional maturity; or, it may be a matter of distinguishing along the lines of material differences, in terms of power, status and access to resources. In either case, though, the idealized adult used as the conventional reference point is viewed as being in a more advantageous position than the child.

The third area in which we may find a degree of consensus concerns the idea of childhood as a time of 'change'. Again, the origins and nature of these change processes may be contested, but there does appear to be wide agreement that there are dynamic forces at play running through children's lives which have a crucial part in shaping their experiences. The source of these dynamics may again be located in very diverse places, for instance, the idea of 'transitions' in childhood and youth can mean very different things according to the conceptual frame adopted. Indeed, as we saw earlier, debates about the history of childhood have often been bound up with the question of whether it is merely the product of certain socio-economic conjunctures, or whether it has 'always' been with us in some form or another. In case we should overlook it, children, too, seem to have held variable views about their own status through the ages. According to one economically active 8-year-old in Victorian England: "'I ain't a child'", although she also maintained that she would not be "'a woman'" until the age of 20 (Mayhew, [1851] 1978).

Thus, arguably, there is some common ground across disciplinary boundaries over the approach to be taken towards the study of childhood. It is accorded some degree of conceptual coherence, it is defined in relation to adulthood, and it is characterized by change and 'transitions' (MacDonald and Marsh, 2005).

Conceptual dilemmas and conflicting positions

On the other side of the coin, however, there are some equally consistent and compelling indications of fundamental disagreements about just 'how' children's lives should be conceptualized and studied.

For instance, there is a major divide between approaches which see childhood as 'real' and those which view it as essentially a socially constructed phenomenon. This is not to suggest that social constructs have no substantive existence or material effects, but rather that childhood viewed in this way prioritizes beliefs and ideologies over its concrete or physical qualities. This dichotomy has sometimes been construed in terms of a disciplinary divide between sociological and biological sciences. Associated with it are a number of other challenges, such as the question of where we stand on the issues of determinism and freedom, or nature and nurture.

Of course, there are difficulties in taking such distinctions to extremes, and opting exclusively for one position or another (Prout and James, 1997); nonetheless, if we wish to attempt some sort of compromise solution, very substantial practical issues arise. For example: 'if we are to see childhood as *both* biological and social ..., what weight should be given to each factor' (Prout and James, 1997, p. 26). Similar tensions can be identified between 'individual' and 'social' orientations towards childhood. Is it best thought of in terms of variations in personal characteristics, such as physical and behavioural attributes, or should it be seen as essentially an interactive production, arising from social systems and inter-personal relationships? Thus, for example, what happens in peer groups is seen by some as a crucial determinant of children's cultures and behaviour, even to the extent of downplaying the impact of parental influences:

> Children learn about themselves by comparing themselves to their groupmates. They vie for status within the group; they win or lose. They are typecast by their peers; they choose or are chosen for different niches. Identical twins do not end up with identical personalities, even if they are members of the same peer group, because they have different experiences within the group.
>
> (Rich Harris, 1999, p. 359)

This argument poses particular problems for psychology as a discipline, it seems, because it faces the kind of choice represented by figures such as Piaget and Vygotsky, about the internal and external aspects of children's mental processes, and how they learn (Carpendale and Lewis, 2006).

This question is associated with a further potential area of conflict which focuses on the kind of change model applied to children's lives. While it may seem relatively non-contentious to think in terms of physical growth and hormonal changes, whether these are seen as developments towards a finished adult state ('becoming') or rather as a continuous and dynamic feature of all human life ('being') is rather more contentious, as Lee (2001) makes clear.While notions of changes throughout children's lives as being 'developmental' are almost axiomatic in some educational and psychological literature (Smith *et al.*, 2003, for example), these are called fundamentally into question by others, perhaps more often of a sociological persuasion, who see children's lives as worthy of recognition and study in their own right:

> The child is conceived of as a person, a status, a course of action, a set of needs, rights or differences – in sum, as a social actor … this new phenomenon, the 'being' child, can be understood in its own right. It does not have to be approached from an assumed shortfall of competence, reason or significance.
>
> (James *et al.*, 1998, p. 207)

Taken to its extreme, this argument might suggest that there is little point in considering the idea of the 'child' as analytically distinct from other life stages, except to the extent that it has come to play such a prominent role in social and scientific discourse. However, this in turn begs the question of just how and why the idea of childhood has assumed such global significance, suggesting a coherent and unified 'state of being' (or becoming!) which can be understood, investigated and provided for as a distinct entity.Where does conceptual unity and pragmatic value come from, and what do we gain by deconstructing it?

Substantive features of childhood: what can we agree on?

In light of our earlier observations, it may be that there are only a very limited number of distinctive aspects of childhood which can be agreed upon across disciplinary and contextual boundaries. These cohere around:

- physiological and neurological changes;
- acquiring knowledge and learning from experience;
- vulnerability and a lack of resources.

It will immediately be clear from this list that it is both quite general and by no means restricted exclusively to that time of life conventionally demarcated as childhood, however, taken together, these characteristics might yet suggest that childhood represents a special case as a form of human existence.

It is obvious, for example, that the period up to around 18 years of age is one in which certain types of growth, hormonal and neurological changes occur which cannot be found in the same form at any other life stage. Puberty, for example, can only be located within the childhood years, even though its precise point of onset is both variable and subject to the influence of environmental factors (Prendergast, 2000, p. 105). These changes have certain determinate consequences, it is suggested, although they will be mediated by social influences and cultural expectations. Shilling (1993, p. 12) believes that it is helpful to think of the body as 'unfinished' at birth, and thereafter subject to a series of biological and social transformations. Each change in the body:

> requires that we adjust to and attend to our body, or that of others in an appropriate and special way, as carers or as cared for, as male or female or as independent or dependent beings. These configurations of size, maturity, dependency, power and value may take very different forms in relation to gender and age.
>
> (Prendergast, 2000, p. 105)

Puberty is conventionally taken as a point of divergence between boys and girls, as it is associated with sexual maturity, and other observable variations, including changes in voice and body shape (Smith *et al.*, 2003). On the other hand, as noted earlier, gender roles and attributes are the subject of close attention from children and adults alike well before these physiological changes take effect.

Importantly, once we recognize the commonality of physical change in childhood, it also becomes clear that certain social processes of differentiation and exclusion have no clear physiological basis. Thus, growth and sexual maturity are features of the lives of disabled children just as they are for others, but their social lives are often found to be sharply differentiated, and these outcomes cannot be accounted for in the same way. While we cannot overlook the extent to which bodily changes are viewed and experienced through subjective processes of interpretation and 'embodiment' (James, 2000, p. 30), there is some value in retaining a hold on the notion of shared aspects of physiological change. The assertion of 'difference' may be somewhat misleading, and may lead to divisive consequences which are much more clearly grounded in ideology and belief than in physical characteristics. Nonetheless children may well articulate self-conscious concerns about their size and body shape in the present, even while they are subject to rapid physiological changes (James, 2000, p. 28). Growth, especially in relative terms, becomes a common feature of children's emerging 'self-consciousness' (James, 2000, p. 27), and this is underpinned by the way in which formal settings such as schools classify and segregate them by age, and thus, implicitly by height as well. In highlighting an acute sense of concern, James notes that, in her research with children, it was always important for them 'to know . . . who is the smallest – indeed the "tiniest" – in the class' (2000, p. 28). Arising from this awareness, and the worries associated with it, children appear to be preoccupied with growing and becoming 'bigger than you' (James, 2000, p. 29). Physical growth and change are clearly a common feature of children's lives; but at the same time, inevitably, these processes are experienced differently, both as between individuals and groups. They are also subject to negotiation and mutual categorization. Notably, for children with disabilities it seems that such shared features of their lives *as* children recede rapidly into the background, to be superimposed by another powerful ascribed identity, associated with impairment and a fixed state of dependency (permanent childhood?), in which growth and sexual maturity are not readily recognized (Middleton, 1999). For all children, though, there remains a simultaneously individual and collective task, of negotiating and making sense (for themselves and others) of the 'ever-changing nature of their bodies' and, crucially 'of the self' which they represent to others (James, 2000, p. 36).

As well as physical change, we can also conclude that 'learning' is a constant feature of children's experience. This is not to suggest that it is exclusive to childhood, or qualitatively different, necessarily, from the ways in which adults learn. It is, however, quantitatively different in the sense that children have relatively fewer prior reference points, and more limited experience on which to draw than adults. It is not a lack of competence which limits children's ability to make sense of what they encounter, so much as the absence of comparative material on which to draw. As already indicated, in some ways children's capacities to absorb information and learn from it may be greater than those of adults for demonstrable neurological reasons (Blakemore and Frith, 2005). It is suggested that there are 'sensitive periods' where the brain has greater capacity for certain types of learning, and that this occurs for essentially functional reasons. In relation to facial recognition, for instance:

> Windows for fast learning exist, but experience itself closes these windows. This is useful. At first a broad range of all sorts of faces and voices can be distinguished, but later on some of these distinctions become less relevant and are 'lost'.
>
> (Blakemore and Frith, 2005, p. 30)

Different and to some extent contrasting models of learning have been developed, such as those of Piaget ([1926] 1959) and Vygotsky (1986). However, lying beneath apparent conflicts there is a common set of assumptions about the centrality of learning processes in children's early years. While some have been critical of what is termed the 'blank sheet' model of children's learning (Moss and Petrie, 2002, p. 118), there may after all be some truth in this presumption. There are, of course, good grounds for criticizing approaches which take an entirely one-sided view of 'transmitting to, or depositing within, the child a predetermined and unquestionable body of knowledge and values, with a prefabricated meaning' (Moss and Petrie, 2002, p. 118). However, even if we think of the child as 'a partner, a co-constructor of knowledge' (Moss and Petrie, 2002, p. 119), with both adults and peers, it remains the case that s/he has limited prior experience and evidence on which to draw. To the extent that children are empiricists (Gopnik, 1996), then, their learning is shaped by the amount of source material on which they can draw. At the same time, this does not imply that they have any less competence than older people when it comes to making sense of what they observe and creating ideas, knowledge and understanding. Moss and Petrie argue that the common ground is to be found in the concept of the child as an 'active learner', who is able to 'problem solve'. S/he is not simply engaged in the process of organizing and manipulating an existing set of 'stable and objective concepts', but is rather to be found producing her/his own ideas and hypotheses, probably more so than older people, and then testing these against other assumptions and evidence: 'When this happens, the child is in a position to view her own constructions in relation to scientific constructions, and make her own choices and meanings' (Moss and Petrie, 2002, p. 121). Indeed, in view of her/his relatively limited prior experience, there might be a case here for actively encouraging independent exploration and discovery in order to provide a rich and varied range of evidence on which to base her/his sense-making processes. Wyness (2000), as noted previously, has called into question the ways in which formal education in schools is organized and structured to restrict children's opportunities to 'explore', and set their own learning agendas: 'Behaviour, dress and speech codes limit what pupils can do in class' (2000, p. 90). In this constrained context, there is no doubt that children are still learning, but what they are learning may derive less from the formal curriculum, and more from the relations of authority, power and inequality which are being brought to bear in shaping their days and the substance of their timetabled activities.

It is power relations such as these which bring us to the third area where we can claim that there is a degree of common ground concerning what childhood comprises. Children's relative physical size and strength, their relative lack of experience (learning), and their relative powerlessness combine to create a sense of vulnerability and threat of harm to which they are all exposed. The notion of childhood vulnerability is, of course, a very well-established and pervasive paradigm, influencing much media content, and official discourses around risk, safety and child protection (Parton, 2006), although clearly any critical analysis has to resist the temptation to accept this simply as a 'given' (Kitzinger, 2004).

Jenks (1996) observes that contemporary perceptions are shaped, first, by the 'discovery' of child abuse in the 1960s, and then in the dramatic growth in its reported range and incidence. This seems to be very much a phenomenon of our time, related to changes in 'patterns of personal, political and moral control in social life' (1996, p. 86) which have influenced our perceptions of childhood, rather than necessarily its concrete reality. These concerns may have crystallized around particular tragic events such as the deaths of Dennis O'Neill, Maria Colwell, Victoria Climbié or 'Baby P', although they do not necessarily represent changes in underlying levels of risk and vulnerability. Christensen (2000) is also concerned about the 'cultural meanings' of a concept such as vulnerability, which necessarily creates a picture of 'an active, protecting and responsible adult' and 'a passive and unprotected child' (2000, p. 39). What we may be observing here is a kind of magnifying effect, whereby an observable characteristic, such as illness or harm, may provide the basis for and accentuate prior assumptions about risk, weakness and dependency.

While the language of vulnerability may thus be problematic because it tends to emphasize children's purported lack of agency and competence, it nonetheless highlights the connection between widely held beliefs and underlying issues to do with physical capacity, relative inexperience and limited resources. This relationship is highlighted by other risks to which children may be disproportionately exposed, such as levels of violence towards and exploitation of street children, or injuries occurring as a result of traffic accidents. We know, for instance, that the age distribution of certain forms of harm is not random, and that those under 18 are particularly susceptible in some respects, including abuse, accidental injury, and criminal victimization.

Some authors (Jenks, 1996; Mason and Falloon, 2001) attribute adverse outcomes such as abuse to inequalities of power between children and adults: 'These inequalities mean that adults are able to respond to children with physical, behavioural and emotional actions, in ways that are denied to children' (Mason and Falloon, 2001, p. 106). Thus, for example, the exercise of physically harmful means of punishment (smacking) is not merely a reflection of adults' greater size or strength, but it is also rooted in 'legitimated' but unequal relations of authority and control, according to these authors.

Other forms of harm, though, including sexual exploitation and abuse, are sometimes attributed to children's relative 'inexperience' and unpreparedness. The idea of 'vulnerability', though, has become quite pervasive, extending its classificatory scope to encompass as many as 4 million UK children in poverty (Parton, 2006, p. 115). This indicates that there is an interplay between children's physical status, their levels of experience and social factors which combine to reinforce the perception that they are distinctively 'at risk' in certain ways:

> [the notion of] vulnerability ... is useful for understanding not only illness in childhood, or other episodes where children may be injured, but also for understanding some basic conceptions of modern childhood itself. Children's vulnerability may be partly associated with their biological being, but it is also a construction of the way in which children perceive themselves and are perceived by others.
>
> (Christensen, 2000, p. 57)

We are thus offered another organizing concept ('vulnerability') which helps to generate a consensual view of the physical (and other) risks which are specific to childhood as a category, and which relate to their physicality, limited experience and lack of resources, on the one hand, and their distinctive relationships with the adult world, on the other.

Aspects of 'difference' in childhood

Having considered a number of aspects of childhood which exhibit a degree of uniformity, it will now be important to consider the extent to which these are mediated by other factors which reflect 'difference' along a number of dimensions. For present purposes, it will be helpful to consider this question in relation to three broad headings: physical, temporal and spatial variations, following the themes introduced earlier (Chapters 2, 3 and 4).

1 Physical variations in childhood

Inevitably, each child is different in purely physical terms, rooted in potentially infinite variations in genetic make-up. It is equally clear that physical difference is associated with fault-lines of major sociological significance, such as those represented by gender, ethnicity and disability. These distinctions run right to the core of children's lives. It is obvious, for example, that the demarcation between children on grounds of gender has major implications for the way in which they are categorized and treated. Prendergast's (2000) discussion of the onset of menstruation connects this experience with a process by which the physical and the conceptual notions of gender are intertwined:

> Each girl learns that menstrual experience must be constantly present in their thoughts in order that it remains invisible to the outside world ... This constant carrying of the body in the mind, and at the same time rendering aspects of the embodied self as invisible, the mindfulness of having to forget what you know, constitute an embodied mapping of gender itself.
>
> (Prendergast, 2000, p. 123)

The author makes no distinction between the body and mind or body and 'self' (Prendergast, 2000, p. 124), and thereby underlines the argument that differences based on gender are fundamental and inevitable aspects of childhood.

It might be argued, too, that disability and ethnicity act as physical determinants of variations in children's lived experience to the extent that tangible markers of difference also have specific consequences in terms of perceptions and social interaction. Studies of the implications of ethnicity, for instance, have identified that children from a relatively early age show a 'preference' for 'play partners' from a similar ethnic group (Smith *et al.*, 2003, p. 197), although this does not imply 'racial prejudice' (2003, p. 198).

For children with disabilities or chronic health problems, their self-perception may be impacted upon by physical factors, and James observes that the task for them of managing the 'signs of illness' may itself become an 'emotionally intense and intensive activity (2000, p. 34). Children affected in this way appear to have a distinctive and more self-conscious relationship with their physical being, which may assume great significance in terms of their own and others' perceptions and behaviour. Although James quite properly makes the point that all children are likely to be involved to some extent in 'managing' their bodily functions and appearances, this does appear to become a more pressing matter for some: 'I used to hide my hands. I didn't want anyone looking at them because they were not as smooth as anyone else's' ('Pauline', quoted in James, 2000, p. 35).

It seems that physical variations, especially those which are easily observable, may operate in two ways to shape differences between childhoods. First, they influence the way in which children experience and express themselves in bodily terms; and, second, they appear also to be significant in helping to shape social interactions and relationships. This kind of distinction cuts across, and perhaps obscures shared experiences of physical growth and learning. Disabled children, for example, may find themselves being treated as dependent for much longer than their peers, at least partly because their physical status suggests and reinforces underlying assumptions. As identified previously, it is just this kind of concern which has been articulated by young people who feel that their rights to 'grow up', or to be treated as equal citizens, have not been recognized due to their impairments. For them, the state of childhood may appear, indeed, to be fixed and timeless.

2 Temporal aspects of childhood

There are other ways, too, in which physicality might be seen as a determinant of difference as between childhoods. This is especially notable, as seen in earlier chapters, in the case of historical accounts which have variously sought to explain the appearance, transformation and disappearance of childhood over time (Cunningham, 2006). These accounts are able to trace changes in the ways in which childhood is defined legally, organized socially, and experienced physiologically. It is noted, for example, that children's health and life expectancy have improved very substantially in developed countries such as the UK (Cunningham, 2006, p. 190), with very dramatic increases in survival rates for those in the first year of life. At the same time, it is pointed out with a degree of irony that:

> No generation before our own has had to concern itself with the obesity of children. In 1997, 9.6 per cent of children [in the UK] were obese; by 2003 it had risen to 13.7 per cent. Nine out of every ten school children, it is said, are set to become 'couch potatoes'.
>
> (Cunningham, 2006, p. 242)

Other significant changes in children's physical lives are also reported, such as the earlier onset of puberty, and earlier sexual maturity. Cunningham argues that 'a change of this magnitude is likely to alter the contours of childhood' (2006, p. 13). So, as the physiological aspects of childhood have changed historically, there have been consequential changes in the 'stages' of childhood, bringing the notion of fixed patterns of development into question. Some, indeed, have suggested that there is a kind of evolutionary process in play, here, which has behavioural and psycho-social as well as physiological consequences (Smith *et al.*, 2003). Lee agrees that 'time is an important source of human variation' (2001, p. 137), although he contrasts the two dimensions of historical change and 'the personal and experiential resonances of growing up'. This distinction reflects alternative 'ways of thinking' about childhood, one of which treats 'chronological age' as the key distinguishing factor between two types of humans', that is, children and adults; while the other would suggest that what is more significant is the way in which ideas of 'growing up' are contingent and historically specific. Thus we encounter a number of paradoxical observations: change is a constant feature of childhood; it has both internal and external dimensions, which can be at odds; the constancy of change itself guarantees diversity in children's lives.

In practical terms, as Uprichard (2007, p. 8) notes, these tensions are recognised, and accommodated by children themselves: 'well, I'll be different when I'm older, well sort of, but things will be different anyway, and so will me friends, and you [pointing to researcher]' (quoting Guillaume, age 7). Following Lee (2001), she also suggests that acknowledging children as 'beings' *and* 'becomings' is an important conceptual building block, in terms of generating a rounded and responsive sense of what childhood is, and the ways in which it is negotiated. For Uprichard, to 'reinstate' the idea of 'becoming' into attempts to understand children's lives is definitely not to 'say that the biological base of childhood is a forceful determinant' (2007, p. 9), but is rather to establish a clearer base for understanding children as beings in the present who are also 'future oriented', and whose lives involve an active process of negotiating the tension between these two poles. This, in her view, allows us to bridge disciplinary differences in the ways we consider the 'child', while also allowing us to stay true to the processes children themselves undergo in constructing their own lives. In this way, common biological trajectories can be understood and negotiated in the specific and varied contexts and transitions which they will experience as discrete individuals.

From this brief discussion we may conclude that aspects of time and change oblige us to recognize that diversity is an inevitable and deep-seated feature of childhood, and that we must therefore seek to develop conceptual frameworks which take account of this. However, it has also been suggested that this should not be at the expense of recognized and accepted features of the experience of being a child, such as ageing, and 'anticipation' (Uprichard, 2007, p. 8), which are clearly viewed as central to their lives by children themselves.

3 The spatial determinants of childhood

Finally, in this context, we should briefly consider the importance of 'space' as an aspect of diversity in childhood. As we have seen already, in discussing children's 'geographies' (Holloway and Valentine, 2000), there is a considerable amount of evidence available on the variable meanings and impacts of their environments. This evidence also acts as a powerful reminder that we should, as far as possible, avoid applying fixed ethnocentric, or 'developed world', models of childhood as prescriptive benchmarks. Reflection on this point suggests that it is hard to avoid the conclusion that the highly variable conditions in which they grow up must be fundamental in shaping children's experiences; common ground is hard to identify. Children who become enforced contributors to the family economy from a very early age have, in effect, been 'adultized', as have those who care for other family members. Many of the conventional markers of development, through education and changing forms of social organization are simply not relevant to them. Indeed, in parallel with our observations about temporal factors, we can see that external variations in the environmental context have very significant implications for the localized and specific aspects of children's use of space – where they are almost constantly involved in poorly paid work settings, for instance, they have virtually no opportunity to take over 'spaces' (Moss and Petrie, 2002) of their own, and to make their own worlds and social relationships.

I have already discussed the impact of urban environments in children's lives (Kong, 2000), but there are other aspects of children's spaces which should also be considered, notably, the ways in which these intentionally or unintentionally operate as sites for shaping their ideas about what is normal and what is possible. As Leonard (2007) observes, spaces and places are not neutral, but are almost inevitably inscribed with powerful messages and meanings for children. Thus, settings which may conventionally be associated with ideas of freedom or security are capable of quite other interpretations:

> The once innocent spaces of childhood such as streets, parks and other public places have become redefined as areas where children are in potential danger from other children or from some of the adults usually defined as their protectors. Even the private spaces of childhood such as family homes have re-emerged as places of power and sites where the abuse of children by adults connected with them becomes a distinct possibility.
>
> (Leonard, 2007, p. 432)

Once again, this observation strikes at conventional assumptions about the structure of children's lives. It does, of course, offer some endorsement for the idea developed earlier that vulnerability is a constant, but at the same time it forces us to recognize that the consequences of this for children will be highly variable. There are very few constants in these terms; ostensibly 'safe' places become sites of risk and fear. For some children, it may be unwise to stray too far from home. In Northern Ireland, children who live in 'interface areas' (historical sites of communal and sectarian conflict) set limits to their movements and will not go into areas where 'their homes are not located' (Leonard, 2007, p. 433). For others, it is the home itself where their lives will be overshadowed by the threat or actuality of abuse. And for some, nowhere is safe, external conflict is replicated within the 'household' (Leonard, 2007, p. 443).

For Leonard, the intensely personal nature of these experiences is also mediated by other factors such as 'class, gender and ethnicity' (Leonard, 2007, p. 443), but the crucial point for her is that environmental factors play a highly significant part in differentiating children's lives, and these are reflected in their behaviour as well as their understandings. Not only is the experience of children living in conflict zones highly specific, but the consequences in terms of learning and social relationships are also distinctive, it is suggested. As competent actors, children are found to be capable of demonstrating 'a level of competence in managing and negotiating safety in high-risk environments' (Leonard, 2007, p. 444). Like others who are exposed to risks, such as street children, it could be argued children in situations of conflict acquire sophisticated skills which others might not need and therefore do not acquire. Does this degree of specificity therefore make a convincing case that we should think primarily in terms of 'difference' rather than uniformity when we think about children and their childhoods?

Conclusion: the meaning of childhood?

In light of these observations, it is increasingly difficult to support the argument that the concept of childhood represents a clear or coherent entity. It seems rather that it is hugely shaped by an array of contextual factors which are both powerfully influential and diverse in their impact. It is difficult, therefore, to find a compelling justification for attempts to explain childhood in terms which suggest a unified phenomenon, even though we have been offered an array of organizing concepts such as 'development' (Smith *et al.*, 2003) or 'generation' (Alanen, 2001). These tend to lead to self-justifying and circular conclusions that childhood is a distinctive category simply *because* it has been defined in those terms. Beyond this, though, there is very little substantive justification for this delineation.

The available grounds for distinguishing children as a group in definitive terms are limited, and with the exception of certain physiological events, even these are not exclusive to childhood. Can we, nonetheless, conclude that childhood has essential common features? Is it characterized by certain key attributes and processes (gaining experience, learning, physical growth, for example), although these are bound to interact with other, equally powerful, sources of divergence (such as genetic variations, social setting, or historical context)?

It may be unsurprising that it is difference rather than uniformity which has become the more compelling starting point for our attempts to understand and respond to the issues affecting children's lives, almost irrespective of disciplinary perspective: 'Instances of childhood would, therefore, be understood as empirical effects of an open-ended process in which the different elements through which they are constructed have come into play' (Prout, 2005, p. 144).

However, this does not mean that there is no basis for or no point in identifying common ground, or generalizable features of the phenomenon. Prout (2005) argues that it is just such elements, together constituting 'juvenility', which justify continued attempts to understand childhood in its own right:

> In this perspective childhood can be seen not as an epiphenomenon of biology but as a translation of it into culture. All childhoods are, in part, constituted through such extended juvenility and all human cultures have to negotiate with it.
>
> (Prout, 2005, p. 111)

On the other hand, it is the concrete specificity of this interaction that ensures that childhood still 'emerges as a very diverse phenomenon', in his view.

From another perspective, it is seen as important to distinguish between those aspects of childhood which are 'external and contingent' (Alanen, 2001, p. 20), such as adult-originated and highly prescriptive developmental pathways, as well as material circumstances, such as poverty and geographical environment; and those which are 'internal' and reflect the ways in which children live and grow, and negotiate and renegotiate their relationships with the 'social world', on the other. This takes us back to an analytical framework which distinguishes between the ways in which childhood is objectified by institutions and ideologies in order to establish a measurable and manageable social category, on the one hand; and a varied set of intra- and inter-personal and subjective processes by which children themselves develop and share a sense of common identities and interests, interactively with these external forces, on the other. Thus, for instance, the impact of the education system (in the developed world, especially) can be seen to be multi-faceted; it identifies and categorizes children according to explicit (and purportedly 'objective') criteria; it delineates their progress *through* childhood and towards 'completion'; it provides the mediating mechanism through which children develop a sense of themselves and their own identities, and the nature of their relationship to others (on the basis of, say, age, behaviour, 'special needs', or academic level); and, sometimes, as is also apparent, it provides the context for the identification of common cause and the articulation of various forms of resistance.

11

Conclusion:

What Should We Do About Children (and Childhood)?

Knowledge about childhood and its uses

In this final chapter, I want to take the opportunity to reflect on what we have learnt about children and childhood, and to look ahead, in the sense of considering how these observations can and should be applied, not only to improve our understanding, but also to improve children's lives. How we address of the subject is clearly not just an academic issue, but is also of critical importance given the extent of interest and activity directed towards them, both by statutory agencies concerned with education and well-being, and by other powerful forces, too, such as the markets and the media; and, of course, because of what they represent to us all.

A very wide range of interests and disciplines have turned their attention to this topic, but at the same time there is little sense of common ground emerging, either in relation to *how* we should think about childhood, or *what* we should do about children (and their problems). Indeed, much debate on the subject is highly polarized (individual vs social; victim vs threat; competent vs not-competent), and many prescriptive judgements emerge from highly partial perspectives. What we have learnt in preceding chapters is that, by any account, this is a complex and contested subject. It may be that partial (in both senses of the word) answers are the best we can achieve at this point; but, in recognizing this, we should also be modest in laying claims to speak on the subject with any degree of authority. In addition, too attempts to determine a basis for meta-analysis (Corsaro, 1997; James *et al.*, 1998; Lee, 2001) should be applauded because they do at least hold out the promise of an inte-grated and productive approach. It is also clear that there is growing recognition of the importance of inter-disciplinary exchange (Smith *et al.*, 2003; Blakemore and Frith, 2005; Carpendale and Lewis, 2006).

Despite such efforts to establish constructive dialogue, there remain substantial concerns about the influence of narrow and inflexible dis-courses of childhood, not just in terms of the way children them-selves are thought about and studied, but more crucially, in the ways that they are treated. In what follows, then, I will address the impor-tant question of how to introduce a proper note of uncertainty and a degree of flexibility into areas of discussion and intervention which often appear to assume that childhood is a 'done deal', and that we already know all that we need to know to make well-informed and beneficial decisions for and on behalf of our children.

The problem of partial thinking

The importance of taking a broad view of children and their needs is encapsulated in the issue of vulnerability, which was recognized in the previous chapter as being a consistent theme. The reasons for this can be located in children's physical immaturity, and their lack of knowledge, experience and other material resources. What this does not suggest, however, is that they should *only* be viewed through the lens of vulnerability, or that this should imply a lack of competence. This is powerfully illustrated for us by Kitzinger (1997) in her dis-cussion of sexual abuse and children. She suggests that consideration of this subject is 'deeply embedded' in our underlying assumptions about what childhood 'is and what it should be'. Recognition of the existence of sexual abuse, and its impact on children, seems also to involve an implicit acceptance of a particular construction of the 'child', which is notable for certain key omissions:

> the very term 'child abuse' allows an evasion of the issue of power because it takes the nature of 'the child' for granted: 'child abuse' is prem-ised on the notion of the child, rather than say young(er), small(er), or weak(er) persons.
>
> (Kitzinger, 1997, p. 184)

Even as the term identifies a significant and very real risk to children, its specificity also helps to underpin a particular conceptualization of children, as being relatively powerless and lacking competence to define and articulate their own needs and wishes. This leads Kitzinger to the challenging conclusion that it is 'childhood as an institution that makes children "vulnerable"' (Kitzinger, 1997, p. 184). Without necessarily accepting this assertion uncritically, we can see that a particular construction of childhood may well lead to an incomplete understanding of abuse and its implications for children. If we deny children's competence, for example, it becomes easier to assume that their complex and conflicting feelings about an abuser are merely the product of immature thought processes, rather than an active and perfectly valid attempt to make sense of contradictory experiences and emotions and challenge what is happening to them. For Kitzinger, the consequences of reframing child abuse also necessitate a critical examination of wider power relationships, which are institutionalized in many forms of adult–child interaction. We need therefore to 'explore ways of openly discussing power with children' (Kitzinger, 1997, p. 183) in order to enable them to identify and resist those structures and relationships which subordinate them to adult definitions and control.

In this sense, childhood is a creative and collaborative project which depends on the lived processes through which material circumstances, social structures and relationships are articulated and continually renegotiated. Even apparent certainties in children's lives become provisional, in the sense that they are subject to interpretation and management in various ways. In parallel to this, even what may seem to be fixed and determinate physiological changes are now known to be subject to variation depending on how children's lives are managed or controlled, as in the case of delayed puberty in female gymnasts, for example (Georgopoulos *et al.*, 1999).

The construction of childhood

Much recent debate has focused on the 'social construction' of childhood which has been described as an 'emergent paradigm' (James and Prout, 1997, p. 3). However, it has also been acknowledged that 'social constructionism does run the risk of abandoning the embodied material child' (James *et al.*, 1998, p. 28), while more recently attempts have been made to articulate an integrated framework for understanding based on the idea of childhood as 'a heterogeneous assembly' (Prout, 2005, p. 57), leading to the suggestion that we should think in terms of a 'multiplicity' of childhoods (2005, p. 144) whose only common feature is the term itself, it would seem. The problem with this formulation of course is that, unlike either 'social' or 'natural' models, this approach offers no basis for distinguishing childhood as either a conceptual or material entity. Thus, for example, 'There is, in this sense, no difference in principle between understanding childhood and adulthood' (Prout, 2005, p. 144). The difficulty here is that as well as dispensing with the idea of children's lives as inherently different from those of adults, we also run the risk of bypassing the essential practical questions as to why the notion of childhood exists at all, how it is adapted to shape the lives of children, and whether these material and social practices are justifiable or acceptable (Alanen, 2001).

It is important to recognize the value of history here, in that this allows us to identify two essential considerations: childhood is clearly subject to quite dramatic change over time, both in the way it is defined and how it is lived; and, at the same time, the changing definitions of the term over time are clearly related to shifts in the material aspects of children's lives. While the appearance (Ariès, 1962) and 'disappearance' (Postman, 1994) of childhood may both be contested discourses, they also derive from and represent historically specific and concrete variations in the substantive experience of being a 'child'. This observation directs us towards an investigative approach which is grounded in this material reality, and seeks to develop explanatory accounts rooted in experience. Mayall (2002), for example, is an advocate of attempts to derive understanding through attending to 'children's own accounts of their lives', and pursuing research which focuses on 'real life situations, at home and in institutional settings' (2002, p. 22). She argues that this also represents a shift towards an emphasis on the 'present tense' as opposed to previously dominant 'future-oriented' developmental methodologies. Children are studied for and in themselves, rather than in terms of their future potential, or their current 'defects' and disadvantages, according to her preferred model.

Recent developments have reflected this changing emphasis, with a clear commitment to promoting children's active involvement in the research process where 'their perspectives, views and feelings are accepted as genuine, valid evidence' (Woodhead and Faulkner, 2000, p. 31; see also Christensen and James, 2008). Of course, it is not just a matter of recognizing and validating the 'evidence' that children provide; if we are to follow through the logic of participation and power-sharing, then children also need to be engaged in deciding what questions will be asked, how they will be addressed and what 'meanings' are generated from research with and about them:

> the assumptions ... of what reality is and how it can be known, need to be brought to the surface. Therefore, as researchers, children need to engage, and critique, different ways of 'seeing'. This includes the difficult task of foregrounding their own interpretive frameworks...
>
> (Warren, 2000, p. 134)

We know, too, from earlier observations that children are neurologically equipped, sometimes particularly well (Blakemore and Frith, 2005), to carry out this sort of investigative activity.

Although their horizons may be situated and limited, children are able to develop a fairly clear view of what childhood is, and how it can be improved upon, through their participation in research. Mayall (2002, p. 135) reflects on young people's accounts of their lives to suggest that they have a 'common domain of childhood, which they experience positively, as a distinctive period of life'. Interestingly, they also seem to see this as a time when they are provided with 'protection' and 'learning', as well as 'privilege and fun'. The perceptions of this particular group of London children share elements with the 'universal' features identified in the previous chapter. Interestingly, too, they are found to have relatively little difficulty in identifying themselves as both 'beings' and 'becomings' (Lee, 2001), even though this balance may be difficult to sustain in practical terms in a highly 'future-oriented regime' such as a school (Mayall, 2002, p. 138).

Unsurprisingly, in view of what we know about structures of power, they do express clear concerns about 'their subordinate position in child–adult relations' (Mayall, 2002, p. 135), and their lack of 'participation rights' (Mayall, 2002, p. 136). These (unequal) intergenerational relationships and the associated distribution of resources also seem to be common features of childhood, and should probably be seen as another locus of uniformity, but at the same time, as one which is likely to be contested by children themselves through various forms of resistance and challenge, both overt and 'hidden'.

Thinking critically: childhood, power and social justice

The exploration of children's experience, whether that of Mayall, or others in very different contexts (Holloway and Valentine, 2000) confirms that there is a degree of tension between children's perceptions of what childhood could and should be, and their lived experiences, especially concerning the ways in which generational relationships are realized. The dominant constructions of childhood are experienced as disempowering, whether this is because children's lives are shaped and structured according to a forward-looking educational agenda, or because they are routinely problematized to the extent that they do not comply with prescribed behavioural norms; for instance, by becoming 'street children' (Beazley, 2000).

The important point here is that these constructions do have a material impact. They may be historically specific, but their paradigmatic qualities ensure that they have the capacity to impact directly on children's lives on a number of levels. By purporting to represent 'natural' qualities of childhood, social constructions are capable of exercising a persuasive, 'hegemonic' (Gramsci, 1971) authority, which may, indeed, account for children's grumbling acquiescence to the dictates of schooling (Mayall, 2002).

The task of challenging prevailing assumptions is not straightforward, though: 'if children are not used to being consulted or expressing an opinion it may take some time for them to participate fully, if at all' (Hyder, 2002, p. 321). As noted previously, there is relatively limited evidence that childhood is substantively or substantially different from any other life stage, or that it can easily be defined according to a number of common features, so we must look elsewhere to develop an understanding of the mechanisms which seek to shape and delineate it according to specific (developmental) criteria, and which are successful to the extent that children comply with these normative expectations. Childhood is primarily a *political* construction, which is subject to debate, challenge and change. This, then, is a matter of power, and the shape and content of children's experience is at least partly determined according to prevailing power relationships. Children's capacity to make sense of and to shape the world:

> is inherently linked to the 'powers' (or lack of them), of those positioned as children, to influence, organize, coordinate and control events taking place in their everyday worlds. In researching such positional 'powers', they are best approached as possibilities and limitations of action, 'determined' by the specific structures (regimes, orders) within which persons are positioned as children.
>
> (Alanen, 2001, p. 21)

This point is valuable not least because of its implications for quite unexpected disciplines such as neuroscience. If it is true that there are 'sensitive periods' (Blakemore and Frith, 2005, p. 30), where children are more receptive to certain types of learning than others at specific times in their lives, and if what is learnt at this points actually sets a precedent for their future skills and attributes, then the way in which 'power' is exercised in relation to them is of critical importance. For example, the evidence indicates 'that early sensory deprivation can have lasting consequences, possibly very subtle ones' (Blakemore and Frith, 2005, p. 31) in terms of children's capacities as well as the substantive content of their learning. Contemporary studies are also beginning to demonstrate the complex but consistent links between child poverty and 'neurocognitive development' (Farah *et al.*, 2006). In light of these observations, it becomes all the more important that proper attention is paid to children's circumstances, their perceptions, the ways in which they articulate these and how others respond to them. Their viewpoint is important, and should be accorded validity not just as an abstract affirmation of 'children's rights', but because it offers significant insights into what it means to be a 'child'.

Balancing perspectives?

The preceding discussion represents an attempt to give due weight to children's perceptions and experience, but it is important to avoid the suggestion that their understanding of their lives should always carry greater weight than those obtained in other ways, or from other perspectives, as illustrations from brain science hopefully substantiate. However, it is clear that until relatively recently children's perspectives have been relatively undervalued, and this omission ought to be addressed. As we have noted, children have their own fairly well-developed views about what childhood is, and where they stand in relation to it. Those who are denied opportunities through exploitation and poverty still articulate very clearly their thirst for education and opportunity, recognizing that these essential elements of their lives are being denied them. In this way, the value they put on education and skills development is at least as great as those who draw the same conclusion from within academic disciplines such as education research. At the same time, notably, children also make the case for time and space to be themselves: 'It's a good laugh it is, yea, we have a really good laugh some of time, we can just giggle and be together here, there's no trouble, you can just be yourself' (Carol, quoted in Skelton, 2000, p. 97).

Children, too, are able to identify the need for security and protection which stems from their specific vulnerabilities, needs which are similarly identified by those concerned with their 'developmental' progress. However, it is not always the case that their analysis of these problems or their proposed solutions are given recognition, and it is worthwhile pausing and asking ourselves why this might be. Is it because we are right and they are wrong? Or, are there other, more suspect reasons for this imbalance? Perhaps children's views are too challenging, and we resist uncomfortable messages coming from them. Of course, a considerable amount of intellectual capital is invested in conventional forms of analysis and prevailing assumptions, and it is difficult to hold in our minds the key point that these are provisional truths rather than absolute certainties. Timimi's (2005) detailed critique of ADHD (Attention Deficit Hyperactivity Disorder) and the social and psychological assumptions incorporated within this label is a powerful reminder of the limitations of uncritical one-sidedness, for example. 'Naughtiness' is, instead, a product of what he describes as 'Western culture', and precisely because of this, it is impossible for that culture to take responsibility for problem behaviour – and so explanations are located *within* the child himself which is 'a convenient way of keeping' these 'in a Western-individualized and "scientific" framework' (Timimi, 2005, p. 32).

We may be able to conclude that arguments for children's voices to be heard, and their views recognized, are not simply based on a leap of faith, or on a political commitment to a rights perspective. Rather, it is because their knowledge and understanding provide an important counterpoint to other sources and perspectives on their lives. We should not expect children to have an advanced knowledge of brain chemistry, of course, but, by contrast, this type of science can be substantially enriched through drawing on their lived experience *and* their insights. This recognition is an important corrective to: 'the principles of certainty by which people within Western culture "know" that children are natural, universal creatures who, eventually, simply 'grow up' (James *et al.*, 1998, p. 196).

This is not to imply that the idea of childhood is ultimately mythical, not least because its very pervasiveness across geographical and cultural distances and over time suggests that we must take it seriously. It is, however, to argue that its status is contingent and provisional, and that its universal characteristics (such as age-bounded physical growth, learning and experience, and vulnerability) form the basis for a constantly changing series of social, psychological and, indeed, moral interpretations of its nature, meaning and consequences. James *et al.* (1998, p. 200) have suggested that these tensions and dynamics can be helpfully examined in relation to four key 'sociological dichotomies' (structure/agency; identity/difference; continuity/change; global/local) which capture the sense of childhood as both a constant, commonly understood object of concern, and simultaneously an ever-changing, disputed subject characterized by diversity and uncertainty. In this sense, indeed, it is appropriate to think of childhood as fundamentally 'unfinished'. It is, and should be, a subject of continuing investigation from a range of disciplinary perspectives, but this should also be recognized as a work in progress, which will necessarily remain incomplete.

It is appropriate to end on a practical note, though. Recognizing the implications of 'growth' and 'learning' as central and immutable features of children's lives should lead us to think in terms of creating the right conditions for these. However, the sheer diversity of children's origins and circumstances should also oblige us to accept that the ways in which these aims are realized must also be flexible and sensitive to difference. Acknowledging this offers support for the further development and more vigorous implementation of instruments such as the United Nations Convention on the Rights of the Child, which specifies a universally applicable framework recognizing both children's inherent vulnerability, and their 'evolving capacities' (Lansdown, 2005) for autonomous learning and self-expression. If applied effectively (and as yet, most countries have failed to do so in key respects), the convention could offer a robust mechanism for challenging at the same time *structural, ideological* and *conceptual* constraints which limit children's lives and undervalue their childhoods. This is a practical approach to the challenge of applying universal principles in diverse circumstances. Street children facing exploitation and harm would benefit from the protections offered, just as children in the developed world would gain from the recognition of their participation rights, and the opportunity to challenge narrow and restrictive 'deficit' models of 'development'. In the end, these aspirations for practical measures of social justice should be the key frame of reference for all our attempts to investigate, analyse and understand children and childhood better.

References

Ainsworth, M. (1962) 'The effects of maternal deprivation: a review of findings and controversy in the context of research strategy', in Ainsworth, M., Andry, R., Harlow, R., Lebovici, S., Mead, M., Prugh, D. and Wootton, B. (eds), *Deprivation and Maternal Care: A Reassessment of Its Effects*, Geneva, Switzerland: World Health Organization, pp. 97–159.

Alanen, L. (2001) 'Explorations in generational analysis', in Alanen, L. and Mayall, B. (eds) *Conceptualizing Child–Adult Relations*, London: RoutledgeFalmer, pp. 11–22.

Alanen, L. (2004) 'Theorizing children's welfare', paper presented at WELLCI Network Workshop 1: New perspectives on childhood, University of Leeds, 12–13 Nov.

Aldgate, J. (2006) 'Children, development and ecology', in Aldgate, J., Jones, D., Rose, W. and Jeffery, C. (eds) *The Developing World of the Child*, London: Jessica Kingsley, pp. 17–34.

Aldgate, J. and Jones, D. (2006) 'The place of attachment in children's development', in Aldgate, J., Jones, D., Rose, W. and Jeffery, C. (eds) *The Developing World of the Child*, London: Jessica Kingsley, pp. 67–96.

Aldgate, J., Jones, D., Rose, W. and Jeffery, C. (eds) *The Developing World of the Child*, London: Jessica Kingsley.

Aldridge, J. and Becker, S. (2002) 'Children who care: rights and wrongs in debate and policy on young carers', in Franklin, B. (ed.) *The New Handbook of Children's Rights*, London: Sage, pp. 208–22.

Anderson, C. (2004) 'An update on the effects of playing violent video games', *Journal of Adolescence*, 27, pp. 113–22.

Anderson, C., Berkowitz, L., Donnerstein, E., Huesmann, L., Johnson, J., Linz, D., Malamuth, N. and Wartella, E. (2003) 'The influence of media violence on youth', *Psychological Science in the Public Interest*, pp. 81–110.

Ariès, P. (1962) *Centuries of Childhood*, New York: Vintage Books.

Baldwin, S. and Hirst, M. (2002) 'Children as carers', in Bradshaw, J. (ed.) *The Well-Being of Children in the UK*, London: Save the Children, pp. 153–66.

Baron-Cohen, S. (2001) 'Theory of mind in normal development and autism', *Prisme*, 34: 174–83.

Baron-Cohen, S. (2004) 'The cognitive neuroscience of autism', *Journal of Neurology, Neurosurgery and Psychiatry*, 75(7): 945–8.

Barrett, M. (2003) 'Meme engineers: children as producers of musical culture', *International Journal of Early Years Education*, 11(3): 195–212.

Bartholow, B., Bushman, B. and Sestir, M. (2006) 'Chronic violent video game exposure and desensitization to violence: behavioural and event-related brain potential data', *Journal of Experimental Social Psychology*, pp. 532–39.

Bartlett, R., Gratton, C. and Rolf, C. (2005) *Encyclopaedia of International Sports Studies*, London: Routledge.

Baxter, J. (2005) *The Archaeology of Childhood*, Walnut Creek, CA: AltaMira Press.

Beazley, H. (2000) 'Home sweet home?: Street children's sites of belonging', in Holloway, S. and Valentine, G. (eds) *Children's Geographies: Playing, Living, Learning*, London: Routledge, pp. 194–210.

Becker, S., Aldridge, J. and Dearden, C. (1998) *Young Carers and Their Families*, Oxford: Blackwell.

Beckett, C. (2002) *Human Growth and Development*, London: Sage.

Beck-Gernsheim, E. (2002) *Reinventing the Family*, Cambridge: Polity.

Benedict, R. (1961) *Patterns of Culture*, London: Routledge & Kegan Paul.

Bennett, A. (1991) *A Working Life: Child Labour Through the Nineteenth Century*, Poole: Waterfront Publications.

Berger, P. and Luckman, T. (1967) *The Social Construction of Reality*, Harmondsworth: Penguin.

Bhatti, G. (1999) *Asian Children at Home and at School*, London: Routledge.

Birn, A-E (2007) 'Child health in Latin America: historiographic perspectives and challenges', *Historia, Ciências, Saúde*, 14(3): 677–708.

Bjorklund, D. and Pellegrini, A. (2000) 'Child development and evolutionary psychology', *Child Development*, 71(6): 1687–708.

Blakemore, S-J. and Choudhury, S. (2006) 'Development of the adolescent brain: implications for executive function and social cognition', *Journal of Child Psychology and Psychiatry*, 47(3): 296–312.

Blakemore, S-J. and Frith, U. (2005) *The Learning Brain*, Oxford: Blackwell.

Boden, S. (2006) '"Another day, another demand": how parents and children negotiate consumption matters', *Sociological Research Online*, 11(2). Available at: http://www.socresonline.org.uk/11/2/boden.html, accessed 15 July 2009.

Bonoli, G., George, V. and Taylor-Gooby, P. (2000) *European Welfare Futures: Towards a Theory of Retrenchment*, Cambridge: Polity.

Bowlby, J. (1953) *Child Care and the Growth of Love*, Harmondsworth: Penguin.

Boyle, R. and Hibberd, M. (2005) *Review of Research on the Impact of Violent Computer Games on Young People*, Stirling: Stirling Media Research Institute.

Bradshaw, J. (2002) 'Conclusion', in Bradshaw, J. (ed.) *The Well-being of Children in the UK*, London: Save the Children, pp. 363–72.

Bradshaw, J. (2005) *Child Benefit Packages in 22 Countries*, DWP Research Report No. 174, Leeds: The Stationery Office.

Bronfenbrenner, E. (1979) *The Ecology of Human Development*, Cambridge, MA: Harvard University Press.

Brown, S. (2005) *Understanding Youth and Crime*, 2nd edn, Maidenhead: Open University Press.

Browne, K. and Hamilton-Giachristis, C. (2005) 'The influence of violent media on children and adolescents: a public-health approach', *Lancet*, 365: 702–10.

Bruner, J., Jolly, A. and Sylva, K. (1976) *Play: Its Role in Development and Evolution*, New York: Basic Books.

Buckingham, D. (2000) *After the Death of Childhood*, Cambridge: Polity.

Buckingham, D. and Bragg, S. (2005) 'Opting in to (and out of) childhood: young people, sex and the media', in Qvortrup, J. (ed.) *Studies in Modern Childhood*, Basingstoke: Palgrave Macmillan, pp. 59–77.

Buckingham, D. and Tingstad, V. (2007) 'Consuming children: commercialisation and the changing construction of childhood', *Barn*, 2: 49–71.

Buckley, H. and O'Sullivan, E. (2007) 'The interface between youth justice and child protection in Ireland', in Hill, M., Lockyer, A. and Stone, F. (eds) *Youth Justice and Child Protection*, London: Jessica Kingsley, pp. 61–74.

Butler, I., Robinson, M. and Scanlan, L. (2005) *Children and Decision Making*, London: National Children's Bureau.

Butler-Sloss, E. (1988) *Report of the Inquiry into Child Abuse in Cleveland 1987*, London: HMSO.

Byron, T. (2008) *Safer Children in a Digital World*, Report of the Byron Review, Nottingham: Department for Children, Schools and Families.

Carney, T. (1999) 'Liberalism or distributional justice? The morality of child welfare laws', in King, M. (ed.) *Moral Agendas for Children's Welfare*, London: Routledge, pp. 53–73.

Carpendale, J. and Lewis, C. (2004) 'Constructing an understanding of mind: the development of children's social understanding within social interaction', *Behavioural and Brain Sciences*, 27: 79–96.

Carpendale, J. and Lewis, C. (2006) *How Children Develop Social Understanding*, Oxford: Blackwell.

Casey, B., Tottenham, N., Liston, C. and Durston, S. (2005) 'Imaging the developing brain: what have we learned about cognitive development?', *TRENDS in Cognitive Science*, 9(3): 104–10.

Christensen, P. (2000) 'Childhood and the cultural constitution of vulnerable bodies', in Prout, A. (ed.) *The Body, Childhood and Society*, Basingstoke: Macmillan, pp. 38–59.

Christensen, P. and James, A. (eds) (2000) *Research with Children: Perspectives and Practices*, London: Falmer.

Christensen, P. and James, A. (2001) 'What are schools for? The temporal experience of children's learning in Northern England', in Alanen, L. and Mayall, B. (eds) *Conceptualizing Child–Adult Relations*, London: RoutledgeFalmer, pp. 70–85.

Christensen, P. and James, A. (2008) *Research with Children: Perspectives and Practices*, 2nd edn, London: Routledge.

Cohen, S. (1972) *Folk Devils and Moral Panics*, London: Paladin.

Coleman, J. and Hendry, C. (1999) *The Nature of Adolescence*, 3rd edn, London: Routledge.

Cook, D. (2005) 'The dichotomous child in and of commercial culture', *Childhood*, 12: 155–9.

Corby, B. (1993) *Child Abuse: Towards a Knowledge Base*, Buckingham: Open University Press.

Corrigan, P. (1979) *Schooling the Smash Street Kids*, London: Macmillan.

Corsaro, W. (1997) *The Sociology of Childhood*, Thousand Oaks, CA: Pine Forge.

Couchman, H. (2006) 'Give us our voice in class', *The Guardian*, 23 October.

Cumberbatch, G. (1995) *Media Violence: Research Evidence and Policy Implications*, Birmingham: The Communications Research Group, Aston University.

Cunningham, H. (1995) *Children and Childhood in Western Society since 1500*, London: Longman.

Cunningham, H. (2005) *Children and Childhood in Western Society since 1500*, 2nd edn, Harlow: Pearson Longman.

Cunningham, H. (2006) *The Invention of Childhood*, London: BBC Books.

Daniel, B., Wassell, S. and Gilligan, R. (1999) *Child Development for Child Care and Protection Workers*, London: Jessica Kingsley.

Daniel, P. and Ivatts, J. (1998) *Children and Social Policy*, Basingstoke: Palgrave.

Darwin, C. (1877) 'A biographical sketch of an infant', *Mind*, 2: 285–94.

Davies, B. (1986) *Threatening Youth*, Buckingham: Open University Press.

Davis, H. and Bourhill, M. (1997) ''Crisis': The demonisation of young people', in Scraton, P. (ed.) *'Childhood' in 'Crisis'*, London: University College Press, pp. 28–57.

De Block, L. (2004) 'Children in communication about migration', *New Perspectives for Learning – Briefing Paper 48*. Available at: http://www.pjb.co.uk/npl/BP%2048%20Final%20CHICAM.pdf, accessed 30 June 2008.

De Mause, L. (ed.) (1976) *The History of Childhood*, London: Souvenir.

Department for Education and Skills (2003) *Every Child Matters*, London: DfES.

Department of Health (2000) *Framework for the Assessment of Children in Need and their Families*, London: The Stationery Office.

Dow, P. (2004) '"I feel like I'm invisible": children talking to ChildLine about self-harm', *Submission to the National Inquiry into Self-harm among Young People*, London: ChildLine.

Dowker, A. (2006) 'What can functional brain imaging studies tell us about typical and atypical cognitive development in children?', *Journal of Physiology – Paris*, 99(4): 333–41.

Drotner, J. (2005) 'Media on the move: personalized media and the transformation of publicness', *Journal of Media Practice*, 6(1): 53–64.

Durkheim, E. (1947) *The Division of Labour in Society*, New York: Free Press.

East, K. and Campbell, S. (2000) *Aspects of Crime: Young Offenders 1999*, London: Home Office.

Eide, B. and Winger, N. (2005) 'From the children's point of view: methodological and ethical challenges', in Clark, A., Kjørholt, A. and Moss, P. (eds) *Beyond Listening: Children's Perspectives on Early Childhood Services*, Bristol: Policy Press, pp. 71–90.

Ennew, J. (2002) 'Outside childhood: street children's rights', in Franklin, B. (ed.) *The New Handbook of Children's Rights*, London: Routledge, pp. 388–403.

Erikson, E. (1995) *Childhood and Society*, New York: Vintage.

Esping-Andersen, G. (1990) *The Three Worlds of Welfare Capitalism*, Oxford: Polity Press.

Esping-Andersen, G. (1999) *Social Foundations of Postindustrial Economics*, Oxford: Oxford University Press.

Fahlberg, V. (1994) *A Child's Journey Through Placement*, London: British Agencies for Adoption and Fostering.

Farah, M., Shera, D., Savage, J., Betancourt, L., Giannetta, J., Brodsky, N., Malmud, E. and Hurt, H. (2006) 'Childhood poverty: specific associations with neurocognitive development', *Brain Research*, 1110: 166–74.

Feilzer, M. and Hood, R. (2004) *Differences or Discrimination?*, London: Youth Justice Board.

Ferguson, H. (2004) *Protecting Children in Time*, Basingstoke: Palgrave.

Fionda, J. (2005) *Devils and Angels: Youth Policy and Crime*, Oxford: Hart.

Foley, P., Roche, J. and Tucker, S. (2001) 'Children in society: contemporary theory, policy and practice', in Foley, P., Roche, J. and Tucker, S. (eds) *Children in Society: Contemporary Theory, Policy and Practice*, Basingstoke: Palgrave, pp. 1–6.

Foucault, M. (1979) *Discipline and Punish*, Harmondsworth: Penguin.

Fox Harding, L. (1996) *Family, State and Social Policy*, Basingstoke: Macmillan.

Fox Harding, L. (1997) *Perspectives in Child Care Policy*, 2nd edn, Harlow: Addison-Wesley Longman.

Franklin, B. (1995) 'The case for children's rights: a progress report', in Franklin, B. (ed.) *The Handbook of Children's Rights: Comparative Policy and Practice*, London: Routledge, pp. 3–25.

Franklin, B. (2002a) 'Children's rights: an introduction', in Franklin, B. (ed.) *The New Handbook of Children's Rights*, London: Routledge, pp. 1–12.

Franklin, B. (ed.) (2002b) *The New Handbook of Children's Rights*, London: Routledge.

Freedman, J. (2001) 'Evaluating the research on violent video games'. Available at: http://culturalpolicy.uchicago.edu/conf2001/papers/freedman.html, accessed 31 March 2008.

Freeman, M. (2002) 'Children's rights ten years after ratification', in Franklin, B. (ed.) *The New Handbook of Children's Rights*, London: Routledge, pp. 97–118.

Freud, S. (1977) *On Sexuality*, Harmondsworth: Pelican.

Garland, D. (2001) *The Culture of Control*, Oxford: Oxford University Press.

Gauntlett, D. (1998) 'Losing sight of the ball?: Children, media and the environment in a video research project', paper presented to the International Broadcasting Symposium, University of Manchester. Available at: http://www.theory.org.uk/david/videocritical.pdf, accessed 30 June 2008.

Georgopoulos, N., Markou, K., Theodoropoulou, A., Paraskevopoulou, P., Varaki, L., Kazantzi, Z., Leglise, M. and Vagenakis, A. (1999) 'Growth and pubertal development in elite female rhythmic gymnasts', *The Journal of Clinical Endocrinology & Metabolism*, 84(12): 4525–30.

Giddens, A. (1991) *Modernity and Self-Identity*, Cambridge: Polity.

Goldson, B. (1999) 'Youth (in)justice: contemporary developments in policy and practice', in Goldson, B. (ed.) *Youth Justice: Contemporary Policy and Practice*, Aldershot: Ashgate, pp. 1–27.

Goldson, B. (2001) 'The demonisation of children', in Foley, P., Roche, J. and Tucker, S. (eds) *Children in Society: Contemporary Theory, Policy and Practice*, Basingstoke: Palgrave, pp. 34–41.

Goldson, B. and Muncie, J. (2006) 'Critical anatomy: towards a principled youth justice', in Goldson, B. and Muncie, J. (eds) *Youth Crime and Justice*, London: Sage, pp. 203–31.

Gopnik, A. (1996) 'The scientist as child', *Philosophy of Science*, 63: 485–514.

Gorin, S. (2004) 'Understanding what children say about living with domestic violence, parental substance misuse or parental health problems', *Joseph Rowntree Findings*, 514, York: Joseph Rowntree Foundation.

Gramsci, A. (1971) *Selections from the Prison Notebooks*, London: Lawrence & Wishart.

Gregg, B. (2003) 'Changing homelessness for children'. Available at: www.shelter.org.uk, accessed 25 Feb. 2009.

Haines, K. and O'Mahony, D. (2006) 'Restorative approaches, young people and youth justice', in Goldson, B. and Muncie, J. (eds) *Youth Crime and Justice*, London: Sage, pp. 110–24.

Hanawalt, B. (1993) *Growing up in Medieval London*, Oxford: Oxford University Press.

Hattenstone, S. (2000) 'They were punished enough by what they did', *The Guardian*, 30 October.

Healy, J. (2004) *Your Child's Growing Mind*, 3rd edn, New York: Broadway Books.

Hendrick, H. (1994) *Child Welfare: England, 1872–1989*, London: Routledge.

Hendrick, H. (1997) 'Constructions and reconstructions of British childhood: an interpretative survey, 1800 to the present', in James, A. and Prout, A. (eds) *Constructing and Reconstructing Childhood*, London: RoutledgeFalmer, pp. 34–62.

Hendrick, H. (2003) *Child Welfare: Historical Dimensions, Contemporary Debate*, Bristol: Policy Press.

Hengst, H. (2005) 'Complex interconnections: the global and the local in children's minds and everyday worlds', in Qvortrup, J. (ed.) *Studies in Modern Childhood*, Basingstoke: Palgrave Macmillan, pp. 21–38.

Heywood, C. (2001) *A History of Childhood*, Cambridge: Polity.

Hill, M., Lockyer, A. and Stone, F. (2007) 'Introduction: the principles and practice of compulsory intervention when children are "at risk" or engage in criminal behaviour', in Hill, M., Lockyer, A. and Stone, F. (eds) *Youth Justice and Child Protection*, London: Jessica Kingsley, pp. 9–38.

Hodge, B. and Tripp, D. (1986) *Children and Television*, Cambridge: Polity.

Holland, P. (2004) *Picturing Childhood: The Myth of the Child in Popular Imagery*, London: I.B. Taurus.

Holloway, S. and Valentine, G. (eds) (2000) *Children's Geographies: Playing, Living, Learning*, London: Routledge.

Holt, J. (1974) *Escape from Childhood*, Harmondsworth: Pelican.

Home Office (2003) *Youth Justice – The Next Steps*, London: Home Office.

Houlbrooke, R. (1984) *The English Family, 1450–1700*, London: Longman.

Howe, D. (2001) 'Attachment', in Horwath, J. (ed.) *The Child's World*, London: Jessica Kingsley, pp. 194–296.

Hyder, S. (2002) 'Making it happen – young children's rights in action: the work of Save the Children's Centre for Young Children's Rights', in Franklin, B. (ed.) *The New Handbook of Children's Rights*, London: Routledge, pp. 311–25.

James, A. (2000) 'Embodied being(s): understanding the self and the body in childhood', in Prout, A. (ed.) *The Body, Childhood and Society*, Basingstoke: Macmillan, pp. 19–37.

James, A. and James, A. (2004) *Constructing Childhood*, Basingstoke: Palgrave.

James, A., Jenks, C. and Prout, A. (1998) *Theorizing Childhood*, Cambridge: Polity.

James A. and Prout, A. (1997) 'Introduction', in James, A. and Prout, A. (eds) *Constructing and Reconstructing Childhood*, London: RoutledgeFalmer, pp. 1–6.

Jenks, C. (1996) *Childhood*, Routledge, London.

John, M. (2003) *Children's Rights and Power*, London: Jessica Kingsley.

Johnson, M. (2008) 'Brain development in childhood: a literature review and synthesis for the Byron Review on the impact of new technologies on children'. Available at: http://www.dcsf.gov.uk/byronreview/pdfs/Johnson%20Brain%20Development%20Literature%20Review%20for%20the%20Byron%20Review.pdf, accessed 19 Jan. 2009.

Jones, C. (2008) Paper presented at Childhood Conference, University of Sheffield, June 8–10.

Katsurada, E. (2007) 'Attachment representation of institutionalized children in Japan', *School Psychology International*, 28(3): 331–45.

Kelly, E. (2007) 'The long–term effects of homelessness on children', Available at: http://npch.org/Microsoft%Word%20–%20Elizabeth%20Kelly%20revised%20child%20homelessness%20paper.pdf, accessed 25 Feb. 2009.

Kempe, R. and Kempe, C. (1978) *Child Abuse*, London: Fontana.

Khabbache, H. (2005) 'The development of the child's conception of the word: theory of mind', *Journal of Arab Children*, 25(7): 38–61.

Khoo, E., Hyvönen, U. and Nygren, L. (2002) 'Child welfare or child protection', *Qualitative Social Work*, 1(4): 451–71.

212

King, M. (1999) 'Images of children and morality', in King, M. (ed.) *Moral Agendas for Children's Welfare*, London: Routledge, pp. 15–32.

King, M. (2007) 'The Sociology of Childhood as Scientific Communications: observations from a social systems perspective', *Childhood*, 14: 193–213.

King, M. and Piper, C. (1990) *How the Law Thinks about Children*, Aldershot, Arena.

Kitzinger, J. (1997) 'Who are you kidding? Children, power and the struggle against sexual abuse', in James, A. and Prout, A. (eds) *Constructing and Reconstructing Childhood*, London: RoutledgeFalmer, pp. 165–89.

Kitzinger, J. (2004) *Framing Abuse*, London: Pluto Press.

Kline, S. (2005) 'Is it time to rethink media panics?' in Qvortrup, J. (ed.) *Studies in Modern Childhood*, Basingstoke: Palgrave Macmillan, pp. 78–98.

Kong, L. (2000) 'Nature's dangers, nature's pleasures: urban children and the natural world', in Holloway, S. and Valentine, G. (eds) *Children's Geographies*, London: Routledge, pp. 257–71.

Kroll, B. and Taylor, A. (2000) 'Invisible children? Parental substance abuse and child protection: dilemmas for practice', *Probation Journal*, 47(2): 91–100.

Kunkel, D., Wilcox, B., Cantor, J., Palmer, E., Linn, S. and Dowrick, P. (2004) *Report of the APA Task Force on Advertising and Children*. Available at: http://www.apa.org/releases/childrenads.pdf, accessed 30 June 2008.

Laming, H. (2003) *Report of the Inquiry into the Death of Victoria Climbié*, London: Department of Health.

Langer, B. (2005) 'Research note: consuming anomie: children and global commercial culture', *Childhood*, 12: 259–71.

Lansdown, G. (2005) *The Evolving Capacities of the Child*, Geneva: UNICEF Innocenti Research Centre.

Lappi-Seppala, T. (2006) 'Finland: a model of tolerance?' in Muncie, J. and Goldson, B. (eds) *Comparative Youth Justice*, London: Sage, pp. 177–95.

Laslett, P. (1977) *Family Life and Illicit Love in Earlier Generations*, Cambridge: Cambridge University Press.

Lavalette, M. (2005) '"In defence of childhood": against the neo-liberal assault on social life', in Qvortrup, J. (ed.) *Studies in Modern Childhood*, Basingstoke: Palgrave Macmillan, pp. 147–66.

Lavalette, M. and Cunningham, S. (2002) 'The sociology of childhood', in Goldson, B., Lavalette, M. and McKechnie, J. (eds) *Children, Welfare and the State*, London: Sage, pp. 9–28.

Lee, N. (1999) 'The challenge of childhood: distributions of childhood's ambiguity in adult institutions', *Childhood*, 6: 455–74.

Lee, N. (2001) *Childhood and Society*, Maidenhead: Open University Press.

Lenroot, R. and Giedd, J. (2006) 'Brain development in children and adolescents: insights from anatomical magnetic resonance imaging', *Neuroscience and Biobehavioural Reviews*, 30: 718–29.

Leonard, M. (2007) 'Trapped in space? Children's accounts of risky environments', *Children & Society*, 21: 432–445.

Lewis, A. and Lindsay, G. (2000) *Researching Children's Perspectives*, Buckingham: Open University Press.

Livingstone, S. (2003) 'Children's use of the internet: reflections on the emerging research agenda', *New Media and Society*, 5: 147–66.

Livingstone, S. and Bober, M. (2004) 'Taking up online opportunities? Children's uses of the internet for education, communication and participation', *E-Learning*, 1(3): 395–419.

Livingstone, S. and Bovill, M. (1999) *Young People: New Media*, London: London School of Economics.

Lorenz, E. (1993) *The Essence of Chaos*, Washington, DC: University of Washington Press.

MacDonald, R. and Marsh, J. (2005) *Disconnected Youth? Growing Up in Britain's Poor Neighbourhoods*, Basingstoke: Palgrave Macmillan.

MacDougall, J. and Chantrey, D. (2004) 'The making of tomorrow's consumer', *Young Consumers*, 5(4): 8–18.

McKechnie, J. and Hobbs, S. (1999) 'Child labour: the view from the North', *Childhood*, 6: 89–100.

McNally, S. (2006) 'Has Labour delivered on the policy priorities of "education, education, education"?' Available at: http://cep.lse.ac.uk/briefings/pa_education.pdf, accessed 19 Jan. 2009.

McNeal, J. (2007) *On Becoming a Consumer*, Oxford: Butterworth-Heinemann.

Mannheim, K. (1952) *Essays on the Sociology of Knowledge*, London: Routledge and Kegan Paul.

Marsh, J. (2007) 'Digital beginnings: conceptualisations of childhood', paper presented to the *WUN Virtual Seminar*, 13 Feb. Available at: http://wunnet.org/download.php?File=2488_Childrenpaper13Feb.pdf8mimetype=application/pdf, accessed 30 June 2008.

Marsh, J., Brooks, G., Hughes, J., Ritchie, L. and Roberts, S. (2005) *Digital Beginnings: Young Children's Use of Popular Culture, Media and New Technologies*, Sheffield: University of Sheffield.

Mason, J. and Falloon, J. (2001) 'Some Sydney children define abuse: implications for agency in childhood', in Alanen, L. and Mayall, B. (eds) *Conceptualizing Child–Adult Relations*, London: RoutledgeFalmer, pp. 99–113.

Matthews, H., Taylor, M., Percy-Smith, B. and Limb, M. (2000) 'The unacceptable *flâneur*: the shopping mall as a teenage hangout', *Childhood*, 7: 279–94.

Matthews, S. (2007) 'A window on the "new" sociology of childhood', *Sociology Compass*, 1(1): 322–34.

Mayall, B. (2002) *Towards a Sociology for Childhood*, Maidenhead: Open University Press.

Mayall, B. (2008) 'Conversations with children', in Christensen, P. and James, A. (eds) *Research with Children: Perspectives and Practices*, 2nd edn, Abingdon: Routledge, pp. 109–124.

214

Mayhew, H. (1985) *London Labour and the London Poor*. London: Penguin.

Mead, M. (1973) *Coming of Age in Samoa*, New York: HarperCollins.

Merton, R. (1957) *Social Theory and Social Structure*, Glencoe, IL: Free Press.

Middleton, L. (1999) *Disabled Children: Challenging Social Exclusion*, Oxford: Blackwell.

Mooney, C. (2000) *Theories of Childhood: An Introduction to Dewey, Montessori, Erikson, Piaget and Vygotsky*, St. Paul, IL: Redleaf Press.

Morss, J. (1995) *Growing Critical: Alternatives to Developmental Psychology*, London: Routledge.

Moss, P. and Petrie, P. (2002) *From Children's Services to Children's Spaces*, London: RoutledgeFalmer.

Mullender, A., Hague, G., Imam, U., Kelly, L., Malos, E. and Regan, L. (2002) *Children's Perspectives on Domestic Violence*, London: Sage.

Muncie, J. (2002) 'A new deal for youth? Early intervention and correction-alism', in Hughes, G., McLaughlin, E. and Muncie, J. (eds), *Crime Prevention and Community Safety: New Directions*, London: Sage, pp. 142–62.

Muncie, J. and Goldson, B. (2006) 'States of transition: convergence and diversity in international youth justice', in Muncie, J. and Goldson, B. (eds) *Comparative Youth Justice*, London: Sage, pp. 196–218.

Nakagawa, M., Lamb, M. and Miyaki, K. (1992) 'Antecedents and correlates of the strange situation behavior of Japanese infants', *Journal of Cross-Cultural Psychology*, 23(3): 300–10.

Newman, T. (2000) 'Workers and helpers: perspectives on children's labour 1899–1999', *British Journal of Social Work*, 30: 323–38.

Nieuwenhuys, O. (2005) 'The wealth of children: reconsidering the child labour debate', in Qvortrup, J. (ed.) *Studies in Modern Childhood*, Basingstoke: Palgrave Macmillan, pp. 167–83.

O'Kane, C. (2008) 'The development of participatory techniques', in Christensen, P., and James, A. (eds) *Research with Children: Perspectives and Practices*, 2nd edn, Abingdon: Routledge, pp. 125–55.

Packman, J. with Randall, J. and Jacques, N. (1986) *Who Needs Care?*, Oxford: Basil Blackwell.

Papadopoulos, T. (1996) '"Family", state and social policy for children in Greece', in Brannen, J. and O'Brien, M. (eds) *Children in Families: Research and Policy*, London: Falmer, pp. 171–88.

Pahl, J. (1989) *Money and Marriage*, Basingstoke: Palgrave.

Parton, N. (1985) *The Politics of Child Abuse*, London: Macmillan.

Parton, N. (2006) *Safeguarding Childhood*, Basingstoke: Palgrave.

Pearson, G. (1983) *Hooligan: A History of Respectable Fears*, Basingstoke: Macmillan.

Peper, J., Brouwer, R., Boomsma, D., Kahn, R. and Hulshoff Pol, H. (2007) 'Genetic influences on human brain structure: a review of brain imaging studies in twins', *Human Brain Mapping*, 28: 464–73.

Phipps, S. (2001) 'Values, policies and the well-being of young children in Canada, Norway and the United States', in Vleminckx, K. and Smeeding, T. (eds)

Child Well-being, Child Poverty and Child Policy in Modern Nations, Bristol: The Policy Press, pp. 79–98.

Piaget, J. (1959) *The Language and Thought of the Child*, London: Routledge.

Pilcher, J., Pole, C. and Boden, S. (2004) 'New consumers? Children, fashion and consumption', paper presented at 'Knowing Consumers: Actors, Images, Identities in Modern History', University of Bielefeld, 27/28 Feb.

Pinchbeck, I. and Hewitt, M. (1969) *Children and English Society*, vol. 1, London: Routledge & Kegan Paul.

Pollock, L. (1983) *Forgotten Children*, Cambridge: Cambridge University Press.

Poster, M. (1979) *Critical Theory of the Family*, London: Pluto Press.

Postman, N. (1994) *The Disappearance of Childhood*, New York: Vintage Books.

Prendergast, S. (2000) '"To become dizzy in our turning": girls, body-maps and gender as childhood ends', in Prout, A. (ed.) *The Body, Childhood and Society*, Basingstoke: Macmillan, pp. 101–24.

Prout, A. (2005) *The Future of Childhood*, London: RoutledgeFalmer.

Prout, A. and James, A. (1997) 'A new paradigm for the sociology of childhood? Provenance, promise and problems', in James, A. and Prout, A. (eds) *Constructing and Reconstructing Childhood*, 2nd edn, London: RoutledgeFalmer, pp. 7–33.

Punch, S. (2000) 'Children's strategies for creating playspaces: negotiating independence in rural Bolivia', in Holloway, S. and Valentine, G. (eds) *Children's Geographies*, London: Routledge, pp. 48–62.

Put, J. and Walgrave, L. (2006) 'Belgium: from protection towards accountability?' in Muncie, J. and Goldson, B. (eds) *Comparative Youth Justice*, London: Sage, pp. 111–26.

Qvortrup, J. (1994) 'Introduction', in Qvortrup, J., Bardy, M., Sgritta, G. and Wintersberger, H. (eds) *Childhood Matters: Social Theory, Practice and Politics*, Avebury, Aldershot, pp. 1–23.

Qvortrup, J. (1997) 'A voice for children in statistical and social accounting: a plea for children's right to be heard', in James, A. and Prout, A. (eds) *Constructing and Reconstructing Childhood*, 2nd edn, London: RoutledgeFalmer, pp. 85–106.

Qvortrup, J. (2005) 'Varieties of childhood', in Qvortrup, J. (ed.) *Studies in Modern Childhood*, Basingstoke: Palgrave Macmillan, pp. 1–20.

Rich Harris, J. (1999) *The Nurture Assumption*, London: Bloomsbury Publishing

Ritzer, G. (2004) *The McDonaldization of Society*, London: Sage.

Robinson, L. (2007) *Cross-Cultural Child Development for Social Workers: An Introduction*, Basingstoke: Palgrave.

Rose, W., Aldgate, J. and Jones, D. (2006) 'Developmental progression', in Aldgate, J., Jones, D., Rose, W. and Jeffery, C. (eds) *The Developing World of the Child*, London: Jessica Kingsley, pp. 163–84.

Rutter, M. (1981) *Maternal Deprivation Reassessed*, 2nd edn, Harmondsworth: Penguin.

Save the Children (2003) 'Invisible children?: Towards integration of children's rights in EU and Member States' development co-operation rights', Conference Report, Brussels. Available at: http://savethechildren.net/ alliance/where_we_work/europegrp_pubs.html, accessed 30 June 2008.

Schor, J. (2004) *Born to Buy*, New York: Scribner.

Scraton, P. (ed.) (1997) *Childhood' in 'Crisis'*, London: Routledge.

Scraton, P. and Haydon, D. (2002) 'Challenging the criminalization of children and young people: securing a rights-based agenda', in Muncie, J., Hughes, G. and McLaughlin, E. (eds) *Youth Justice: Critical Readings*, London: Sage, pp. 311–28.

Seabrook, J. (2007) 'Children of the market'. Available at: http://commentisfree. guardian.co.uk/jeremy_seabrook/2007/06/children_of_the_market.html, accessed 18 Feb. 2008.

Seidman, S. (1998) *Contested Knowledge*, 2nd edn, Oxford: Blackwell.

Shah, A. (2008) 'Beyond consumption and consumerism: children as consumers'. Available at: http://www.globalissues.org/TradeRelated/ Consumption/Children.asp?p=1, accessed 18 Feb. 2008.

Sharland, E. (2006) 'Young people, risk taking and risk making: some thoughts for social work', *British Journal of Social Work*, 38(2): 247–65.

Shilling, C. (1993) *The Body and Social Theory*, London: Sage.

Skelton, T. (2000) ''Nothing to do, nowhere to go?': Teenage girls and "public" space in the Rhondda Valleys, South Wales', in Holloway, S. and Valentine, G. (eds) *Children's Geographies: Playing, Living, Learning*, London: Routledge, pp. 80–99.

Skevik, A. (2003) 'Children of the welfare state: individuals with entitlements, or hidden in the family?', *Journal of Social Policy*, 32(3): 423–40.

Skidmore, C., Cuff, N. and Leslie, C. (2007) *Invisible Children*, London: The Bow Group.

Smart, C., Neale, B. and Wade, A. (2001) *The Changing Experience of Childhood: Families and Divorce*, Cambridge: Polity Press.

Smith, D. (2004) *The Links Between Victimization and Offending*, Edinburgh: Centre for Law and Society, University of Edinburgh.

Smith, F. and Barker, J. (2000) 'Contested spaces: children's experiences of out of school care in England and Wales', *Childhood*, 7: 315–33.

Smith, P., Cowie, H. and Blades, M. (2003) *Understanding Children's Development*, 4th edn, Oxford: Blackwell.

Smith, R. (2000a) 'Order and disorder: the contradictions of childhood', *Children & Society*, 14(1): 3–10.

Smith, R. (2000b) 'Whose childhood? The politics of homework', *Children & Society*, 14(5): 316–25.

Smith, R. (2007) *Youth Justice: Ideas, Policy, Practice*, 2nd edn, Cullompton: Willan.

Smith, R. (2008) *Social Work with Young People*, Cambridge: Polity.

Solberg, A. (1997) 'Negotiating childhood: changing constructions of age for Norwegian children', in James, A. and Prout, A. (eds) *Constructing and Reconstructing Childhood*, London: RoutledgeFalmer, pp. 126–44.

Squires, P. and Stephen, D. (2005) *Rougher Justice: Anti-Social Behaviour and Young People*, Cullompton: Willan.

Steeds, L., Rowe, K. and Dowker, A. (1997) 'Deaf children's understanding of beliefs and desires', *Journal of Deaf Studies and Deaf Education*, 2(3): 185–95.

Strandell, H. (1997) 'Doing reality with play', *Childhood*, 4: 445–64.

Taine, H. (1877) 'On the acquisition of language by children', *Mind*, **2**: 252–9.

Taylor, J. McGue, M. and Iacono, W. (2000) 'Sex differences, assortative mating, and cultural transmission effects on adolescent delinquency: a twin family study', *Journal of Child Psychology and Psychiatry*, 41(4): 433–40.

Thomas, N. (2000) *Children, Family and the State*, Bristol: The Policy Press.

Thompson, P., Cannon, T., Narr, K., van Erp, T., Poutanen, V-P., Huttunen, M., Lönnqvist, J., Standertskjöld-Nordenstam, C-G., Kaprio, J., Khaledy, M., Dail, R., Zoumalan, C. and Toga, A. (2001) 'Genetic influences on brain structure', *Nature Neuroscience*, 4(12): 1–6.

Thorne, B. (1993) *Gender Play: Boys and Girls in School*, New Brunswick, NJ: Rutgers University Press.

Timimi, S. (2005) *Naughty Boys: Anti-Social Behaviour, ADHD, and the Role of Culture*, Basingstoke: Palgrave Macmillan.

Tirassa, M., Bosco, F. and Colle, L. (2006) 'Rethinking the ontogeny of mindreading', *Consciousness and Cognition*, 15: 197–217.

Tracey, I. (2005) 'Functional connectivity and pain: how effectively connected is your brain?', *Pain*, 116: 173–4.

Turmel, A. (2008) *A Historical Sociology of Childhood*, Cambridge: Cambridge University Press.

Turner, B. (1984) *The Body and Society*, Oxford: Basil Blackwell.

UNICEF (2005) *Child Labour Today*, London: UNICEF.

Uprichard, E. (2007) 'Children as "beings and becomings": children, childhood and temporality', *Children & Society*, 22(4): 303–13.

Urry, J. (2000) *Sociology Beyond Societies: Mobilities for the Twenty-First Century*, London: Routledge.

Valentine, G. (2004) *Public Space and the Culture of Childhood*, Aldershot: Ashgate.

Vygotsky, L. (1986) *Thought and Language*, Cambridge, MA: MIT Press.

Warren, S. (2000) 'Let's do it properly: inviting children to be researchers', in Lewis, A. and Lindsay, G. (eds) *Researching Children's Perspectives*, Buckingham: Open University Press, pp. 122–34.

Weber, M. (1957) *The Theory of Social and Economic Organisations*, Chicago: Free Press.

West, A. (2003) *At the Margins: Street Children in Asia and the Pacific*, Poverty and Social Development Papers, No. 8, Manila: Asian Development Bank.

Whiting, B. (1963) *Six Cultures: Studies of Child Rearing*, New York: Wiley.

Whiting, J. and Child, I. (1953) *Child Training and Personality*, New Haven, CT: Yale University Press.

Whitty, G and Wisby, E. (2007) *Real Decision Making? School Councils in Action*, London: Institute of Education, University of London.

Winn, M. (1984) *Children without Childhood*, Harmondsworth: Penguin.

Wintersberger, H. (2005) 'Work, welfare and generational order: towards a political economy of childhood', in Qvortrup, J. (ed.) *Studies in Modern Childhood*, Basingstoke: Palgrave Macmillan, pp. 201–20.

Woodhead, M. and Faulkner, D. (2000) 'Subjects, objects or participants? Dilemmas of psychological research with children', in Christensen, P. and James, A. (eds) *Research with Children*, London: Falmer, pp. 9–35.

Woodhead, M. and Faulkner, D. (2008) 'Subjects, objects or participants? Dilemmas of psychological research with children', in Christensen, P. and James, A. (eds) *Research with Children*, 2nd edn, Abingdon: Routledge, pp. 10–39.

Wyness, M. (2000) *Contesting Childhood*, London: Falmer.

Zelizer, V. (1994) *Pricing the Priceless Child: The Changing Social Value of Children*, Princeton, NJ: Princeton University Press.

Zelizer, V. (2005) 'The priceless child revisited', in Qvortrup, J. (ed.) *Studies in Modern Childhood*, Basingstoke: Palgrave Macmillan, pp. 184–200.

Zirakzadeh, C. (1989) 'Traditions of protest and the high-school student movements in Spain and France in 1986–87', *West European Politics*, 12(3): 220–37.

Index